QUANTITATIVE BUSINESS ANALYSIS CASEBOOK

QUANTITATIVE BUSINESS ANALYSIS CASEBOOK

Samuel E. Bodily
Darden Graduate School of Business Administration
University of Virginia

Robert L. Carraway
Darden Graduate School of Business Administration
University of Virginia

Sherwood C. Frey, Jr.
Darden Graduate School of Business Administration
University of Virginia

Phillip E. Pfeifer
Darden Graduate School of Business Administration
University of Virginia

IRWIN

Chicago • Bogotá • Boston • Buenos Aires • Caracas
London • Madrid • Mexico City • Sydney • Toronto

Irwin Book Team

Publisher: *Tom Casson*
Senior sponsoring editor: *Richard T. Hercher, Jr*
Developmental editor: *Wanda J. Zeman*
Marketing manager: *Colleen Suljic*
Project editor: *Jean Lou Hess*
Production supervisor: *Dina Genovese*
Manager, prepress: *Kim Meriwether David*
Designer: *Bethany Stubbe*
Compositor: *Times Mirror Higher Education Group, Inc., Imaging Group*
Typeface: *10/12 Times Roman*
Printer: *R. R. Donnelley & Sons Company*

Times Mirror
Higher Education Group

Library of Congress Cataloging-in-Publication Data

Quantitative business analysis casebook / Samuel E. Bodily . . . [et al.].
    p.   cm.
  ISBN 0–256–14714–0
   1. Decision-making—Case studies.   I. Bodily, Samuel E.
  HD30.28.0357   1996
  658.4'03—dc20   96–3991

Printed in the United States of America
1 2 3 4 5 6 7 8 9 0 DO 3 2 1 0 9 8 7 6

To student-centered learning and to the MBA students of the Darden Graduate School of Business Administration, University of Virginia, who have enriched us with their personalities and energized our teaching with their enthusiasm for learning.

This book contains a set of cases that have proven to be effective pedagogical tools for MBA and executive education audiences in the general area of quantitative business analysis, including decision analysis, statistics, and management science. As such, the cases in this book can be used to complement virtually any existing MBA (or undergraduate, for that matter) curriculum, providing practice in the application of the most commonly used quantitative tools and techniques in realistic business settings.

This book can be much more than this; it can provide the basis for moving away from the traditional technique-driven, compartmentalized, quantitative methods course to a course that is

- decision and action oriented, not technique and numbers driven;
- integrated in both form and pedagogy within a business curriculum, not compartmentalized;
- managerially exciting, not methodologically dull.

Such a course would contain all of the usual topics of existing quantitative courses. Students in such a course will develop the skill and the perspective to use quantitative techniques artfully to gain insight into the resolution of practical business problems. They not only master the specific techniques, but also develop the ability to garner information from commonly available sources and to recognize when a particular technique is appropriate, when additional analysis is called for, and when to end the analysis and make the decision. The most widely applicable methodologies of decision and risk analysis, probability and statistics, competitive analysis, and management science are thus integrated with personal judgment and intuition in a way that is meaningful to MBA and executive learners alike.

A key characteristic of such a course is field-based (i.e., they actually happened) cases drawn from all the functional areas of business. The cases provide realistic, unstructured, business settings wherein the methodologies of the course can be usefully and creatively applied to the decisions of the practicing manager. The case studies serve as vivid answers to the question, Why do I need to learn this? A common theme cutting across all cases, and indeed across the entire course, is the need to make real *decisions.* The cases thus avoid being academic exercises, but assume the vitality of business itself. Thus, *decision analysis* becomes an accurate descriptor of all the cases in this book and is a critical framework from which this new type of quantitative methods course hangs.

Just what is a case? The answer must recognize that cases play a variety of roles in a course. They may be focused on understanding core tools and concepts, on applying methodology appropriately, on defining the limits of good practice, or on inventing new methods and adapting existing ones for the problem at hand.

Some cases in this book are highly structured, focused on a single issue, with needed data laid out. These cases can be used to develop methodology; the cases are not intended merely to present institutional information and provide practical enrichment. Such a case is more than a problem or exercise; it requires some initial assumptions, which may lead to alternative answers, and the analysis must be explained by the student in the case context.

Some of the cases are appraisal cases, where the analysis is partly or wholly done. The student will evaluate the work, applying what has been learned about good practice, and perhaps push the analysis further.

Finally, and more commonly in this book, many cases are unstructured, with multiple issues and data challenges (missing or incomplete data, choices among data, or data preparation needed). In these cases, the student must diagnose the situation, perform the analysis, and explain the use of the analysis and its limits. The intent here is not to produce apprehension, but to show that skills can be confidently applied to realistic situations. Some of the student's fear that may arise when using cases comes from concern that there is a single right answer and that the student will be unable to find it. If students can see that many reasonable assumptions may be made (some more reasonable than others, to be sure) and that they can do analyses (some more insightful than others), they will find their own way and complement their efforts with ideas that emerge in class.

What makes a strong case? A leading characteristic is a *decision orientation. Relevancy* is key; students recognize that the resolution of the situation matters to them. A strong case demonstrates a *need to know* something not currently known. It involves the *practice of skills,* including new and recently acquired skills. And it requires some *internalization* of concepts and the *articulation* of the reasoning process. Students will see that they are involved in situations that can be key to their careers.

In addition to these characteristics, these cases provide integration with other courses. Issues come up from other disciplines that provide bridges to other courses. If these issues are not immediately put aside in class and built upon, the course is not pigeon holed: "That's *quant,* not management, and therefore not for me." These cases provide many opportunities for joint class sessions, where the regular instructor can be joined by a professor of accounting, ethics, economics, finance, marketing, operations, or human resources to bring together two streams of concepts and to solidify the role of quantitative analysis in each of the business functions.

This casebook's dedication to student-centered learning places both added responsibility and ownership of the learning process upon students who use the book and leads to improved skill retention and less complaining.

The cases are organized alphabetically, not according to a particular methodological approach. This organization allows flexibility in the use of the cases and preserves student responsibility to determine what should be done with each case. Of course, the cases are not to be taught in alphabetical order. The *Instructor's Manual* describes the typical use of each case and provides sample course outlines.

The cases have been used in a one-year course in quantitative analysis or quantitative methods at the first-year MBA level. Many of them have also been used in executive education in short, non-degree programs. They would fit nicely in courses more narrowly focused in decision analysis, management science, or forecasting and regression. For short courses, any subset of these cases can be selected for custom publishing by Irwin.

The cases cover the following topics:

Decision Analysis (both as a methodology in its own right and as a general framework for the course and decision making): Decision Diagrams (trees), Discrete Probability, Expected Value, Sensitivity Analysis, Risk Preference, Value of Information and Control

Discounted Cash Flow Analysis: Relevant Flows, Present Value, NPV, and IRR

Continuous Probability and Probability Distributions: Subjective Assessment, From Data, Analytical Distributions

Risk Analysis with Many Uncertain Quantities: Monte Carlo Simulation, Spreadsheet Modeling with Add-ins

Sampling

Time Series Forecasting

Regression Modeling

Multi-Objective/Multi-Stakeholder Analysis

Competitive Analysis and Negotiation

Optimization: Linear Programming, 0-1 Integer Programming.

We assume virtually no prerequisites. Although calculus is not needed, some algebra is assumed, but rarely getting as far, for example, as solving two equations in two unknowns. Although no prior probability or statistics is presumed, some familiarity can help the student. The principal requirements are clear thinking, the ability to conceptualize, and the ability to cut to the core of an issue.

Even though this case book is software neutral, the electronic spreadsheet is assumed to be a fundamental tool available to the student. The spreadsheet is a very helpful way for instructors to provide the right amount of help to students. Spreadsheets containing data from case exhibits and, sometimes, the setup for analysis are available with the *Instructor's Manual.* They may also be downloaded from the QBA Casebook home page accessible through the Darden School's home page (http://www.darden.virginia.edu/) on the internet. It will be necessary to use @Risk or Crystal Ball, and the Solver within Excel or What'sBest! to do some of the cases. Other software tools, such as TreePlan or DPL, may be useful to students in the course but are not necessary.

A complete instructor's manual, with sample course outlines and an extensive teaching note for each case, is available from Irwin. To the instructor's advantage, the authors have put as much effort and time into the teaching notes as the cases. Each note is the product of many teaching meetings and discussions of pedagogy.

The production of this casebook reaffirms our commitment to what we have been doing with cases for many years. We are glad to see that others in our discipline are also interested in using cases, as evidenced by many sessions on the topic at the meetings of such professional societies as the Institute for Operations Research and the Management Sciences, and the Decision Sciences Institute. We welcome the interest and hope that our efforts may be useful elsewhere.

Please provide feedback (especially about successes and failures with these cases), new case ideas, and innovative ways of teaching. Write to any of the authors at Darden Graduate Business School, University of Virginia, Box 6550, Charlottesville, VA 22906-6550, or send E-mail.

Samuel E. Bodily (bodilys@virginia.edu)
Robert L. Carraway (rlc6g@virginia.edu)
Sherwood C. Frey, Jr. (scf@virginia.edu)
Phillip E. Pfeifer (pep8s@virginia.edu)

A C K N O W L E D G M E N T S

We thank the students at the Darden School for their comments and contributions during the development and refinement of these cases. We gratefully acknowledge the resources of the Darden School for case writing support in the form of research assistants, travel expenses, and summer salaries. Many individuals contributed to specific cases including the following:

Edward R. Case	*T. Rowe Price*
Dana Clyman	*Athens Glass Works, Harimann International*
John L. Colley, Jr.	*Oakland A's (A)*
Glenn A. Ferguson	*Edgcomb Metals (A)*
James V. Gelly	*Lesser Antilles Lines*
Lonnie Gorban	*Lightweight Aluminum Company*
C. William Hosler	*Foulke Consumer Products, Inc.; Sleepmore Mattress Manufacturing: Plant Consolidation*
James C. McLean	*American Lawbook Corporation*
Donna M. Packard	*Jade Shampoo (A) and (B)*
Michel Schlosser	*Dhahran Roads (A) and (B)*
Douglas L. Schwartz	*Roadway Construction Company*
Steven R. Scorgie	*The Waldorf Property*
George R. Stearns	*Piedmont Airlines (A)*
Ann C. Stephans	*Oakland A's (A)*
William T. Stewart	*Edgcomb Metals (A)*
Hasmeeth S. Uppal	*Harimann International*
Larry Weatherford	*CyberLab (A), (B), and Supplement; Shumway, Horch, and Sager (A); Sprigg Lane (A), Wachovia Bank and Trust Company N.A. (B): Supplement*

We acknowledge Harvard Business School Publishing for their permission to use the following cases: C. K. Coolidge, Inc. (A), Freemark Abbey Winery, Maxco, Inc., and the Gambit Company.

We thank the many companies and individuals who willingly cooperated with the field research needed for the cases. We are pleased to note that there are many managers who recognize the educational value of field-based course materials and, as a result, who generously contributed their time and experience. Some of the companies are named in the cases; others for a variety of reasons chose to have their material disguised. Although the cases in this book are written as fact, almost all of them have some facts disguised. In some, individual names have been changed; in others, some of the numbers are changed. Some are written from general experience, without a specific sponsoring company. We are pleased if the cases appear to be totally realistic, but the reader should be aware that names, numbers, and situations are not all real.

We benefited (as will the users) from the efforts of Darden editors Bette Collins, Stephen Smith, and Elaine Moran.

Finally, we thank the Irwin editors Dick Hercher, for approving this project, and Wanda Zeman, for shepherding it along.

C O N T E N T S

QUANTITATIVE BUSINESS ANALYSIS CASEBOOK

CASE 1
AMERICAN LAWBOOK CORPORATION (A)

Ed Troy glanced briefly out the window of his downtown office toward the busy street below, then returned his gaze to the three Publication Proposals on his desk (Exhibit 1). He had just finished filling in his assessment of the first year's sales potential for these titles (Exhibit 2). As director of educational and professional publishing for the American Lawbook Publishing Company (AL), he was ultimately responsible for choosing which of these titles the company would offer for use in American law schools in the fall of 1982.

Law school professors were normally offered a complimentary examination copy of every book published for classroom use in their fields. When deciding whether or not to "adopt" any of these books, a professor might consider the reputation and background of the author; the breadth and organization of topics covered; the length of individual chapters and of the book itself; whether an innovative pedagogical approach was used; the availability of auxiliary teacher's notes; the style and readability of the prose; whether cases and examples were up to date; the aesthetics of the typeface, layout, and binding; the retail price that their students would have to pay (usually in the range of $25 to $35); and similar considerations.

As a graduate of the Duke University Law School, and a veteran of the law school publishing business, Troy had a strong intuitive understanding for the many factors that influenced the performance of a new book. Indeed, everyone at AL recognized that Troy was the person most qualified to synthesize the available information on a new title into a subjective forecast of first-year sales. Troy, however, was never entirely comfortable with the task. He maintained that AL needed a more systematic approach for evaluating and weighing the critical factors affecting sales, assessing the risks, and ranking different proposals. He was therefore concerned not just with the disposition of these three proposals but with the more fundamental questions of what marketing information should be collected and how it should be analyzed to guide future publishing activities. Since law school publishing would always retain a substantial element of risk, he believed it was essential to know the odds against which one was playing.

Law and Law School Publishing

The American Lawbook Corporation was founded in Boston, Massachusetts, in 1897 and had grown to employ over 350 people, including approximately 70 lawyer-editors. The company specialized in the editing, annotation, and printing

---

EXHIBIT 1   Three Publication Proposals

Proposal One: Casebook in Admiralty Maritime Law

Authors:	Thomas Schoenbaum, J. D. Michigan 1965, Professor of Law, Tulane University
	A. N. Yiannapoulos, J. S. D. Berkeley 1956, Professor of Law, Tulane University
Pages:	800
Enrollment:*	Percentage of students with opportunity . . . . <u>0.5816</u>
	Percentage of students enrolling . . . . <u>0.0317</u>
	Estimated national enrollment 2,139
Books in field:†	2 case, 1 text

Proposal Two: Casebook in Administrative Law

Authors:	Donald P. Rothschild, LL.M. Harvard 1965, Professor of Law, George Washington University
	Charles H. Koch, LL.M. Chicago 1975, Professor of Law, College of William and Mary
Pages:	950
Enrollment:*	Percentage of students with opportunity . . . . <u>0.9269</u>
	Percentage of students enrolling . . . . <u>0.1202</u>
	Estimated national enrollment 12,929
Books in field:†	10 case, 3 text

Proposal Three: Casebook in Criminal Law

Authors:	Robert Misner, J.D. Chicago 1971, Professor of Law, Arizona State University
Pages:	450
Enrollment:*	Percentage of students with opportunity . . . . <u>0.9407</u>
	Percentage of students enrolling . . . . <u>0.2798</u>
	Estimated national enrollment 30,544
Books in Field:†	14 case, 6 text

---

* First Percentage is the percentage of all law students attending those schools that offer a course for which the book is suited.

Second percentage is the average percentage of those students with the opportunity who actually enroll in the course.

Estimated national enrollment is the total enrollment at all American Bar Association–approved law schools (116,047) multiplied by the two percentages.

† Number of comparable books, including this one, competing for adoption in this subject area.

---

of the statutory output of state legislatures. Having submitted a winning bid to perform this service for a state, a law publisher generally became the only source from which attorneys in that state could obtain an up-to-date copy of the state code—a necessity for general legal practice. As there was relatively little turnover among code publishers, the business tended to be characterized by consistent and predictable profitability.

EXHIBIT 2   Ed Troy's Assessment of First-Year Sales

Proposal	Proposed Retail Price	Fractiles				
		0.05	0.25	0.50	0.75	0.95
1. Schoenbaum & Yiannapoulos $35		10	400	600	1,000	2,000
2. Rothschild and Koch $30		200	800	1,000	2,000	6,000
3. Misner $25		10	200	500	1,100	4,000

In 1968, AL merged with the Tinline-Geary Publishing Company of Cincinnati, Ohio, and shortly thereafter the activities of both companies were consolidated in Boston. Among the Tinline-Geary properties were an existing line of casebooks and treatises for the law school market, including several titles under contract but not yet published.

In contrast to code publishing, law school publishing proved to be a strikingly unpredictable business. It was quite possible for the large prepublication investment in a new title (frequently in the range of $30,000 to $50,000) to be lost through an indifferent sales response. Moreover, whereas AL was a major publisher of state codes and a monopoly supplier in most of its markets, the law school course markets were commonly saturated with many published offerings of a number of much larger companies.

West Publishing Company of St. Paul, Minnesota, and Foundation Press of Mineola, New York, dominated the law school publishing business. West owned Foundation, and together they held an estimated 60–65 percent of the total law school market. Little, Brown of Boston accounted for another 15 percent and was the publisher of choice for many Harvard Law School professors. The third largest firm, The Michie Company of Charlottesville, Virginia, held about 5 percent of the market. AL was the largest of several small firms that made up the remainder of the estimated $15 million annual law school market.

In addition to code and law school books, AL also published what were referred to as author books. These books were written on law-related subjects and were sold primarily to practicing lawyers. AL found author books an attractive way to smooth the demand on its production facilities. Whereas code and law school books required rigid time schedules, author books could be published at any time.

Genesis of a Law School Publication

Law school curricula offered publishers an astonishing variety of publishing options. While only six to eight courses (such as contracts or torts) were required at all schools, many others (e.g., evidence or future interests) were tested on most state bar examinations and were therefore widely attended. Enrollment in the hundreds of other subject areas could range from dozens in an admiralty course to a handful studying Zairan tribal legal systems.

Courses might be taught with one or more teaching approaches, including traditional lecture methods. The "case" approach was the study of court cases with their judicial decisions and opinions. The "problem" approach was akin to the case method used in graduate business schools. In the Socratic method, professors attempted to stimulate intellectual curiosity and tenacity among students by directing repeated and probing questions toward individual class members.

Reliance on a particular teaching method strongly influenced a professor's choice of type of book. Most prevalent in law schools was the "casebook" or "coursebook" containing edited cases and opinions linked by the author's commentary and questions. "Problem" books were used less commonly and primarily in courses with a practical bent, such as tax or estate planning. Textbooks, "treatises," "hornbooks," and "handbooks," the distinctions among which were not rigorous, were most often used as supplemental materials.

The initial inspiration to write—for example, a casebook in environmental law—most frequently arose with a professor who was dissatisfied with existing teaching materials in that field. His or her proposal, which ranged from single paragraphs to 1,000-page typed manuscripts, could reach the publisher's office in several ways. First, "law school travelers" visited campuses to promote good will and solicit new manuscripts. At AL, Donald Layton, the administrative editor for law school publications, performed this function.

Second, AL employed an advisory board of prominent legal academicians who reviewed proposals, suggested authors, and occasionally submitted proposals. Finally, and most often, professors who had assembled sets of teaching materials for their own courses mailed proposals to one or more publishers. Such unsolicited proposals were received at AL several times each week.

Many proposals could be rejected immediately. To illustrate, a book might be proposed for an arcane field not currently studied in American law schools (e.g., French administrative law). Alternatively, the subject area might be already dominated by one or more universally acclaimed works. Occasionally, sample chapters would exhibit a dismaying lack of clarity or grammatical accuracy.

Proposals that offered initial promise were subjected to review by advisory board members, by their colleagues, and by the AL staff. Since this process could last several months, it was not unusual for many proposals to be "under consideration" at any given time.

Production of a Law School Publication

Unlike many publishing houses, but in common with West/Foundation, AL maintained its own in-house composition, pressroom, and bindery facilities. This total production capacity was believed to provide AL advantages in cost and quality control, as well as considerable scheduling flexibility.

Once a proposal was approved and contracted for publication, AL waited for the submission of a completed manuscript. The manuscript copy was then edited, arranged into pages and chapters, and sent to the manufacturing plant. Edited materials were electronically typeset, and the resulting "camera copy" was photographed and made into printing plates. High-speed printing on a web offset press and hard- or soft-cover binding yielded a finished book.

Several weeks before a book was printed and bound, prepublication announcements, which included an offer of a complimentary copy, were mailed to all professors teaching an appropriate course. Every attempt was made to provide potential adopters with a review copy before professors informed law school bookstores of their text selections, which normally occurred in mid to late spring.

Performance Measurement for New Publications

Specific objectives for the performance of published law school titles were derived from corporate return on sales (ROS) and return on investment (ROI) goals. The custom at AL was to pursue these ROS/ROI goals through the intermediate objective of a 40 percent gross margin on individual products. (Troy had also adopted a goal of a 10 percent annual growth rate in sales dollars for law school publications and usually required a one-year payback on investments in new products.)

Most AL products (code books) were sold through competitive bidding to markets with well-defined sizes and purchase rates. To achieve a 40 percent gross margin, costs were estimated, prices set to yield the desired margin, and a skillful selling job performed to justify what might be a premium price on the basis that publishing the code books was an irreplaceable service. Because academic titles faced a highly uncertain market, however, the standard AL "profit planning" formulas were not easily applicable to law school publications titles. Since assuming responsibility for this product line, Troy had evaluated the profit potential of new titles in the following manner:

1. Proposals were reviewed for quality and timeliness by the advisory board.
2. Total costs for an approved proposal were estimated by using a formula supplied by the manufacturing department:

Editorial	120 hrs/500 pages @ $12.80/hr
Prepress	$17.50/page
Print/bind	$4.25/copy

3. Sales revenues were estimated by multiplying the likely manufacturer's selling price by an estimated sales volume. This estimate was derived from a subjective assessment of the size of the market in question and the relative strengths of competitors' titles.
4. Total costs were compared with sales revenues to estimate total profits.

Troy worried about the reliability of this approach. Among recently published titles, many were doing significantly better or worse than had originally been predicted. While their aggregate performance was respectable, he was sure that those results could be improved dramatically if the potential for individual titles could be identified more accurately. To do so, Troy felt that the procedures used for estimating both costs and sales should be scrutinized.

Cost Estimation

Troy had several reservations about the cost formula supplied by manufacturing, all of which were related to the unusual cost structure of law school titles. The production process through plate-making was very labor intensive, and prepress costs were unaffected by the number of copies ultimately produced. The variable

---

EXHIBIT 3 Labor Hours and Material Costs (1981 dollars) for Recent AL Titles

	Copies	Pages	Edit (hours)	Composition (hours)	Press (hours)	Bindery (hours)	Paper (dollars)	Bindery (dollars)
1	2,525	1,400	1,002.0	1,931.1	61.2	296.5	$4,465.2	$ 813.4
2	1,552	328	159.7	537.1	13.9	108.6	863.5	379.9
3	1,539	734	480.1	790.1	22.4	127.5	2,347.5	612.5
4	1,967	1,328	680.4	1,827.1	46.7	227.7	3,408.3	671.7
5	3,043	1,352	620.6	1,852.9	87.6	394.0	7,169.6	1,102.6
6	2,081	656	456.3	876.3	25.6	134.7	1,969.6	615.7
7	3,034	1,176	737.1	2,079.5	62.0	417.6	2,391.7	1,002.2
8	3,075	944	312.1	983.4	51.4	290.0	4,154.5	1,211.0
9	3,010	960	453.9	1,032.2	51.7	242.3	5,711.7	1,087.8
10	3,025	1,156	701.5	1,710.6	47.8	264.5	5,545.4	1,114.4
11	2,046	520	223.7	686.5	22.5	134.0	1,924.3	780.6
12	3,048	872	844.1	1,163.6	44.1	239.0	4,597.5	1,046.7
13	2,025	440	326.4	672.2	23.1	109.5	1,944.7	785.9
14	1,015	1,218	1,017.3	1,671.5	28.1	141.5	1,802.7	525.1
15	9,009	262	193.1	304.9	52.5	231.1	4,146.5	3,672.5
16	2,042	704	499.8	1,015.2	27.4	130.5	3,854.2	797.2
17	2,067	752	510.7	1,100.1	36.9	138.3	5,043.7	859.7
18	3,654	368	202.1	772.1	28.4	206.8	3,081.0	1,386.4
19	1,091	344	231.1	736.1	10.4	67.5	504.7	349.5
20	2,083	532	337.8	969.0	20.2	128.0	1,999.9	841.8
21	1,583	1,236	915.8	1,424.4	32.0	194.8	4,948.2	705.3
22	1,080	376	266.4	665.3	23.5	83.5	892.5	442.2
23	2,046	998	507.2	1,457.3	44.5	204.8	4,197.3	876.1
24	2,105	672	559.4	863.5	19.0	121.9	2,278.0	849.8
25	1,031	960	842.2	1,971.2	30.9	107.4	2,437.2	571.6

printing and binding expenses were quite small and resulted mainly from paper costs. Because law school course enrollments were relatively small, press runs were short. Prepress costs thus became by far the largest component of the total investment required to publish a new title.

Troy had found law school professors, as authors, to be somewhat capricious in their dealings with publishers. It was not unusual for a professor's late delivery of manuscript copy to cause AL to miss the late-spring coursebook review period. Moreover, the professor might then insist on costly revisions to accommodate late statutory and judicial developments in the book's field. Troy was concerned that the manufacturing formula might not acknowledge how expensive and how variable the prepress investment in a new law school title might really be.

In addition, the manufacturing formula did not provide for costs associated with wholesale discounts, which averaged 20 percent off suggested list price; authors' royalties, which averaged 20 percent of sales net of wholesale discounts; or promotion costs, which ranged from $1,000 to $5,000 per new title. Troy wondered how best to incorporate all these costs into the publication decision.

Toward that end, he had requested that accounting prepare some data on the costs of past AL law school publications. Those data, including labor hours accumulated by those titles in editorial, prepress, pressroom, and bindery categories, plus average 1981 dollar rates charged each category of labor hour, are presented in Exhibits 3 and 4.

EXHIBIT 4   1981 Average Hourly Labor and Overhead Rates

Rate Category	1981 Direct Labor $ Rates	1981 Budgeted Hours	1981 Overhead $ Rates*	1981 Total Dollar Rates
Editorial	$5.20	157,500	$ 5.67	$10.87
Composition	5.76	150,550	8.75	14.51
Total pressroom	7.52	15,700	10.96	18.48
Total bindery	5.55	75,750	11.21	16.76

* A detailed study had not been undertaken to determine what percentage of AL overhead rates represented "direct" costs. However, if the portion of overhead expenses representing overtime premiums and supplies is considered "direct" and the portion including depreciation, taxes, and the like is considered "nondirect," the breakdown of overhead costs was as follows:

	Direct (%)	Nondirect (%)
Editorial	59	41
Composition	51	49
Pressroom	31	69
Bindery	42	58

Moreover, the performance of law school publications was measured on the basis of profit after allocation of full costs, not divisional cash flow.

Sales Estimation

Predicting sales for individual titles posed considerably greater difficulty than did estimating costs, for a far less deterministic process was involved. Not merely the number of students enrolled in a course, the number of competing texts, and the month of publication, but a host of less-quantifiable factors influenced the sales potential of a particular volume. The effective sales life of a law school book had been estimated at an average of three years, however, and, as a general rule, Troy assumed that total sales would be double those achieved in the first year.

To investigate these questions, and to develop the best approach for evaluating current and future publication proposals, Troy had commissioned a survey of course enrollments at American Bar Association–approved U.S. law schools. He hoped to use data from this survey along with other information regarding sales of existing AL law school titles (consolidated in Exhibit 5) to search for patterns in sales.

Marketing Research

Although AL had never undertaken a market survey for a new law school book, the company had conducted surveys for author books. Quite recently, as a matter of fact, Troy had received the results of a mail survey of Kentucky law offices (Exhibit 6), in which 47 percent of those responding indicated they would buy *Kentucky Contract Law* if AL went ahead with publication. Considering the conclusions of the study, Troy was fairly confident that this percentage could be applied to the 3,840 known "law-practice units" in Kentucky to forecast approximate sales of 1,805 for this new title.

He wondered whether a similar survey could be justified for a textbook. Certainly $340, the cost of this recent survey, did not seem a large amount to pay for the additional information on potential sales. Perhaps an even more thorough survey might be justified, with a personal interview of each and every law school professor who taught a course for which the proposed text could be used. Although such a survey would be considerably more expensive than the Kentucky example, it would tell Troy almost exactly what the first year's sales would be.

EXHIBIT 5   Sales Data for Recent AL Titles

	Estimated Market[a]	*Percent Opportunity*[b]	*Percent Enroll*[c]	*Number Books*[d]	*Months*[e]	*Sales*[f]
1 . . .	4,909	74.85%	5.65%	3	16	1,324
2 . . .	13,222	97.44	11.69	8	14	946
3 . . .	1,510	26.90	4.84	2	12	667
4 . . .	2,172	64.47	2.90	5	21	741
5 . . .	4,945	78.17	5.45	8	18	2,509
6 . . .	192	7.16	2.31	1	17	531
7 . . .	750	11.72	5.51	1	16	409
8 . . .	25,525	97.89	22.47	15	12	1,547
9 . . .	21,259	89.83	20.39	15	11	1,451
10 . . .	3,333	38.32	7.49	2	11	1,151
11 . . .	6,294	73.88	7.34	5	10	310
12 . . .	19,774	99.08	17.20	11	20	3,436
13 . . .	41,405	100.00	35.68	16	16	421
14 . . .	5,378	59.18	7.83	6	16	628
15 . . .	26,510	100.00	22.84	5	15	7,198
16 . . .	2,696	74.17	3.11	5	15	977
17 . . .	37,460	100.00	32.28	11	15	497
18 . . .	1,059	7.90	11.55	1	14	2,027
19 . . .	3,938	65.65	5.17	3	12	507
20 . . .	4,020	62.97	5.50	6	11	273
21 . . .	2,628	67.01	3.38	12	11	692
22 . . .	8,337	95.52	7.52	5	20	1,612
23 . . .	21,505	96.52	19.20	4	18	1,418
24 . . .	5,257	83.57	5.42	8	18	1,401
25 . . .	39,892	98.74	34.81	11	17	1,317

[a] *Estimated Market* is total law school enrollments times Percent Opportunity times Percent Enroll.

[b] *Percent Opportunity* is the percentage of all law school students with the opportunity to take the course for which the book was written.

[c] *Percent Enroll* is the average percentage of students who, given the opportunity, take the course for which the book was written.

[d] *Number of Books* is the number of competing texts, including this one.

[e] *Months* is the number of months for which the title was available for sale towards use in its first July-through-June academic year.

[f] *Sales* is total copies sold in the first year.

Exhibit 6   Mail Survey Report, March 31, 1982

Proposed book: *Kentucky Contract Law,* by Samuel K. Kline, Jr.
Market: Kentucky lawyers

No. of attorneys 6,618   Sole practitioners 3,110
Law firms 2–9 730   Total law-practice units (LPUs) 3,840

Survey:
Total no. mailed 400
Responses 115
Percent responses 28.8%

	Number	Percent
Respondents indicating would buy	54	47%
Respondents indicating book useful but would not buy (or not sure)	36	21
Respondents indicating not buy	25	22

Statistical Analysis

If *n* samples are drawn (independently and without replacement) from a population of size *N,* the standard error (*SE*) of the resulting sample proportion ($\bar{P}$) is given by the following formula:

$$SE = [\bar{P}(1-\bar{P})/n]^{1/2} \, [(N-n)/N]^{1/2}$$

The minimum number of samples (*n*) required to obtain a desired standard error (*SE*) is given as

$$n = N/[4(N)(SE^2) + 1]$$

Conclusions

In this example, *N* = 3,840. If we desire a standard error (*SE*) less than 0.05, we require

$$n = 3,840/[4(3,840)(0.05^2) + 1]$$

$$= 97.5$$

Since the realized sample size was 115, the standard error will be less than 0.05 for all estimated proportions.

There are two caveats to the use of these survey results. First, the 400 attorneys and firms surveyed were randomly selected from our computer file of American Lawbook customers, not the practicing bar at large. This could cause a bias in favor of sales. However, the American Lawbook Corporation list of 2,056 customers should be representative of the bar generally.

Secondly, the survey was made in early 1982. If conditions should change significantly (e.g., by the publication of a competing book), the survey results would be invalid.

Upon the assumptions and caveats stated and results analyzed, we can conclude that 47 percent plus or minus 5 percent, or 1,805 plus or minus 90, LPUs would buy *Kentucky Contract Law.*

We can further conclude that 68 percent plus or minus 5 percent, or 2,611 plus or minus 130, LPUs believe this book would be useful to the Kentucky bar. These potential sales do not include other customers who would be likely to purchase this book, including libraries, state agencies, small and large corporations in the energy industry, public utilities, and the like. The survey also makes no allowance for the additional sales that would be made by personal contact and selling by our market representatives.

EXHIBIT 6   *Continued*

Kentucky Contract Law Survey

1. Total of population being surveyed (LPUs) (estimated) 3,840
2. Total responses required for 5 percent standard error   97
3. Total surveys mailed to achieve responses:

	Sent	*Received*
1st mailing, Dec. 1, 1981	400	60
2nd mailing, Feb. 22, 1982	340	55

4. Costs of survey:

		Cost
a.	Secretarial time*: 2 days at $6.00/hr.	$ 96
b.	Postage, 740 mailings at $0.20	148
c.	Return postage, 115 at $0.25	29
d.	Photocopying, 740 × 3 pages at $0.03	67
	Total	$340

*Secretarial time and costs on future comparable surveys can be reduced to one day and $48.

CASE 2
AMERICAN LAWBOOK CORPORATION (B)

Ed Troy hired an MBA student for the summer to help him tackle the general problem of selecting law school books to be published by the American Lawbook Corporation. After hearing the basic components of the problem, the student became very excited about the possibility of using regression analysis to estimate the cost of a new title. Given permission to pursue this idea, the student returned in two weeks with a report on his results.

"As you can see in the table in Exhibit 1, I put together the total direct cost of each of the 25 recent AL titles," began the student. "And then I ran a regression to explain these costs using the number of copies printed and the number of pages per copy. The regression results were fantastic. I've summarized them in Exhibit 2. We obtained an adjusted R-square of 90.5 percent, and the t-statistics for both coefficients were significant at the 95 percent level.

"Next I tried to forecast first year's sales using the data we compiled from our survey of law schools. The results here are not as fantastic, but I don't think you can expect to predict sales as well as you can predict costs. The explanatory variable is market-per-book, defined as the estimated market divided by the total number of competing books. The resulting model shown in Exhibit 3 has an adjusted R-square of 23.3 percent and a t-statistic significant at the 95 percent level. The coefficient tells me that on average each new book gets 52 percent of its share of the market."

Troy did not know quite how to react to these new cost and sales equations and the student's enthusiastic reporting. There was quite a difference between this regression equation and the manufacturing formula AL had been using to estimate the cost of a new title. Troy wondered if these new equations would indeed give a more accurate indication of the costs and profit potential of new law school titles.

EXHIBIT 1   Total Direct Costs (1981 dollars) for Recent AL Titles

Titles	Copies	Pages	Total Cost (dollars)
1	2,525	1,400	$37,289.0*
2	1,552	328	9,362.9
3	1,539	734	16,691.2
4	1,967	1,328	31,414.3
5	3,043	1,352	37,510.1
6	2,081	656	17,099.8
7	3,034	1,176	35,906.0
8	3,075	944	21,618.1
9	3,010	960	24,277.6
10	3,025	1,156	33,373.1
11	2,046	520	13,252.8
12	3,048	872	27,684.6
13	2,025	440	13,815.8
14	1,015	1,218	29,865.7
15	9,009	262	15,528.2
16	2,042	704	20,936.9
17	2,067	752	23,333.4
18	3,654	368	16,516.0
19	1,091	344	11,158.5
20	2,083	532	17,165.7
21	1,583	1,236	30,387.1
22	1,080	376	11,524.3
23	2,046	998	26,887.7
24	2,105	672	18,192.6
25	1,031	960	31,793.6

*Calculated as follows:

	Hours	Direct Labor $ Rates	Direct OH $ Rate	Total Dollars
Edit	1,002.0	$5.20	$3.35	$ 8,567.1
Composition	1,931.1	5.76	4.46	19,735.8
Press	61.2	7.52	3.40	668.3
Bindery	296.5	5.55	4.70	3,039.1
Paper				4,465.2
Bindery				813.4
Total				$37,288.9

Exhibit 2   Regression Results for Total Direct Costs

Variable	Coefficient	Std. Error	T
Copies	0.94	0.36	2.62
Pages	23.68	1.56	15.21
Constant	1,394.90	1,744.00	0.80

Adjusted R-square 0.9053
Std. dev. of residuals . . . 2,702.27
Sample size   25

Prediction equation:

$$TDC = 1394.90 + 0.94 \text{ (Copies)} + 23.68 \text{ (Pages)}$$

Correlation matrix:

	TDC	Copies	Pages
TDC	1.000		
Copies	−0.003	1.000	
Pages	0.941	−0.175	1.000

Exhibit 3   Regression Results for First Year's Sales

Variable	Coefficient	Std. Error	T
Market-per-book	0.52	0.18	2.88
Constant	503.40	38.80	1.30

Adjusted R-square 0.233
Std. dev. of residuals   . . . 1,247
Sample size   25

Prediction equation:

$$FYS = 503.40 + 0.52 \text{ (Market-per-book)}$$

Correlation matrix:

	FYS	MPB	Market	Books
FYS	1.000			
MPB	0.515	1.000		
Market	0.243	0.734	1.000	
Books	0.027	0.164	0.698	1.000

Case 3
Amore Frozen Foods
Macaroni and Cheese Fill Targets

Tom Jenkins, manager of quality services at Amore's frozen foods plant in Cortland, New York, thought the summer of 1984 might be the time to return the fill target for Amore's 8-ounce frozen macaroni and cheese pie to 8.22 ounces. Amore had been filling each aluminum tin to an uncharacteristically high target of 8.44 ounces ever since problems with underweight macaroni and cheese appeared in New York City in 1978. The higher target had protected Amore from fines levied against several producers for underweight product, but at the expense of an extra 0.022 ounces of macaroni and cheese in each pie.

Cortland Production Facility

The production facility in Cortland, New York was originally a cold storage warehouse for locally grown apples and peaches. When these forms of agriculture dwindled, a former Cortland State University student associated with the Duncan Packing Company of Louisville, Kentucky, suggested that the company purchase and convert the warehouse for use as a frozen foods production and storage facility. The Duncan Packing Company had been founded in 1940 and prospered as a supplier of canned goods to the United States military. With the end of World War II, the company decided to expand into frozen foods and chose the Cortland apple and peach storage facility as part of that expansion.

By 1954, Duncan Packing Company sales of frozen meat and fruit pies reached $11 million. The company employed 925 people in its facilities in Cortland (126,000 square feet) and Webster City, Iowa (116,000 square feet). Duncan was acquired a year later, 1955, by the American Baking Company, which changed the name to Duncan Frozen Foods. The International Communications Corporation acquired American Baking in 1968 and in 1981 sold Duncan to the Amore Corporation (a subsidiary of K. J. Kyburg Industries, Inc.). At that time, Duncan's annual sales of $187 million represented a significant expansion by the Amore Corporation (primarily involved in canned foods) into the higher-margined areas of processed and frozen foods.

By 1984, the Cortland facility had grown to 500,000 square feet and employed 1,250 people. It produced 30,000 cases a day of finished products that carried the names Amore, Duncan, and Won Ton. Exhibit 1 lists the products made in the Cortland facility.

15

EXHIBIT 1   Cortland Products

— Beef, chicken, and turkey pot pies
— Full line of frozen dinners (13 varieties)
— Two-pound entrees (10 varieties)
— Casseroles (macaroni and cheese, and spaghetti and meat)
— Boil-n-Bag (10 varieties)
— Donuts (4 varieties)
— Full line of Food Service meals—primarily in-flight service for airlines

---

EXHIBIT 2   Standard Cost Breakdown

Item	Dollars per Dozen
Ingredients:*	$1.82
Cheese	
Macaroni	
Packaging:	0.62
Tins	
Cartons	
Case	
Direct labor	0.07
Indirect labor	0.13
Overhead	0.36
Total	$3.00

*At the 8.44-ounce target.

Macaroni and Cheese Production

The Cortland facility produced 60,000 dozen 8-ounce frozen macaroni and cheese pies each month on a line staffed with 25 workers making about $6 an hour. When this line was not making macaroni and cheese, it produced any number of other similar products.

Raw materials entered the preparation area where the cheese sauce was made and the macaroni cooked and cooled. The two were then blended in horizontal mixers and pumped to the filling line. At the filling line the aluminum trays were placed on a conveyor, mechanically filled with the macaroni and cheese, and then placed in cartons. The product was then cased (24 pies to the case), frozen, and placed in storage for distribution. The line operated at a speed of 1,000 dozen pies every 20 minutes. It took nine minutes for the mixed macaroni and cheese to end up packaged, cartoned, and cased, and another 40 minutes to freeze the cased product.

Exhibit 2 gives the standard cost breakdown for a dozen 8-ounce macaroni and cheese pies as estimated by the accounting department. Pies sold at a wholesale price of $4.50 per dozen, $1.50 above the $3.00 standard cost per dozen.

Fill Targets

The practice in the food and beverage industry was to set a target weight or volume to which each container or package was filled. Because of the variability associated with the physical mechanisms that actually filled each package, fill targets were always set above the amount stated on the package. Industry practice was to set targets at one standard deviation above the package amount so about 85 percent of all packages would be in compliance. Exhibit 3 gives a detailed table of normal probabilities used to determine the percentage of underweight packages. The filling device for macaroni and cheese at Amore's Cortland plant could fill amounts that were normally distributed around the target value with a standard deviation of 0.22 ounces. Industry practice would then dictate a fill target for an 8-ounce macaroni and cheese pie of 8.22 ounces.

During the energy crisis of the late 70s, Amore (then Duncan Frozen Foods) discovered that cost-conscious supermarkets were turning off their freezers when they went home for the evening. The effect on frozen macaroni and cheese was to cause a softening of the product and a subsequent weight loss due to dehydration. Local government inspectors discovered several examples of underweight macaroni and cheese for which some producers were fined several thousand dollars. In particular, inspectors from the Bureau of Weights and Measures of New York City levied fines of up to $15 for each 8-ounce package of frozen macaroni and cheese found to be substantially underweight.[1] Despite the industry's presentation of evidence that improper storage of the product led to dehydration that caused the underweight product, the fines were not rescinded. In response to these problems, Amore quickly raised the target to 8.44 ounces in 1978, a full two standard deviations above the package weight. This unusually high target protected Amore from most of the problems brought on by the energy crisis. In 1984, with energy costs at normal levels, fines for substantially underweight frozen macaroni and cheese were virtually nonexistent in the industry.

Weight Control System

The United States Food and Drug Administration (FDA) was the arm of the federal government responsible for monitoring the practices of the food and beverage industry. One part of the FDA's activities required each food packager to submit a program designed to ensure that packages contained the stated amounts (weights) of product.

For Amore's macaroni and cheese pies, the FDA had approved a weight control system that required a sample of five pies be taken every 20 minutes. The five pies were selected consecutively at the beginning of a 20-minute run by a quality control technician, who then spent almost the entire 20 minutes

---

[1]The guidelines for levying fines varied with locality. In general, fines were imposed if an average of some number of pies fell under the package amount. It was possible, however, for one significantly underweight pie (e.g., one weighing less than 7.5 ounces) to warrant a fine.

EXHIBIT 3   Normal Probabilities

	0.00	0.01	0.02	0.03	0.04	0.05	0.06	0.07	0.08	0.09
	0.	0.	0.	0.	0.	0.	0.	0.	0.	0.
-3.2	00069*	00066	00064	00062	00060	00058	00056	00054	00052	00050
-3.1	00097	00094	00090	00087	00084	00082	00079	00076	00074	00071
-3.0	00135	00131	00126	00122	00118	00114	00111	00107	00104	00100
-2.9	00187	00181	00175	00169	00164	00159	00154	00149	00144	00139
-2.8	00256	00248	00240	00233	00226	00219	00212	00205	00199	00193
-2.7	00347	00336	00326	00317	00307	00298	00289	00280	00272	00264
-2.6	00466	00453	00440	00427	00415	00402	00391	00379	00368	00357
-2.5	00621	00604	00587	00570	00554	00539	00523	00508	00494	00480
-2.4	00820	00798	00776	00755	00734	00714	00695	00676	00657	00639
-2.3	01072	01044	01017	00990	00964	00939	00914	00889	00866	00842
-2.2	01390	01355	01321	01287	01255	01222	01191	01160	01130	01101
-2.1	01786	01743	01700	01659	01618	01578	01539	01500	01463	01426
-2.0	02275	02222	02169	02118	02068	02018	01970	01923	01876	01831
-1.9	02872	02807	02743	02680	02619	02559	02500	02442	02385	02330
-1.8	03593	03515	03438	03362	03288	03216	03144	03074	03005	02938
-1.7	04457	04363	04272	04182	04093	04006	03920	03836	03754	03673
-1.6	05480	05370	05262	05155	05050	04947	04846	04746	04648	04551
-1.5	06681	06552	06426	06301	06178	06057	05938	05821	05705	05592
-1.4	08076	07927	07780	07636	07493	07353	07215	07078	06944	06811
-1.3	09680	09510	09342	09176	09012	08851	08691	08534	08379	08226
-1.2	11507	11314	11123	10935	10749	10565	10383	10204	10027	09853
-1.1	13567	13350	13136	12924	12714	12507	12302	12100	11900	11702
-1.0	15866	15625	15386	15151	14917	14686	14457	14231	14007	13786

Note: Row and column headings give number of standard deviations from mean, and table entry gives the probability that a normally distributed uncertain quantity will be less than the specified number of standard deviations from the mean.

* Read: There is a 0.00069 probability that a normally distributed uncertain quantity is more than 3.200 standard deviations below the mean.

weighing and checking various attributes of the sample. The technician cost the company close to $12 an hour with fringe benefits. The pies were taken from the line after being cartoned and just prior to being cased and frozen. To weigh a macaroni and cheese pie, the technician placed the completed pie (complete with tin and carton) on one side of a balance scale and a tin, a carton, and a "tare" bottle (a standard weight constructed to weigh exactly the target weight of 8.44 ounces) on the other. The scale then read in units of 50ths of an ounce above or below the target. A reading of +28 thus meant the pie weighed 9 ounces (28/50 of an ounce above the target of 8.44 ounces).

Light samples, those that averaged less than −11 (8.22 ounces), were reported immediately to the line supervisor for corrective action. The workers had enough experience to easily respond to any unusual situation, so the worst that could happen was that the line ran below target for 20 minutes before it was noticed and corrected. Exhibit 4 shows an example of a weight control reporting sheet for the macaroni and cheese line, with reaction lines drawn at plus and minus 11.

Although it was Amore's company policy to react to samples averaging less than 8.22 ounces, the FDA-approved system required formal action only if the sample average weight was less than 8 ounces. In such cases, the entire 20-minute production had to be either fixed (weighed individually with extra ingredient added to all those found underweight, carton destroyed), reworked (ingredient reused, tins and cartons destroyed), or sold as underweight. To avoid the costs of fixing or reworking, Amore usually chose to send the entire 20-minute

---

EXHIBIT 4   Example Weight Control Report

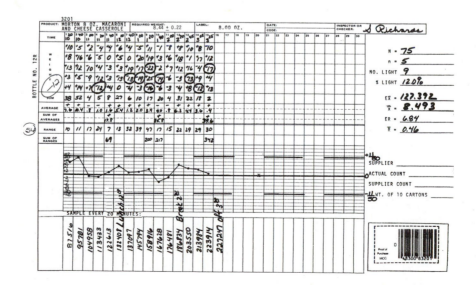

production to the company-operated Thrift Store on those rare occasions that the sample average weight fell below 8 ounces. In the first six months of 1984, only one such run was sent to the Thrift Store.

Thrift Store

The company-operated Thrift Store, located across the road from the main plant, sold a variety of underweight and second-quality frozen food merchandise to the general public. The selection of products available for sale was dictated by the "mistakes" made in the plant. However, any product that presented a potential health hazard, no matter how remote, was destroyed immediately.

Underweight macaroni and cheese was stamped with a 7-ounce label and sold fairly briskly at $3.60 per dozen. The local demand was such that approximately 60 dozen were sold each week when macaroni and cheese pies were available. This limited local demand and relatively high energy costs of storage led to an inventory policy that limited the amount of stored macaroni and cheese pies to 1,000 dozen pies. If more became available, the oldest cases in inventory were donated to charity.

CASE 4
ATHENS GLASS WORKS

In early August 1993, Christina Matthews, the product manager for nonglare glass at the Athens Glass Works (AGW), met with Robert Alexander, the controller of the Specialty Glass Division, to review the product's performance and prepare a pricing recommendation for the coming quarter. Once approved by the division president, the price would be announced and, as was customary in this segment of the glass industry, adhered to for at least 90 days.

The flat-glass industry was a $10.0 billion industry worldwide, of which $2.7 billion was generated in the United States. Approximately 57 percent of domestic production was for the construction industry, 25 percent for the automotive industry, and the remaining 18 percent for specialty products ranging from the mundane, like mirrors, to a wide variety of high-tech applications. Among the many technical applications of specialty glasses were solar panels, laminated and tempered safety glasses, heat- and bullet-resistant glasses, electrical and insulating glasses, phototechnical and photosensitive glasses, aerospace glass, and cookware. Nonglare glass was a fairly simple specialty product designed to reduce the glare of reflected light. It was used primarily to frame and protect artwork.

With 1992 sales of $195 million, Athens Glass Works was a midsized, regional glass company serving several niche markets in the southeastern United States. For a number of reasons, AGW enjoyed a dominant market position for nonglare glass in its region: (1) AGW was known for its fast, reliable service; it was willing to deliver glass on short notice at no extra charge in any of a variety of cut-to-order sizes, including the industry-standard delivery size (48-by-96-inch sheets) and all of the standard picture-frame sizes. (2) AGW provided an exceptionally high-quality nonglare glass with little light loss and virtually no blemishes. (3) AGW operated its own fleet of delivery vehicles so delivery times were well managed and shipping charges were kept low. And (4) AGW's salaried sales staff was widely acknowledged for its helpful, courteous service and customer orientation.

The production of nonglare glass, like many other coated-glass products, began with flat glass, the output of one of Specialty Glass's sister divisions. The flat glass was treated by the Specialty Glass Division with a patented coating that provided the desired optical characteristics. This process required specialized equipment that was usable only in the production of nonglare glass. The finished, treated glass was then cut to order and shipped.

The business outlook for nonglare glass, like that for flat-glass products in general, had been flat for the past several years. As a result, last September, in response to increased corporate pressure to improve margins, Christina and

This case was prepared in conjunction with Professor Dana Clyman (Darden). Copyright © by the University of Virginia Darden School Foundation, Charlottesville, Virginia. All rights reserved.

EXHIBIT 1   Sales Volume and Price History of Nonglare Glass

		Sales Volume (000 square feet)		Price ($ per square foot)	
Year	Quarter	AGW	Competitors	AGW	Competitors
1991 3		241	443	$2.05	$2.05
1991 4		313	592	2.05	2.05
1992 1		204	381	2.15	2.15
1992 2		269	513	2.15	2.15
1992 3		251	456	2.15	2.15
1992 4		238	672	2.36	2.15
1993 1		139	474	2.36	2.15
1993 2		162	642	2.36	2.15

Robert increased the price of nonglare glass by slightly less than 10 percent, from $2.15 to $2.36 per square foot. This pricing decision was one of many made during the past year in anticipation of the company's considerable capital requirements to fund a recently approved long-term expansion and modernization program. At the time of the price increase, Christina and Robert hoped that competitors would follow AGW's lead and increase their prices as well.

Unfortunately, AGW's competitors held the line on the price of nonglare glass, and Christina believed that AGW's significant loss of market share in the last nine months was due solely to AGW's price change, as little else had changed in the industry during that period. To document the decline, Christina prepared Exhibit 1, which presents the sales-volume and price-history data for nonglare glass in AGW's market region for the past eight quarters. Looking ahead, Christina believed that a reasonable forecast of total regional volume for the fourth quarter of 1993 (usually the best quarter of the year) was 920,000 square feet. Christina believed that if AGW were to return to the $2.15 price, it could regain a major portion of its original market share with sales of 275,000 square feet. On the other hand, if competitive prices were not met, she feared a further decline. Nonetheless, because of AGW's outstanding reputation in the crafts marketplace, she reasoned that a sufficient number of customers would stay with AGW and prevent sales from falling below 150,000 square feet, even at the current price of $2.36 per square foot.

While reflecting on the upcoming meeting with Christina, Robert realized that price would be the major topic of discussion, so he had his staff prepare a schedule of expected costs to produce nonglare glass over a wide range of production levels. This schedule is presented in Exhibit 2.

During their discussion, Christina and Robert together reviewed the historical sales levels and pricing data as well as the anticipated-cost schedule. They began by discussing the cost schedule. Christina noticed that unit costs grew with increasing volumes, but Robert said that the increasing unit costs were

EXHIBIT 2   Nonglare Glass

Estimated Cost per Square Foot at Various Production Volumes

	Production Volume (000 sq. ft.)							
	150	*175*	*200*	*225*	*250*	*275*	*300*	*325*
Material	$0.45	$0.45	$0.45	$0.45	$0.45	$0.45	$0.45	$0.45
Energy	0.38	0.36	0.36	0.35	0.35	0.37	0.37	0.38
Labor	0.32	0.31	0.30	0.31	0.33	0.35	0.36	0.38
Shipping	0.11	0.11	0.11	0.11	0.11	0.11	0.11	0.11
General overhead*	0.08	0.08	0.08	0.08	0.08	0.09	0.09	0.09
Depreciation	0.27	0.23	0.20	0.18	0.16	0.15	0.14	0.13
Manufacturing cost	1.61	1.54	1.50	1.48	1.48	1.52	1.52	1.54
Selling and admin. costs[†]	0.72	0.69	0.67	0.66	0.67	0.68	0.68	0.69
Total cost	$2.33	$2.23	$2.17	$2.14	$2.15	$2.20	$2.20	$2.23

*General overhead includes a variety of corporate expenditures. It is allocated as 25 percent of labor.

[†] Selling and administrative costs include the costs of the sales and administrative support staff. It is allocated as 45 percent of manufacturing cost.

simply the result of the company's cost allocation system. Next, Robert asked whether there was any possibility that competitors might reduce their prices below $2.15 per square foot if AGW returned to that price. Christina replied that she was confident no competitor would do so, because all were facing the same general economic conditions resulting from the long recession and several were in particularly tight financial straits. They then discussed whether the pricing decision for nonglare glass would have any repercussions on other Specialty Glass products; both were convinced it would not. Finally, they explored the implications of AGW's returning to the industry price of $2.15 per square foot. Christina believed recapturing lost market share was essential for AGW to maintain its dominant role in the nonglare-glass niche. Robert, however, was concerned that, at $2.15, the product would show a loss, an outcome that would not be welcomed by senior management.

CASE 5
BUCKEYE POWER & LIGHT COMPANY

Don Peters was manager of the Production Fuels Department of Buckeye Power & Light Company (BP&L), a small utility in southeastern Ohio. BP&L had three steam electric power plants—located in Athens, Zanesville, and Steubenville—whose primary energy source was coal. Each month, coal for these plants was purchased from a heterogeneous collection of vendors in Ohio, Pennsylvania, and West Virginia, ranging in size from small father-and-son operations to large mining companies. Peters was responsible for the monthly coal-procurement process, including how much to purchase from each vendor and which specific plant (or plants) each vendor should supply.

In October 1986, Peters' immediate task was to determine November's coal-procurement schedule. BP&L had recently retained the services of a consulting firm to analyze aspects of its operations, including the coal-procurement process. Peters hoped to use the opportunity of the consultants' analysis to rethink the entire procurement process. He also hoped the report would shed some light on two related issues that had been a source of controversy within the department.

Coal

Compared with oil, natural gas, and nuclear energy, coal was a relatively cheap source of fuel during the 1980s. Coal is a combustible rock formed by the underground compression of partially decomposed plant matter over millions of years. There are four major types of coal, classified according to energy content: lignite (lowest energy content), subbituminous, bituminous (most widely used as a fuel source), and anthracite (highest energy content). Coal's energy content (or thermal value) is measured in British thermal units (Btus). (One Btu is the amount of heat needed to raise a pound of water one degree Fahrenheit.) Pure bituminous coal typically contains on the order of 15,000 Btu per pound (Btu/lb).

There are three major determinants of the quality of coal. One is *total moisture content*. There are two distinct types of moisture associated with coal. *Free* moisture lies on the surface of the coal. Its presence, which depends primarily on conditions in the mine and in transit, is an important parameter in the design of coal-handling and -preparation equipment. *Inherent* moisture is trapped within the pores of the coal itself, and is present even when the surface of the coal appears dry. Both types of moisture reduce energy content.

A second determinant of coal quality is *ash content*. Ash is the incombustible residue that remains after coal is burned. Like moisture, a high ash content increases shipping, handling, and preparation costs while reducing thermal value.

Additional equipment and expense is required periodically to remove ash from a coal-fired furnace. Failure to do so adequately has a long-term impact on the life of a furnace.

The third major determinant of quality is *sulfur content.* When coal is burned, sulfur oxides are released, causing pollution and contributing to the corrosion of vital plant parts. Some sulfur can be removed prior to burning by "washing" the coal. To further control pollution, "scrubbers" can be attached to smokestacks to filter out a substantial number of sulfur oxide particles. During the 1980s, the maximum level of sulfur oxide pollution was regulated by law. Each coal-fired plant was thus forced to restrict the amount of sulfur in the coal it burned on the basis of the specific pollution-control equipment it was using.

BP&L's Coal-Procurement Process

Each month, vendors interested in supplying one or more of BP&L's coal-fired power plants completed an offer sheet specifying the amount of coal they had to sell, along with its quality and price. Quality was expressed in terms of Btu/lb and moisture, ash, and sulfur content. Vendors were asked to quote a per-ton price, transportation included, for each power plant they were willing and able to supply. The Production Fuels Department took all offers, adjusted them for past performance (particularly the amount of coal available for purchase, which was often overstated and had to be adjusted downward), and summarized the results in a document called the Offers Edit Report (see Exhibit 1).

At the same time, each of the three coal-fired power plants submitted its requirements for the upcoming month. Corporate policy dictated that a plant have sufficient Btus on hand each month to satisfy 120 percent of expected demand. Exactly how many Btus to order for the upcoming month thus depended on both the estimated ending inventory of coal in the current month (stated in terms of Btus) and expected demand during the upcoming month.

Each plant also provided minimum acceptable quality standards for moisture, ash, and sulfur content. Each of these was stated in terms of a weighted average of all coal delivered to the plant in the month. For example, 1,000 tons of coal with 2 percent sulfur content and 500 tons of coal with 1 percent sulfur content would produce an overall 1.67 percent sulfur-content level; this number was not allowed to exceed the sulfur standard. The sulfur standards were set by law; moisture and ash standards were left to the discretion of the individual plant managers, who were familiar with the costs associated with handling increased levels of moisture and ash at their respective plants.

The Production Fuels Department was responsible for taking the Offers Edit Report and the plant requirements, summarized in a Plant Requirements Edit Report (Exhibit 2), and arriving at an overall coal-procurement plan. Peters, as manager of the department, had the flexibility to negotiate with both vendors and plant managers to strike a better overall deal for the company. For example, he could

EXHIBIT 1   Offers Edit Report for November

Vendor	Quantity Available (tons)	Btu/Lb	Moisture (%)	Ash (%)	Sulfur (%)	Plant	$/Ton
Willis Bros. . .	2,500	10,980	6.2%	21%	1.2%	Ath	$30.80
MacMillan . . .	9,000	11,590	6.0	20	0.9	Ath	36.80
K. Barnes . . .	3,000	11,550	6.4	18	1.1	Ath	34.00
Foster &	27,000	12,065	6.1	12	1.0	Stb	42.00
Hughes						Zan	41.60
						Ath	45.60
Western	22,500	12,210	6.2	14	0.9	Stb	43.92
						Zan	42.70
						Ath	41.48
Pellham	6,000	11,240	6.8	18	1.8	Stb	33.15
McIntyre	3,000	11,000	6.3	17	2.2	Stb	32.00
Monongahela .	30,000	12,640	5.8	10	0.8	Stb	44.10
Consolidated						Zan	45.36
Pope	3,600	12,570	6.4	10	1.0	Zan	35.00
Lyon Valley . .	2,700	11,950	6.8	12	0.9	Zan	33.12
Crescent Rock .	2,300	12,080	6.6	13	1.1	Zan	32.40

Long-term contracts:
  MacMillan (minimum of 8,000 tons)
  Foster & Hughes (minimum of 20,000 tons)
  Western (minimum of 16,000 tons)
  Monongahela Consol. (minimum of 18,000 tons)

EXHIBIT 2   Plant Requirements Edit Report for November

Plant	Btus (billions)	Maximum Allowable Weighted Average Percent		
		Moisture	Ash	Sulfur
Steubenville	800*	6.0%	15%	1.0%
Zanesville	500	7.0	11	2.0
Athens	600	7.0	18	1.0

* Number of Btus that, when added to October's expected ending inventory, would equal 120 percent of
  November's expected demand.

negotiate price reductions or quantity increases with vendors, or both. Similarly, he could make plant managers aware of particularly restrictive quality requirements and negotiate to have them relaxed. Ultimately, Peters was responsible for approving the overall coal-procurement plan.

Recently, the Production Fuels Department had been struggling with two issues relating to the coal-procurement process: long-term contracts and safety-stock levels.

Long-Term Contracts

Because of a utility's need to have a guaranteed source of fuel, long-term contracts with coal vendors were a long-standing industry practice. A long-term contract with a vendor obligated the utility to buy a minimum amount of coal each month from that vendor at the contract-specified price. The balance of the utility's needs was met by purchasing additional coal on the spot market.

Prior to 1973, BP&L had purchased approximately 65 percent of its coal on long-term contract. The energy crises of the 1970s and resulting surge in demand for coal and coal prices had precipitated an upward trend in this figure. By 1986, BP&L was purchasing 80 percent of its coal on long-term contract (vendors in late 1986 with whom BP&L had long-term contracts and the contract amounts are indicated in Exhibit 1).

As the energy crisis eased, however, the availability of coal became less of a concern. Moreover, by 1986, prices on the spot market were running about $6 per ton less than long-term contract prices. Many people in the Production Fuels Department thought that the percentage of coal purchased on long-term contract should be reduced, perhaps back to the 65 percent level.

Peters estimated that returning to the 65 percent figure would allow BP&L to reduce the amount of coal purchased on long-term contract by 12,000 tons. If such a reduction were to be made, it was not clear to Peters which of the current long-term contracts should be reduced or eliminated.

20 percent Safety Stock

Running out of coal forced a utility to purchase energy from a neighboring utility at a premium price. In August, for example, BP&L had sold 10 billion surplus Btus on an emergency basis to a utility in western Pennsylvania for $20,000. A rash of such purchases by BP&L in the 1970s had driven the company to raise its required safety-stock level from 15 to 20 percent.

Since the safety stock had been increased, however, none of BP&L's plants had ever been forced to purchase outside energy. In fact, over the past three years, actual monthly energy demand had rarely exceeded 110 percent of expected demand. Some BP&L officials attributed this situation to improved forecasting techniques, while others thought it represented a leveling off of demand.

Whatever the reason, many at BP&L were now pushing to reduce the safety-stock level back to 15 percent. Peters recognized that such a reduction would save BP&L carrying costs on the coal needed to supply 5 percent of overall Btu demand. From October's coal-procurement numbers, Peters estimated that the average cost of a billion Btus at each plant were as follows:

Plant	Average Cost of 1 Billion Btus
Steubenville	$1,740
Zanesville	$1,610
Athens	$1,625

He wondered if these were the appropriate costs to use, and, if so, how to balance the cost savings against the increased possibility of running out of coal.

CASE 6
BUCKEYE POWER & LIGHT COMPANY SUPPLEMENT

Early in October 1986, Don Peters, manager of the Production Fuels Department of Buckeye Power & Light Company (BP&L), received a preliminary report from a consultancy commissioned to analyze various aspects of its operations, including the coal-procurement process. The consultants had been given, among other items, the Offers Edit Report and the Plant Requirements Edit Report for the November coal-procurement decision. The section of the report dealing with the coal-procurement process, reproduced below, contains the consultants' recommendations with respect to the November purchase, as well as an explanation of their methodology. Peters was anxious to understand how this approach might help him more aggressively manage the procurement process and resolve the internal debates on long-term contracts and safety-stock levels.

Section of the Consultants' Report Dealing with the Coal-Procurement Process

Attached is a spreadsheet model (Exhibit 1) of the November coal-procurement decision. The model is constructed to facilitate the use of *What'sBest!,* a linear programming (LP) software package for spreadsheets. Based on the information contained in the model, LP can be used to identify the optimal (i.e., minimum cost) procurement and shipping plan. In addition, LP provides valuable ancillary information on related questions of interest, such as how much you would be willing to pay for additional coal from certain vendors, how much your long-term contracts are costing you, and how much the quality restrictions imposed by the various plants are costing the company.

Below is a summary of LP and a guide to interpreting the spreadsheet model.

In LP, a decision is viewed as an allocation of *resources* to potential *uses* of those resources. The allocation is made with a specific *objective* in mind—such as to maximize profit or minimize cost—and is subject to *constraints,* or restrictions, on how the resources can and should be allocated. These constraints may be either environmental in nature (outside the control of the decision maker) or policy (within the control of the decision maker). Within the limitations imposed by these constraints, LP identifies the allocation of resources to uses that achieves the best, or optimal, result in terms of the objective.

In the coal-procurement decision, the resources are the supplies of coal from the various vendors. There are three potential uses of these resources: the Btu requirements of each of BP&L's three coal-fired plants. The objective is to minimize the cost of satisfying these requirements.

EXHIBIT 1

	A	B	C	D	E	F	G	H	I	J	K	L
1	Buckeye Power & Light Company											
2												
3	Total cost											
4		—	—	—								
5	$3,165,119[1]											
6							Maximum		Shadow	Range		
7	Vendor	Steubenville	Zanesville	Athens	Total purchased		available	Slack	price	Decrease	Increase	
8		—	—	—	—		—	—	—	—	—	
9	Willis			2,500	2,500[2]	≤	2,500	0	$1.52	2,500	239	
10	MacMillan			8,000	8,000	≤	9,000	1,000	$0.00	1,000	**********	
11	Barnes			227	227	≤	3,000	2,773	$0.00	2,773	**********	
12	F & H	16,036	3,964	0	20,000	≤	27,000	7,000	$0.00	7,000	**********	
13	Western	1,487	0	14,513	16,000	≤	22,500	6,500	$0.00	6,500	**********	
14	Pellham	0		0	0	≤	6,000	6,000	$0.00	6,000	**********	
15	McIntyre	2,277			2,277	≤	3,000	723	$0.00	723	**********	
16	Monongahela	12,921	7,664		20,585	≤	30,000	9,415	$0.00	9,415	**********	
17	Pope		3,600		3,600	≤	3,600	0	$10.12	3,600	2,594	
18	Lyon Valley		2,700		2,700	≤	2,700	0	$4.94	2,700	346	
19	Crescent		2,300		2,300	≤	2,300	0	$3.62	2,300	228	
20		—	—	—								
21	Total	32,721[3]	20,228	25,240								
22	Total cost	$1,381,502[4]	$802,487	$981,131								
23												

[1] @SUM(B22..D22)
[2] @SUM(B9..D9)
[3] @SUM(B9..B19)
[4] $42.00*B12 + $43.92*B13 + $33.15*B14 + $32.00*B15 + $44.10*B16

30

EXHIBIT 1 (*CONTINUED*)

Contract Requirements

	Vendor	Total purchased		Minimum contract	Surplus	Shadow price	Range Decrease	Increase	
	Willis	2,500[5]		—	—	—	—	—	
	MacMillan	8,000	>	8,000	0	$2.68	2,763	226	
	Barnes	227							
	F & H	20,000	>	20,000	0	$3.15	4,208	345	
	Western	16,000	>	16,000	0	$5.54	2,623	215	
	Pellham	0							
	McIntyre	2,277							
	Monongahela	20,585	>	18,000	2,585	$0.00	*********	2,585	
	Pope	3,600							
	Lyon Valley	2,700							
	Crescent	2,300							

Minimum Plant Btu Requirements

	Plant	Actual		Required	Surplus	Shadow price	Range Decrease	Increase	
				—	—	—	—	—	
	Steubenville	800[6]	>	800	0	$1,653	15	151	
	Zanesville	500	>	500	0	$1,696	17	208	
	Athens	600	>	600	0	$1,472	5	64	

[5] +E9

[6] ((12,065*B12 + 12,210*B13 + 11,240*B14 + 11,000*B15 + 12,640*B16)*(2,000/1,000,000,000))

31

Exhibit 1 Concluded

	A	B	C	D	E	F	G	H	I	J	K	L
49												
50					Minimum Quality Requirements				Shadow	Range		
51			Steubenville									
52					Actual		Allowed	Slack	price	Decrease	Increase	
53			Moisture		1,963[7]	<	1,963[8]	0	$1,048	1	9	
54			Ash		3,812	<	4,908	1,096	$0	1,096	*********	
55			Sulfur		327	<	327	0	$103	27	2	
56												
57			Zanesville									
58												
59			Moisture		1,252[9]	<	1,416[10]	164	$0	164	*********	
60			Ash		2,225	<	2,225	0	$248	7	74	
61			Sulfur		187	<	405	218	$0	218	*********	
62												
63			Athens									
64												
65			Moisture		1,549[11]	<	1,767[12]	217	$0	217	*********	
66			Ash		4,198	<	4,543	346	$0	346	*********	
67			Sulfur		235	<	252	17	$0	17	*********	
68												

[7] .061*B12 + .062*B13 + .068*B14 + .063*B15 + .058*B16

[8] .06*B21

[9] .12*B12 + .14*B13 + .18*B14 + .17*B15 + .10*B16

[10] .15*B21

[11] .010*B12 + .009*B13 + .018*B14 + .022*B15 + .008*B16

[12] .010*B21

32

There are several constraints on the allocation:

Resource Availability.   Each vendor is offering a limited supply of coal. We cannot buy more coal than a vendor has available.

Btu Requirement.   Each plant has a required number of Btus. The coal we ship to each plant must have sufficient thermal value to satisfy that plant's Btu needs.

Contracts.   From certain vendors, we are obligated to purchase a minimum amount of coal.

Quality Restrictions.   Each plant has restrictions on the weighted-average moisture, ash, and sulfur content of incoming coal. We must make sure that the average of all coal we ship to each plant satisfies these requirements.

To apply LP, we must first model the relationship between resources and uses. This is accomplished by first defining a set of spreadsheet cells that represents the allocation of resources to uses. There needs to be one cell for each potential resource-use combination. In the coal-procurement model, there is a cell for each vendor/plant combination (cells B9–E19). For all vendor/plant combinations that are not feasible, the corresponding cell is left blank. The remainder of the cells are allowed to vary in search of a minimum cost allocation. (Because these adjustable cells form the core of the decision, they are referred to as *decision variables* in traditional LP terminology.)

We next must specify the relationship between uses and the objective. Associated with allocating some or all of a particular resource to a specific use is the impact of that allocation on the objective. In the coal-procurement model, purchasing one ton of coal from a particular vendor and shipping it to a specific plant costs us the per-ton offering price for that vendor/plant combination. For a given allocation plan, the total cost of the plan is calculated by multiplying the number of tons assigned to each vendor/plant combination by the associated per-ton cost, and summing these totals across all vendor/plant combinations. In the coal-procurement model, this total is in cell A5 (the sum of cells B22–D22). It is precisely this figure that we are trying to minimize.

The final step in setting up our LP model is to make sure that the optimal allocation does not violate any of the constraints. In the coal-procurement plan, this is accomplished as follows:

Resource Availability.   Cells E9–E19 contain the total number of tons purchased from each vendor, irrespective of plant destination. These totals cannot exceed the vendors' corresponding supplies of coal, contained in cells G9–G19. The "<" symbol between the two is *What'sBest!*'s way of stating that, for example, cell E9 must be "less than or equal to" cell G9. Cells H9–H19 contain the number of tons of coal offered by each vendor but not purchased. (In LP terminology, this is referred to as *slack*.)

Btu Requirement.   To see how this constraint is modeled, consider the Steubenville plant. This plant requires 800 billion Btus; this number is entered in cell G45. Given a particular allocation scheme, cell E45 contains the total number of Btus in the coal shipped to the Steubenville plant. It is calculated by first multiplying each vendor's average Btu/lb by the number of lbs shipped from that vendor to Steubenville and then summing across vendors. The ">" symbol specifies that cell E45 must be greater than or equal to cell G45. The number in cell H45 specifies how many billions of Btus above the required 800 are being sent to Steubenville. (This is often referred to as the *surplus.*)

Contracts.   Cells E29–E39 duplicate the total number of tons ordered from each vendor (also contained in cells E9–E19). The minimum order quantities for each of BP&L's long-term contracts are in cells G30 (MacMillan), G32 (Foster & Hughes), G33 (Western), and G36 (Monongahela). As with the Btu requirements, actual tonnage must exceed the minimum order quantities; hence, the ">" symbols and the surplus column.

Quality Restrictions.   To see how these 9 constraints (3 plants times 3 quality considerations) are modeled, consider the moisture constraint for the Steubenville plant. For a given allocation scheme, the actual number of tons of moisture sent to the Steubenville plant is contained in cell E55. It is found by multiplying the moisture percentage of each vendor's coal by the number of tons shipped by that vendor to Steubenville and then summing these totals across vendors. The total number of tons of moisture allowed in Steubenville is found by multiplying Steubenville's maximum allowable weighted-average moisture percentage (6 percent, from Exhibit 2) by the total number of tons shipped to the plant (cell B21). The use of "<" and the slack cells parallel the resource-availability constraints above.

Using *What'sBest!*, we arrive at the procurement plan outlined in the attached hard copy. Notice that all constraints are satisfied. The algebra underlying the LP solution approach used by *What'sBest!* guarantees that we have found a plan that minimizes total cost (cell A5).

Shadow Prices.   There is one additional bit of valuable information that is provided. For a variety of reasons, it is often useful to know the *value* of resources and the *cost* of restrictions placed on how we are allowed to allocate them. One assessment of value is the amount by which our economic position would be improved if we had one additional unit of resource. For a restriction, an assessment of value is the amount by which our economic position would be improved if we could "relax" the restriction (make it less restrictive). In both cases, the amount by which our position would be improved represents an upper bound on how much we would pay to receive the benefit. *Shadow prices* provide this information.

For example, how valuable is coal supplied by Willis? Notice that, in the optimal procurement schedule, we purchase all of the Willis coal offered. The shadow price for Willis coal (cell I9) is $1.52. The proper interpretation of this number is as follows: If we had one additional ton of Willis coal available (i.e., 2,501 instead of 2,500) at the current price, we could improve our economic position by $1.52. Purchasing an additional ton from Willis would allow us to purchase less from another vendor; the net effect would be an overall cost reduction of $1.52. Analogously, if we had one less ton available from Willis (2,499 instead of 2,500), the net effect of having to purchase additional coal elsewhere would drive up our overall procurement cost (thereby worsening our economic position) by $1.52.

Alternatively, consider the ash restriction at the Zanesville plant. The shadow price is $248 (cell I62). The correct interpretation is as follows: If we could allow one additional ton of ash (over and above the 15 percent of the total currently allowed) to be handled at the Zanesville plant, we could improve our economic position by $248. Relaxing this constraint (allowing more ash to be sent to Zanesville) would allow us to allocate a less-expensive mix of coal to Zanesville, with repercussions echoing throughout the procurement plan. The net effect would be a cost reduction of $248. Analogously, if our ability to handle ash at Zanesville were decreased by one ton (below the 15 percent of the total currently allowed), our cost would increase (thereby worsening our economic position) by $248. Tightening this constraint (allowing less ash to be sent to Zanesville) would force us to send a more expensive mix of coal to the plant.

For each ">" constraint, the interpretation of shadow prices is analogous to the above, adjusting for the fact that *relax* now carries a different meaning. For example, consider the minimum order quantity due to the long-term contract with Foster & Hughes. We are currently purchasing precisely the minimum amount, and the shadow price is $3.15 (cell I32). The proper interpretation: If we could purchase one less ton from Foster & Hughes (i.e., 19,999 instead of 20,000), we could improve our economic position by $3.15 (alternatively, having to purchase an additional ton would worsen our economic position by $3.15). Again, this represents the net effect of purchasing one less ton from Foster & Hughes and some additional coal elsewhere. Relaxing a ">" constraint means reducing the quantity on the right-hand side of the inequality (lowering the hurdle we have to clear), while relaxing a "<" constraint means increasing the right-hand side (raising the bar we have to get under).

Three additional points should be made. First, notice that the shadow price is $0 for any constraint where there is a slack or surplus. The rationale for this is simple: If we are not currently using up all the available quantity of a particular resource, having more of that resource available does not affect our optimal procurement plan and, hence, has no effect on total cost. Analogously, if the weighted average of the coal we are shipping to a particular plant is of better than required quality along any of the relevant dimensions, then relaxing the allowable quality along that dimension will not change the optimal procurement plan and, hence, does not reduce overall cost.

Second, a shadow price tells us the marginal value of relaxing a constraint by *one* unit only (e.g., the cost savings of being allowed to buy *one* less ton of coal on contract from MacMillan or, conversely, the additional cost of having to buy *one* additional ton on contract from MacMillan). This per-unit cost only holds over a limited range. At some point, the per-ton cost savings of being allowed to buy less coal from MacMillan is bound to decrease and, conversely, the per-ton additional cost of having to buy additional coal from MacMillan is bound to increase. *What'sBest!* reports the amount by which the current right-hand side value of any constraint can be increased or decreased and the reported per-unit shadow price still be guaranteed to apply. For example, the $2.68 (cell I30) per-ton cost savings of being allowed to buy less MacMillan coal applies for a reduction of at least 2,763 (cell J30) tons. Once the contract amount is reduced to less than 8,000 − 2,763 = 5,237 tons, the per-ton shadow price associated with an additional reduction may drop. Conversely, the same $2.68 per-ton additional cost of having to buy additional coal from MacMillan holds for at least an additional 226 (cell K30) tons. Once the contract amount is increased to more than 8,000 + 226 = 8,226 tons, the per-ton shadow price of having to buy an additional ton may go up. Hence, the marginal cost of $2.68 of a ton of MacMillan coal purchased on contract is guaranteed to hold over the range of 5,237 to 8,226 tons. To find the new shadow prices (if they do in fact change) outside of this range, the right-hand side of the constraint must be changed to a value outside the range, and the LP reoptimized.

Third and finally, each shadow price can, strictly speaking, be interpreted only within the context of everything else in the model remaining unchanged. For example, the shadow price of $1.52 for Willis coal is based on the assumption that the available quantities from all other vendors and the quality restrictions imposed by the plants do not change. To investigate changes in more than one constraint simultaneously, the model should be rerun. Practically speaking, however, using shadow prices to gauge the net effect of multiple changes is often acceptable as long as the changes are relatively small. For example, shadow prices can be used to investigate the marginal impact of an event that would change several quantities simultaneously.

The model is set up to allow you to make changes and reoptimize using *What'sBest!*. Be careful when doing so to change only those cells that have numbers—not formulas—in them. Do not replace cell formulas with numbers, as this might destroy some of the important LP relationships built into the model. To reoptimize, make whatever changes you wish to make to the model itself, then reoptimize with *What'sBest!*

Case 7
California Oil Company

Carl Shimer, research and development director for California Oil Company (COC), had been studying the proposed construction of a supertanker port and pipeline. The new facility would supply COC's Richmond refinery in the San Francisco Bay area. The port would consist of a single-point mooring two or three miles from shore to unload supertankers. Submarine pipelines would take the oil into a shore-based pumping station, where it would enter the pipeline to the Richmond refinery. After a preliminary screening, four sites had been selected for more detailed evaluation: Moss Landing, Estero Bay, Port Hueneme, and Oso Flaco Dunes. Shimer had to recommend a site to COC's research and development committee.

The major considerations in evaluating the sites were economic, political, and environmental. These were then refined and expanded into 10 criteria (see Table 1). The importance of each criterion was discussed at length at a committee meeting, after which Shimer received the following memo from his assistant:

TO: Mr. C. Shimer, Research and Development Director
FROM: Mr. D. Klopp, Assistant Director of Research and Development
SUBJECT: Tanker Port Selection

At Friday's meeting (April 2), it was decided that 10 criteria be used for evaluating promising sites. The 10 criteria were ranked in order of importance. The list developed on Friday places the "attitude of local politicians" as the *most*

TABLE 1 California Oil Company 10 Criteria Selected for Proposed Supertanker Port Evaluation

Economic	Facilities
	Port characteristics
	Location
	Initial cost
	Annual cost
	Possibilities for future development
Political	Attitude of local populace
	Attitude of local politicians
Environmental	Environmental impact from operation and accidents
	Environmental impact from placement of facilities

Note: Adapted from Elwood S. Buffa and James S. Dyer, *Management Science Operations Research* (New York: John Wiley & Sons, 1977).

Source: Unpublished report by G. Hill, A. Kokin, and S. Nukes. Reproduced with permission.

important factor and "environmental impact from placement of facilities" as the *least* important factor. I have enclosed the ranked criteria with comparative site descriptions for your information.

DATE: April 5, 1978   SIGNED: D. Klopp

With this information, Shimer pulled out his notes from the committee meeting, which held evaluations of each of the sites broken down by the 10 criteria. He placed the criteria in the order suggested by the committee (see Table 2). Shimer examined each criterion and decided the "best" and "worst" situation possible under the circumstances. For example, the "best" outcome for the criterion "attitude of local politicians" would be a favorable vote assured, and the "worst" outcome would be an unlikely favorable vote (see Table 3).

For each criterion, Shimer assigned the "worst" situation a value of 0 and the "best" situation a value of 1. He then hoped to assign values between 0 and 1 for each site characteristic, weighing them by the relative importance of each of the 10 criteria to achieve an overall evaluation of each site (see Figure 1). He anticipated this method would help differentiate between

FIGURE 1   California Oil Company Work Sheet

		Alternatives			
Criterion	*Weight*	*Moss Landing*	*Estero Bay*	*Port Hueneme*	*Oso Flaco Dunes*
Attitude of local politicians					
Initial cost					
Annual cost					
Location					
Possibilities for future development					
Port characteristics					
Attitude of local populace					
Environmental impact from operation and accidents					
Facilities					
Environmental impact from placement of facilities					

TABLE 2   California Oil Company Assessment of Port Sites

Criterion		Alternatives		
	Moss Landing	Estero Bay	Port Hueneme	Oso Flaco Dunes
Attitude of local politicians	Possibly opposed	Possibly favorable	Favorable	Possibly favorable
Initial cost	$40 million less than Estero Bay	The cost-base location	$60 million more than Estero Bay	$5 million more than Estero Bay (estimate)
Annual cost	$2 million per year less than Estero Bay	Base location	$5 million more than Estero Bay	Near cost of base location
Location	Close to Richmond, farther from Elk Hills than base location	Base location	90 miles farther from Richmond than base location	Central location
Possibilities for future development	Area already populated	Rolling terrain will hamper large expansion	Navy interference	Area available, subject to local politicians
Port characteristics	Fair	Good	Excellent	Good
Attitude of local populace	Possible opposition	Vocal opposition	Little effect on population	Little effect on population
Environmental impact from operation/accidents	High impact: area is sandy to marshy, possibly difficult to clean up; possible long-term effects	High impact: tourism and fishing industry will be seriously affected; marshy area and rocky coastline extremely difficult to clean up; possible long term damage to bird sanctuary and oyster beds	Minimal impact: area sandy; easy cleanup; area already industrialized	Minimal impact: area sandy; easy cleanup
Facilities	No	Some	No	No
Environmental impact from placement of facilities	Tank farm highly visible	Tank farm hidden; major restructure of existing creek	Tank farm visible (no nearby population)	Tank farm visible (no nearby population)

39

TABLE 3   California Oil Company Reference Port Descriptions

Criterion	"Worst" Value for Each Criterion	"Best" Value for Each Criterion
Attitude of local politicians	Favorable vote unlikely	Favorable vote assured
Initial cost (Estero Bay cost as base)	$60 million above base	$60 million below base
Annual cost (Estero Bay cost as base)	$5 million above base	$5 million below base
Location (Estero Bay as base)	Near Los Angeles with poor access to the San Joaquin Valley and Richmond	Between the Elk Hills oil field and San Francisco, but closer to Elk Hills with easy pipeline access to San Joaquin Valley
Possibilities for future development	No future development or expansion possible after initial part is completed	No limit on future growth or expansion of facilities
Port characteristics	Very rough seas and more than four miles from shore	Calm seas and one mile from shore
Attitude of local populace	Large, strong, vocal, and effective opposition	Small, weak, and ineffective opposition
Environmental impact from operation/accidents	Oil spill would seriously disrupt the community and harm wildlife; extreme danger due to proximity to military operations or other industry	Oil spill could be cleaned up relatively swiftly with no serious effect
Facilities	No facilities to support supertanker operations	All facilities completed for supertanker port operations
Environmental impact from placement of facilities	Extreme blight on the area and interference with the natural environment	No major adverse effects from placement of facilities

sites rated favorably on high-priority criteria from those with good ratings on low-priority items. At the moment, he favored Moss Landing because it was superior for the criteria ranked second, third, and fourth. Specifically, Moss Landing was

1. The cheapest to build.
2. The cheapest to operate.
3. The closest to Richmond.

CASE 8
C. K. COOLIDGE, INC. (A)

On a Sunday in mid-September 1993, Christine Schilling was in the office of Ralph Purcell, president of C. K. Coolidge, Inc. (CKC). Schilling, recently hired as Purcell's analyst, was presenting the details of an analysis she had prepared on Saturday. Purcell hoped that by the end of the afternoon, aided by Schilling's insights, he would be able to establish a course of action that might hasten the final settlement of a patent suit brought against CKC three years earlier by the Tolemite Corporation and its licensee, Barton Research and Development (BARD).

The Contenders

CKC was founded in Milwaukee, Wisconsin, in 1932 as a commercial outlet for the inventive genius of Dr. Charles K. Coolidge, an astute organic chemist. The company had weathered the Great Depression and then participated in the prosperity associated with World War II and the postwar years. By 1970, annual sales were in the neighborhood of $3 million.

Dr. Coolidge owned and managed the company until 1980, when, desiring to retire, he sold it along with all its patents and products to Arrow Industries, a small Chicago-based conglomerate. CKC continued to prosper as an Arrow subsidiary and by 1993 had annual sales of $10.5 million,[1] 14 percent of the Arrow total. About 10 percent of CKC's sales in 1993 were derived from a chemical component called Varacil, whose manufacturing process was the subject of the patent suit. The remainder of its sales included a wide range of specialty organic chemical products, sold in relatively small volume, primarily to the pharmaceutical industry.

Tolemite, also headquartered in Chicago, was a large chemical and pharmaceutical manufacturer with estimated 1993 sales in excess of $300 million. In 1984, Tolemite had been awarded a patent covering various aspects of a new, low-cost method for synthesizing Varacil. The techniques covered by the patent had been discovered at Tolemite's research facility in 1979 as an offshoot of another project. Because Tolemite was neither a user nor a producer of Varacil, it had decided to offer the use of the patent, under license, to BARD, the principal Varacil producer in the United States.

---

[1] Based on actual sales for January–August and an estimate for September–December.

Copyright © 1993 by the President and Fellows of Harvard College.
Harvard Business School case 894-017
This case was prepared by Donald L. Wallace under the direction of Dr. John S. Hammond III as the basis for class discussion rather than to illustrate either effective or ineffective handling of an administrative situation. Reprinted by permission of the Harvard Business School.

BARD, located in Evanston, Illinois, had begun as a small research company. By 1984, however, it had dropped all research and was involved solely in the production of Varacil. To maintain its position as industry leader, BARD had accepted Tolemite's licensing offer and had converted all Varacil production to the new process. In return for the use of the patent, BARD had agreed to pay Tolemite a 4 percent royalty on all sales of synthetic Varacil. In addition, BARD had received rights to sublicense any other Varacil producers who became interested in the process and to work out individual royalty agreements with producing firms. Under these sublicensing agreements, royalties of 4 percent would go to Tolemite, and any excess would accrue to BARD.

In 1989, five years after Tolemite had received its patent, a research chemist at CKC had, quite independently, discovered a very similar process for synthesizing Varacil. The CKC researchers, however, had not felt that the new processing techniques could be patented. Thus, no patent search had been initiated and production facilities had simply been converted to the new process. At the time, no one at CKC had suspected the degree to which its new process was similar to the one originated by Tolemite and covered by Tolemite's patent. It was with some surprise then that CKC management learned that it was being sued by Tolemite and BARD for patent infringement.

Varacil

Varacil was a chemical substance sold almost exclusively to pharmaceutical manufacturers. Although it appeared in a variety of drug preparations, it represented only a minor fraction of any one drug. The economics of its manufacturing (high fixed and low variable costs plus economies of scale), however, suggested that it be made in relatively long runs involving substantial volume. Thus the major drug companies themselves were not involved in its preparation.

Before 1984, Varacil had been processed from naturally occurring organic chemicals found in animal tissue. As a result of the high cost of these natural chemicals, the cost of Varacil itself had been relatively high. With the advent of synthetic Varacil, this situation was dramatically changed. Variable costs in the manufacture of synthetic Varacil represented only about 15 percent of sales, so the synthetic soon drove the natural product virtually out of the market. (A few Varacil users still specified the natural product in the belief that it had certain superior properties.)

In 1993, the national market for synthetic Varacil amounted to some $9 million in sales. On a unit basis (pounds sold) this market had been relatively stable for several years. As drugs requiring Varacil had been phased out, new ones requiring similar amounts of the compound had always seemed to appear. There was, furthermore, no reason to believe that this stability would be lost over the next several years. Industry unit sales projected thus tended to be quite flat as far as 5 and 10 years out.

On the dollar value side, however, the story was quite different. Prices for Varacil, and industry dollar sales as well, had been in decline for several years.

EXHIBIT 1   Unit and Dollar Sales of Synthetic Varacil by Company

	Bard		Coolidge		All Others	
Year	Lbs.	$	Lbs.	$	Lbs.	$
1984	1,000	153,000	0	0	0	0
1985	5,000	738,000	0	0	0	0
1986	20,000	2,676,000	0	0	0	0
1987	60,000	6,569,000	0	0	0	0
1988	68,000	8,022,000	0	0	0	0
1989	76,000	9,045,000	0	0	0	0
1990	83,000	9,624,000	1,000	111,000	0	0
1991	89,000	9,546,000	6,000	576,000	2,000	213,000
1992	94,000	7,899,000	11,000	936,000	19,000	1,608,000
1993*	100,000	6,000,000	17,000	1,050,000	35,000	2,100,000
1994	100,000	6,000,000	17,000	1,020,000	35,000	2,100,000
1995	100,000	5,700,000	17,000	969,000	35,000	1,995,000
1996	100,000	5,400,000	17,000	918,000	35,000	1,890,000
1997	100,000	4,800,000	17,000	816,000	35,000	1,680,000
1998	100,000	4,500,000	17,000	765,000	35,000	1,575,000
1999	100,000	4,500,000	17,000	765,000	35,000	1,575,000
2000	100,000	4,500,000	17,000	765,000	35,000	1,575,000
2001	100,000	4,500,000	17,000	765,000	35,000	1,575,000
2002	100,000	4,500,000	17,000	765,000	35,000	1,575,000
2003	100,000	4,500,000	17,000	765,000	35,000	1,575,000
2004	100,000	4,500,000	17,000	765,000	35,000	1,575,000

*Estimated.

Note: Total unit sales of Varacil (including the natural product) were roughly 150,000 lbs. annually for the period 1984–93. Sales for 1984–93 were actual; sales for 1994–2004 were projected.

Source: C. K. Coolidge, Inc.

When converting to the synthetic process, each competitor in the industry had tooled up to supply an optimistic share of the market. Then, when market share objectives were not met, prices were slashed in an attempt to keep manufacturing facilities operating at efficient levels and to bring in as much contribution as possible toward fixed costs. This situation was expected to continue for at least five years. Exhibit 1 shows industry unit and dollar sales of synthetic Varacil for the period 1984–93, as well as projections for 1994–2004.

In 1993, there were seven principal competitors in the synthetic Varacil market. BARD, with $6 million in sales, took 67 percent of the market. CKC, with $1,050,000 in sales, was the second largest operator and held a 12 percent share. The remaining five competitors, none of whose Varacil sales exceeded $570,000, then constituted the remaining 21 percent of the market. By 1990, all seven of the principal competitors were manufacturing synthetic Varacil by nearly identical processes. Only BARD, however, was paying royalties to Tolemite.

Background on the Litigation

On June 12, 1990, Tolemite and BARD had jointly filed suit in the Superior Court of the Fifth District of Wisconsin charging CKC with having infringed on Tolemite's patent. To remedy the infringement, Tolemite and BARD were seeking a royalty payment of 20 percent of all of Coolidge's future sales of synthetic Varacil over what remained on the 17-year life of the patent, as well as a lump-sum indemnity to cover past sales.

When confronted with the suit, Purcell had immediately discussed the matter with Aaron Mantiris, general counsel for Arrow Industries. Both men had felt there was considerable evidence indicating that Tolemite's process might not be patentable. At Mantiris's suggestion, CKC had obtained the services of Evans and Blaylock, a well-known and highly reputable firm of patent attorneys in New York. These attorneys agreed with Mantiris on the potential weakness of the Tolemite suit. Thus, in 1990, Evans and Blaylock had begun to prepare a case for CKC's defense.

Tolemite's patent contained 12 claims of originality. To obtain it, Tolemite, like all successful patent applicants, had had to demonstrate to the patent examiners that there was no "prior art," and that there was invention. Prior art could consist of previous patents, applied-for patents, or processes in the public domain—unpatentable but generally known—that were similar. To show invention, it was necessary to demonstrate that the applied-for process was not obvious to a person reasonably knowledgeable about related chemical processes.

Any patent was always subject to later challenge in the courts. All or part of a patent could be overturned on the basis of prior art or absence of invention. As a practical matter, it was sometimes possible to argue the absence of invention years later. Ideas that had seemed novel at the time of the invention often seemed far more obvious at a later date. The patent holder, in defense, attempted to reemphasize the novelty of the ideas at the time of the invention. Nevertheless, there were many instances of patents being successfully challenged. In the matter of synthetic Varacil, Mantiris argued that Tolemite had not, in fact, introduced any novelty. It had merely observed and harnessed a naturally occurring process which, in itself, was not patentable.

A patent holder whose patent was infringed was entitled to sue the infringer for sales and profit wrongfully gotten. In determining the amount to be demanded in a lawsuit, the plaintiff usually calculated these damages in a way most favorable to itself. However, if the plaintiff prevailed in court, the actual damages awarded were often considerably less. In the Varacil matter it was the opinion of both the Evans and Blaylock lawyers and Mantiris that the royalty amount awarded, if CKC lost the suit, would be approximately 10 percent, or about half of the amount demanded.

From 1990 to 1993, a partner in Evans and Blaylock worked intermittently in liaison with Mantiris researching and preparing the case. CKC considered the suit to be little more than a nuisance and was content to drag its feet in hope that Tolemite's case might simply collapse from inertia. Late in 1992, however, a tentative trial date was set for January 1993. Before a firm date could be set, Purcell and Mantiris decided, with the concurrence of the patent attorneys, to make at least a token effort at a pretrial settlement. Their offer amounted to the payment of all future liabilities at a royalty rate of 2.5 percent of sales. This offer was rejected out of hand by Tolemite and BARD. Eventually, the case reached the court docket and a trial date in October 1993 was set.

By September, Purcell was becoming uneasy over the high—and increasing—level of attorneys' fees. These fees had already reached a total of $300,000 and, if the trial were to take place as scheduled, they would surely loom large in comparison with the total value of any successful defense. Furthermore, these legal fees and any future ones would not be recoverable, even if CKC won its case.

In response to this uneasiness about both the progress of the suit and the alarming accumulation of the attorneys' fees, Purcell decided on two immediate actions. First he arranged, through Mantiris, for a meeting in New York City to review the case thoroughly with the patent attorneys. Second, he asked his new analyst, Schilling, to review the case and, he hoped, to bring a fresh viewpoint to bear.

Schilling's Analysis and the Meeting with the Patent Attorneys

Christine Schilling was a recent graduate of the Harvard Business School, who was quite interested in the quantitative analysis of decision problems. Thus her approach to this problem took the form of a decision tree. It recognized two options open to CKC:

1. Go to court and contest the patent, which would cost an additional $150,000 in legal fees and lead to winning the suit with probability X or losing it with probability $1-X$; or
2. Settle out of court for an amount $Y\%$ of past and future sales. She summarized these options in the decision diagram shown in Figure A.

Her analysis sought to determine for any given out-of-court settlement offer Y, how large the probability X of winning the suit would have to be to justify rejecting the offer. To do this break-even analysis she solved the following equation for X, given various values of Y:

$$[\text{Cost of winning}] \, (X) + [\text{Cost of losing}] \, (1-X) = [\text{Cost of settlement at } Y\%]$$

This resulted in the break-even curve shown in Figure B. For all offers above the curve it was preferable to go to court. Offers below the line were worthy of consideration. For example, if CKC personnel felt that the probability of winning was 0.6, then settling up to a 7.5 percent royalty rate (shown by the dotted line in Figure B) could be justified.

Schilling's principal conclusion from this analysis was that, unless the odds on winning the suit were extremely good, any reasonable pretrial settlement was preferable to paying the additional costs and taking a chance on going to court. Purcell, a chemical engineer, was himself well attuned to quantitative analysis and, in fact, liked to support his own arguments with numerical data whenever possible. He was intrigued by Schilling's presentation and invited her to join him and Mantiris on the trip to New York City to meet with the patent attorneys.

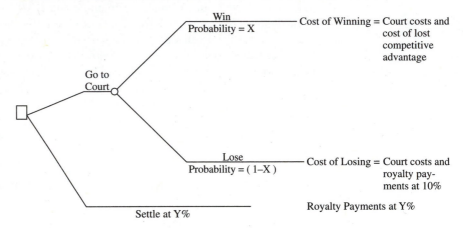

Win
Probability = X
Cost of Winning = Court costs and
cost of lost
competitive
advantage

Go to
Court

Lose
Probability = (1–X)
Cost of Losing = Court costs and
royalty pay-
ments at 10%

Settle at Y%
Royalty Payments at Y%

Note: If CKC wins the suit, BARD would no longer have to pay 4% royalty to Tolemite. Because of the highly competitive nature of the industry, Schilling believed that BARD would pass this savings along to customers, forcing CKC to retaliate. Thus CKC's revenues would be reduced from the status quo by 4% if the suit is won.

FIGURE B   Break-even Curve

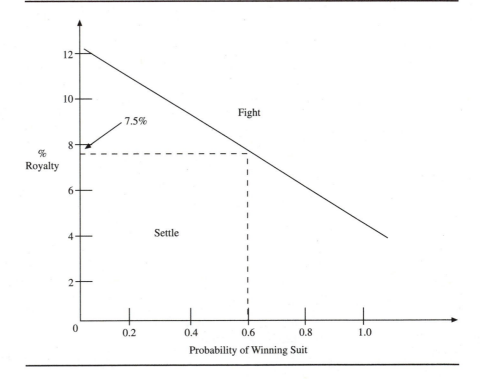

%
Royalty

7.5%

Fight

Settle

Probability of Winning Suit

At that meeting Purcell intended to confront the attorneys with Schilling's analysis and then to obtain their opinion on the benefits of pursuing the case to trial.

In New York the patent attorneys began the meeting by presenting an outline of their case. Everyone attending agreed that the case was indeed a strong one with a high probability of success in the trial phase. The attorneys demurred, however, when asked to give a precise figure for their probability of success in court. At that point, Purcell sketched out Schilling's analysis. He then asked the patent attorneys if they still felt that their probability of success was high enough to merit going to trial. The attorneys were visibly uncomfortable with Schilling's approach. Although they remained convinced of the merits of their case, they agreed that some rethinking was probably necessary before proceeding to trial.

On the flight back to Milwaukee, Purcell discussed with his general counsel and his analyst what had happened at the meeting. As a result of that conversation he decided that Schilling should pursue her analysis further and take into account such things as potential appeals and to appraise the sensitivity of the analysis to the underlying assumptions. All three agreed that settlements well in excess of 2.5 percent would, in all probability, be preferable to a court fight.

Final Analysis

The next day, Saturday, Schilling broadened her analysis as Purcell had requested. The expanded analysis took into account the possibility of appeals by Tolemite or CKC and the additional legal expenses in the event of appeals. The result was the revised break-even curve shown in Figure C, which strengthened the conclusion that any reasonable settlement would be preferable to going to court. (The complete analysis is presented in the Appendix.) On Sunday afternoon Schilling presented her findings to Purcell in an informal meeting and they began to map a strategy for resolving the suit.

APPENDIX
CHRISTINE SCHILLING'S ANALYSIS

Objective: To determine the range of payment Arrow Industries can offer to pay in pretrial settlement relative to future costs and the probability of success in court.

Conclusion: If the likelihood of winning the trial is between 75% and 100% Arrow can pay a pretrial settlement royalty rate of up to 8.5% and save money. In fact, Arrow can afford to pay a royalty rate of 7% even if the probability of winning the trial is 100%, because of the magnitude of future attorneys' fees and subsequent appeals. (See Figure C for the break-even probability curve.)

FIGURE C   **Revised Break-even Curve**

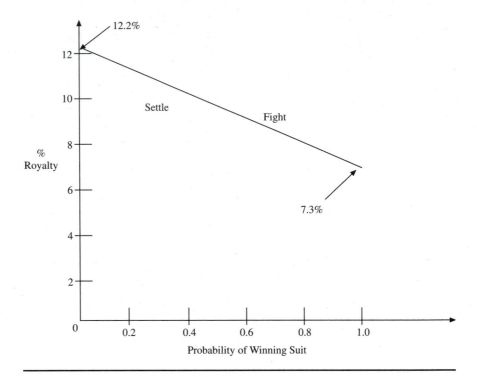

Assumptions:

I.   Expected Proceedings:
    A.   If Arrow wins the trial, there is a 90% chance that Tolemite will appeal.
    B.   If Tolemite wins the trial, there is a 10% chance that Arrow will appeal.
    C.   If Arrow wins the trial, there is a 75% chance that Arrow will win the appeal.
    D.   If Tolemite wins the trial, there is a 75% chance that Tolemite will win the appeal.

II.   Future Attorneys' Fees and Court Costs Will Be:
    A.   For the trial—$150,000
    B.   For the appeal:
        1.   If Arrow wins the trial—$75,000.
        2.   If Tolemite wins the trial—$150,000.

III.   Exposure to Liability:
    A.   Past liabilities:
        1.   If Tolemite wins the trial, it will be awarded 10% of sales 1990–1993—total liability of $267,300.
        2.   Tolemite will settle past liabilities prior to the trial at the same royalty rate applied in future sales. (See III.B.2.)

B. Future royalties:
   1. If Tolemite wins the trial, it will receive 10% of future sales.
   2. The Tolemite pretrial settlement royalty requirement is unknown but will be approached in this analysis as that rate at which Arrow Industries would break even in the alternative of facing the costs and risks of trial. (See Figure C.)

IV. Actual Royalty Costs Involved:
   A. C. K. Coolidge will continue to produce 17,000 pounds of Varacil per year for the next seven years (remaining life of the patent).
   B. The price/pound for Varacil will erode as expected and produce the total sales shown in Table A–1.
   C. In this industry of high fixed and low variable costs, resulting in severe pressure upon price, BARD will have a competitive advantage directly proportional to the royalty differential between itself and CKC. The assumption is that it will lower the price, rather than simply absorb extra profit. The extent of BARD's use of this advantage and its significance on CKC's profitability will be illustrated in the analysis.
   D. The "value of money" to the corporation is approximately 10%.

Analysis: The objective of this analysis is to define, in general terms, the relationship between the future expenses and risks faced in the Tolemite suit with the cost of an immediate settlement. An attempt has been made to break the overall problem into a number of smaller events and action alternatives and to assess reasonable ranges of event probability and consequence; these elements are then related mathematically to obtain a solution.

TABLE A–1   Present Value of Royalties and Lost Competitive Advantage ($ in thousands)

Year	Discount Factor*	Sales	Cost of 10% Royalty Payments and Past Liability Claims		Cost of 4% Lost Competitive Advantage		Cost of Settlement at 8% Royalty	
			Royalty (10%)	NPV[†]	Lost Competitive Advantage (4%)	NPV	Royalty (8%)	NPV
0	1.000	$2,673[‡]	$267.3	$267.3	—	—	$213.9	$213.9
1	0.909	1,020	102.0	92.7	$40.8	$37.2	81.6	74.1
2	0.826	969	96.9	80.1	38.7	31.8	77.4	63.9
3	0.751	918	60.9	69.0	36.6	27.6	73.5	55.2
4	0.683	816	81.6	55.8	32.7	22.2	65.4	44.4
5	0.621	765	76.5	47.4	30.6	18.9	61.2	38.1
6	0.564	765	76.5	43.2	30.6	17.4	61.2	34.5
7	0.513	765	76.5	39.3	30.6	15.6	61.2	31.2
				$694.8		$170.7		$555.3

* Rate = 10%.
[†] Net present value.
[‡] Past sales (1990–93).

FIGURE A–1 Decision Diagram

COSTS

(1) $395,700
(2) $919,800
(3) $320,700
(4) $470,700
(5) $994,800
(6) $844,800
(7) Independent Variable

Arrow Wins (.75)
Arrow Loses (.25)
[$526.6] Tolemite Appeals (.9)
No Appeal (.1)
[506.1] Arrow Wins (X)

Arrow Wins (.25)
Arrow Loses (.75)
[863.7] Arrow Appeals (.1)
No Appeal (.9)
[846.6] Arrow Loses (1-X)

Go to Court
Settle

50

There can be a substantial advantage in this approach in illuminating the basic issues, which generally remained submerged in a single assessment of the entire situation. There is a potential danger in quantification and simplification of complex problems—the result is apparently so precise and straightforward that it can be very easily overlooked that this result is no better than the assumptions on which it is based.

Based on the above assumptions and the decision diagram shown in Figure A–1, the following costs were calculated:

1. Cost associated with Endpoint (1)   (Arrow wins trial, Tolemite appeals, Arrow wins appeal)

Present value of 4% lost competitive advantage (See Table A–1)	=	$170,700
Appeal cost	=	75,000
Trial costs	=	150,000
Total		$395,700

2. Cost associated with Endpoint (2)   (Arrow wins trial, Tolemite appeals, Arrow loses appeal)

Present value of royalty payments and past liability claims at 10% (Table A–1)	=	$694,800
Appeal costs	=	75,000
Trial costs	=	150,000
Total		$919,800

3. Cost associated with Endpoint (3)   (Arrow wins trial, no appeal)

Present value of 4% lost competitive advantage	=	$170,700
Trial costs	=	150,000
Total		$320,700

4. Cost associated with Endpoint (4)   (Arrow loses trial, Arrow appeals, Arrow wins appeal)

Present value of 4% lost competitive advantage	=	$170,700
Appeal costs	=	150,000
Trial costs	=	150,000
Total		$470,700

5. Cost associated with Endpoint (5)   (Arrow loses trial, Arrow appeals, Arrow loses appeal)

Present value of royalty payments and past liability claims at 10%	=	$694,800
Appeal costs	=	150,000
Trial costs	=	150,000
Total		$994,800

6. Cost associated with Endpoint (6)   (Arrow loses trial, Arrow does not appeal)

Present value of royalty payments and past liability claims at 10%	=	$694,800
Trial costs	=	150,000
Total		$844,800

The next step is to find, for a given settlement rate of $Y\%$ royalty, the probability of winning the trial that will make the expected cost of going to court equal to the cost of the settlement. For example, assuming a settlement rate of 8% royalty payments, the present value of the cost of settlement is $555,300 as shown in Table A–1. The break-even probability of winning, X, could be calculated from the following equation:

$$\text{Expected cost of going to court} = \text{Cost of settlement}$$

$$\$506,100X + 846,600\,(1\text{–}X) = \$555,300$$

$$\text{To get: } X = 0.85$$

Solving this equation for different settlement rates resulted in the break-even probability curve shown in Figure C.

H. Franklin Nilson sipped on a tankard of ale and surveyed the guests in the lounge of The Commerce Tavern. As usual, the room was filled, and Nilson was pleased to see that everything was running smoothly. His staff had no particular problems in handling the full house—an empty table at The Commerce was a rarity. Ever since its opening in 1982, Nilson's establishment had enjoyed all the business it could handle. Even though it was mid-October, Nilson was content in the knowledge that The Commerce was booked solid, straight through the holiday season. The first available reservation was for mid-January.

Nilson's thoughts this particular evening drifted to his recent conversation with Anne Hamlet of the Virginia Merchants Bank (VMB). Over the past several weeks, Hamlet had been providing Nilson with information regarding the potential acceptance of credit cards at the tavern. The Commerce Tavern had never accepted credit cards, personal checks, or house charges. Nilson often wondered if this cash-only policy hurt his business. He had been pleasantly surprised to learn that Hamlet and VMB were quite willing to authorize The Commerce to honor MasterCard and Visa cards. He also realized that, if this change in credit policy were to be attractive, the fees levied by VMB would have to be made up by increased business. Nilson always struggled with decisions like this one, and, as he returned to his ale, he decided to think about it later.

The Tavern

For over a decade, The Commerce Tavern had enjoyed the reputation of being one of the finest colonial-cuisine restaurants in Colonial Williamsburg. Located in Merchants Square, a business-and-shopping district at the west end of Duke of Gloucester Street, the tavern was adjacent to the Historic Area but technically outside it. Even so, Merchants Square was a stop on the free bus route through Colonial Williamsburg.

The Commerce Tavern, like all other buildings in Merchants Square, was designed in a late-18th-century style. It was patterned after the typical alehouse of that era: a center entrance with a large room on either side (the public bar to the left and the lounge to the right). The traditional division of rowdiness in the public bar and gentility in the lounge was not maintained at The Commerce. Both rooms provided the guests of the tavern the opportunity for elegant dining in a quiet and intimate atmosphere. The rooms were illuminated only by candlelight, were paneled in hand-rubbed walnut, and were decorated simply with "alehouse artifacts" of colonial times and with flowers of the season. To complete the colonial effect, the service staff dressed in period attire. The Commerce was proud of the colonial charm and ambience it had created in a modern building.

EXHIBIT 1   **Typical Menu**

Commerce Tavern

~ Bill of Fare ~
Choice of entrée denotes price of entire meal

~ Relish Tray ~
Spiced Cantaloupe   Pickled Onions
Moist Quinces   English Chop Pickle

~ Choice of Soups ~
Peanut Soup   Terrapin Stew
Cat Fish Chowder   Mulligatawny Soup

~ Choice of Flesh or Fowl ~
English Steak and Kidney Pie $13.95   Oxford John $14.95
The Kings Roast Beef $15.95   Buttered Shrimp $14.95
Williamsburg Veal Partridges $15.95   Baked Stuffed Sturgeon $13.95

~ Selection of Fresh Vegetables, of the Season ~
~ Green Salad ~

~ Bread Tray, served with creamery butter ~
Williamsburg Buns   Coach Wheels
Sally Lunn   Sweet Potato Buns

~ Choice of Dessert ~
Blanc Mange   Indian Pudding
Regency Trifle   Pumpkin Pye
Plum Ice Cream   Deep Dish Apple Pye

~ Your choice of fine Coffees and Teas ~

Many believed that the dining experience provided by The Commerce was on a par with that of the Kings Arms Tavern and Christiana Campbell's Tavern in the Historic Area. The Commerce had been featured in several gourmet magazines and had received three stars from a popular guidebook. The tavern offered a limited menu of well-prepared, authentic Colonial dishes. The price of an entrée ranged from $13.95 to $15.95 and included relishes, a choice of soups, vegetables of the season, a green salad, breads of the house, and a choice of dessert with a selection of coffees and teas. The bill of fare is shown in Exhibit 1. The tavern offered full

---

EXHIBIT 2   Budget for 1993 (revised 10/5/93)*

Revenues:
Food	$560,000
Wine/liquor	180,000
Total	$740,000

Expenses:
Food	$168,000
Wine/liquor	44,000
Service staff	68,800
Administrative staff	40,000
Utilities	20,000
Trash	2,000
Supplies	10,000
Fringe	13,000
Interest	64,000
Laundry	26,500
Total	$456,300

* Reflects actual revenues and expenses for the first three quarters of 1993 and projections for the final quarter.

bar service emphasizing specialty drinks of imported ales, grogs, and punches priced from $1.75 to $3.50. In addition, The Commerce maintained an extensive wine cellar of domestic and European wines ranging in price from $12 to $36 a bottle.

The Commerce's reputation was so renowned that virtually every table was occupied for each of its two sittings on both Friday and Saturday nights. As a result, approximately 400 guests were served each night. Even though Nilson had experienced considerable public pressure to open the tavern for weekday dining, he had resisted the temptation. Weekday service would interfere with his personal involvement with the tavern, and he believed that operating at full capacity provided very attractive efficiencies. Exhibit 2 presents the tavern's budget for 1993.

Nilson believed that a substantial portion of his patrons came from the Williamsburg area—townspeople as well as faculty and students of the College of William and Mary. Because of the lead time on reservations, less than one-third of his guests were visitors to Williamsburg and most of those diners were returning for another visit. As a result of the strong base of local customers, The Commerce had barely noticed the periodic tourist crises that had virtually crippled most other establishments in the area.

Visa and MasterCard

Virginia Merchants Bank had sent Nilson the standard bank credit-card-participation agreement. This agreement specified in great detail the responsibilities of The Commerce with respect to credit-card transactions. In particular, for each transaction, it was the restaurant's responsibility to (1) check the expiration date of the card, (2) check that the card number did not appear on any restricted- or revoked-card bulletin, (3) check that the card was signed on the back and that the cardholder's signature on the sales slip was similar, and (4) fill out correctly the sales slip furnished by the bank with the required information. On delivery of a sales slip to the bank within three bank–business days of the sales slip's completion, the bank agreed to credit the restaurant immediately for the face amount of the sales slip less a fee computed at the rate that was in effect at that time. The agreement required the bank to give written notice within 30 days of any change in the fee.

Hamlet had informed Nilson during an earlier telephone conversation that the initial rate charged The Commerce would be 4 percent—the rate charged all new participants in the Virginia Merchants Bank Credit Card Agreement. She mentioned that this rate would remain in effect for a year, at the end of which the bank would review the account. The rate would probably be lowered at that time based on the total yearly credit-card sales of The Commerce. If the total credit-card sales for the year were greater than $500,000, the rate would be lowered to 2 percent. If, however, total yearly credit-card sales were less than $200,000, the rate would remain at 4 percent. For totals between $200,000 and $500,000, the rate would be set at 3 percent. Hamlet said that there was no set period for subsequent reviews, but she hinted that this new rate would remain in effect for at least a couple of years.

Hamlet had also sent Nilson credit-card-usage information (see Exhibit 3) that she said might help give a rough idea about which of the three rates (2 percent, 3 percent, or 4 percent) The Commerce would end up paying. Unfortunately, the bank did not have information on total-sales dollars or increases in total sales after credit cards had been accepted at similar restaurants. In Hamlet's words:

> Oh yes, I'm sure that most businesses see an increase in sales after honoring Visa and MasterCard cards, sometimes up to 50 percent. But, as I'm sure you appreciate, our participants hold their total-sales data in confidence and don't share them with me, let alone allow me to distribute them to potential clients. It's tough enough getting cooperation on usage data, let alone total sales. I do remember, however, hearing about a recent article in a restaurant journal that concluded that credit cards were economically attractive if only 1 additional customer in 10 comes to your restaurant because you honor credit cards.

Nilson reviewed the chart provided by Hamlet. He was familiar with all the establishments listed on it. With the exception of the family restaurants, The Laughing Lobster and Bill and Ellen's Family Steak House, each restaurant had a price range comparable to that of The Commerce and distinctive cuisine or decor that would attract patrons similar to those of The Commerce. As a result, credit-card usage at The Commerce could well be like the usage at any of the eight restaurants. Unfortunately, when Nilson focused his attention on the previous year's data, no consistent pattern emerged. The usage

---

Exhibit 3   Credit-Card Usage

	Bills Paid by Credit Card (%)		
Restaurant	*1990*	*1991*	*1992*
Madison Inn	40%	39%	39%
Italian-American menu, partly à la carte, $3.95–$16.95			
Specialties: spare ribs, seafood, fresh-fruit rum cake			
Candlelit			
Lordsmill	38	35	38
Continental-American menu, partly à la carte, $6.25–$12.75			
Specialties: *escalopes de veau,* fresh seafood, veal Oscar			
Contemporary decor, facing the James River			
The Laughing Lobster	19	20	19
Seafood menu, partly à la carte, $4.95–$9.95			
Specialties: fresh seafood, all-you-can-eat specials			
Family restaurant			
Grecian Urn	51	51	52
Continental-American menu, partly à la carte, $6.50–$15.95			
Specialties: shrimp à la Grecque, moussaka			
Owned by chef			
Black Beard's Hold	70	70	69
American menu, partly à la carte, $6.95–$16.95			
Specialties: seafood, steak			
Nautical decor			
Settlement Dining Room	29	29	25
Varied menu, partly à la carte, $6.95–$9.75			
Specialties: veal Oscar, Virginia ham, seafood kabob			
Colonial decor			
Bill and Ellen's Family Steak House	10	12	12
American menu, partly à la carte, $3.95–$7.95			
Specialties: charbroiled steaks			
Family restaurant			
The Salty Dog Inn	43	41	42
Continental-American menu, partly à la carte, $3.95–$12.95			
Specialties: broiled seafood, crab rolled in Smithfield ham			
Owned by chef, waterfront			
Neptune's Seafood Pavilion	44	47	44
Continental-American menu, partly à la carte, $8–$16			
Specialties: lobster Bien Dien rice, seafood shish kabob			
Grecian atmosphere, art collection			
Peyton's Ordinary	60	62	61
Varied menu, partly à la carte, $4.95–$14.95			
Specialties: fresh seafood, Virginia ham			
Colonial-tavern decor, built in 1732			

---

ranged from 25 percent to 69 percent. He observed that a usage rate of 43 percent was the median of the data and that 38 percent and 57 percent seemed to divide the data in half again. These figures certainly left the issue of the extent of credit-card usage at The Commerce rather ambiguous.

Further Investigations

Nilson devoted the next day, Sunday, to obtaining more information about credit cards. He first stopped at the College of William and Mary Business Library to find the article to which Hamlet had referred. He looked up everything he could find on credit cards. The only relevant article appeared in *Food Service Marketing* and did report Hamlet's figure of 1-in-10. As he had feared, the article focused on increases in the number of customers, a phenomenon from which The Commerce would not benefit. The article did point out, however, that the honoring of credit cards might be justified by increased customer spending: The credit-card user need not worry about having sufficient cash to cover the bill or about the impact that the restaurant check might have on a monthly budget.

He then decided to contact several acquaintances in the restaurant business. The information he received was mixed. One friend, Marcia Fitzgerald of The Barnacle, stated that The Barnacle had always honored credit cards and had never considered dropping them. Fitzgerald said, "We have found that credit-card customers almost always spend more than cash customers, and almost half my customers use credit cards." Nilson found this comment rather encouraging.

A second call, to Paul Pickering of The Wayside Inn, brought up an area that Nilson had not considered—the errors that could be made in filling out the sales slip.

> Didn't you read paragraph 3 of the VMB Agreement? If you mess up, you lose. After my hostess accepted three or four expired cards, I had to tell her that the next one was coming out of her pay. Also, you do realize that the bank takes its cut off of the grand total, a total that includes the 4 percent sales tax and tips?

This perspective was rather disconcerting, but Nilson decided that his host and hostess would not make these kinds of mistakes and, regardless, he would institute Paul Pickering's policy from the start. In addition, for those tips charged on credit cards, he would reimburse his staff for the tips less the bank's charge on them. Although he believed they might object to the idea initially, he could argue that the customers would not only spend more when using credit cards but also tip at a higher percentage. Finally, regarding the bank's attaching its fee to the sales tax, Nilson asked himself, "What's 4 percent of 4 percent, anyway?"

A crucial factor in the decision would be the increase in the amount spent on food and drink by someone using a credit card over what he or she might have spent if cash were required. There was no easy way to figure out what this percentage might be: The experience of other restaurants was irrelevant, because of differences in clientele and menu; questionnaires would not measure actual behavior, just expectations; and a trial period was ruled out, because of its disruptive effects. Nilson decided that his only option was to draw on his experience in running The Commerce. Over the years, he had overheard many of his customers' conversations concerning their food and wine decisions and had gained some insight, albeit loosely structured, into how the cash-only policy influenced those choices.

After thinking about those experiences and reviewing his menu and wine list, Nilson believed that the increase in the dollar amount of bills paid by credit card was just as likely to be more than 5 percent as less than 5 percent when compared with bills paid by cash. Nilson also decided that the increase in a year's credit-card sales over what those same customers might have spent using cash would have to amount to something—say, 1 percent at a minimum—but it was inconceivable that the increase could ever reach 15 percent. Approaching a finer estimate, Nilson believed it was three times as likely that the yearly increase would be less than 8 percent as more than 8 percent, and three times as likely to be over 3 percent as under. Having seen the year-to-year consistency in credit-card usage in Hamlet's data, Nilson thought that the increased spending experienced in the first year would hold for several years.

As Nilson reviewed the results of his inquiries of the past few days, he saw clearly that the decision hinged on the trade-off between the increase in sales and the discount taken by the bank. He decided to evaluate this opportunity—just as he evaluated projects in his other businesses—by using a 20 percent hurdle rate and by considering the next three years only.

It then occurred to Nilson that he might want to back out of the arrangement—say, after a year—if it did not turn out to be profitable. On Monday, he called Hamlet to see if there was any penalty for such an action. She replied,

> Well, the bank will not reimburse you for unused sales slips, but we will buy back, for $15, the credit-slip imprinter you originally purchased for $25. Other than that, there is really no other penalty, except perhaps a few confused and angry customers.

CASE 10
CYBERLAB: A NEW BUSINESS OPPORTUNITY FOR PRICO (A)

The Precision Instrument Corporation (PRICO) was a major manufacturer of equipment used in the research laboratory. CyberLab, a new venture in the field of lab robotics, had just offered 30 percent of CyberLab equity to PRICO in exchange for $1 million in capital and a marketing agreement. Under the plan, PRICO would market all of CyberLab products through its existing international distribution system. CyberLab had a patent pending on its robot system and had just finished construction of a small manufacturing facility in New Milford, Connecticut. It also had operational prototypes for all its products, but now needed a capital infusion to develop a major manufacturing facility and to provide working capital for expanded operations. Some aspects of the CyberLab proposal were attractive to James Campbell, president of PRICO, but others were downright frightening. A significant new market could be harvested by his company, or the million dollar investment could vanish down a rat hole. Campbell needed to understand the financial soundness of PRICO's opportunity.

The Inception of CyberLab

Cyberlab had started in 1985 as a result of the frustration of Dr. H. Meltzer, a biochemist working at the New York Psychiatric Institute. Dr. Meltzer was preparing and testing human enzymes[1] in bioassays.[2] Preparing samples was taking an inordinate amount of time and expense; human enzymes were extremely expensive, and manual sample preparation tended to waste enzyme. Dr. Meltzer was looking for an automated system that could prepare his samples, but none existed with the accuracy and reliability he needed for his tests. When he outlined his needs to his son, Walter Meltzer thought a system could be developed and the project began.

Two years later, the CyberLab system prototype was complete. Walter had designed the prototype with the idea that, eventually, all the components that needed machining could be subcontracted, and the remaining parts could be purchased from readily available sources.

---

[1]Enzymes are complex protein substances that are essential to life. They act as catalysts in promoting reactions at cell temperatures without undergoing destruction in the process.

[2]A bioassay is the determination of the relative effective strength of a new substance by comparing its effect on a test organism with that of a standard substance.

This case was prepared in conjunction with Research Assistant Larry Weatherford (Darden). It was based on a Supervised Business Study by Thomas E. Johnstone (Darden Class of 1988). Some numbers and the name of the interested party have been disguised.

Laboratory Robotics

Francis Zenie, president of a major lab-robot developer and manufacturer (Zymark Corporation), summed up the need for laboratory automation: "You've got 10 or 20 years of advancements in instrumental data measurements and data reduction, but our interviews revealed that people are still preparing samples like they did in the Dark Ages." Zymark personnel spent six months interviewing laboratory chemists and chemical-industry personnel by asking "What is your biggest problem?" The most common answer: sample preparation prior to analysis. Zymark correctly identified a need for new technology and introduced the first laboratory robot in 1982.

Laboratory technicians worked in the 2-D environment: *d*ull and *d*emanding. Preparing lab samples was tedious and required a high level of concentration. Humans could work as quickly as robots, but robots could maintain their work pace indefinitely (excluding maintenance and downtime) and were not prone to such errors as mixing up samples. The advantage of robotics lay in the increased output, enhanced consistency of preparations, and lower labor costs. Most robots currently on the market operated on a workstation principle, with the station arranged in a circle about an arm fixed in the center. The arm moved the sample to the stations for various preparations and tests. The CyberLab 800, however, worked in three dimensions and the arm was controlled by a computer, such as the IBM PC. Programming involved numerous commands to control each movement. Starting and stopping the arm in the same place was the critical factor. It allowed the arm to "find" the sample and move it to the next station. Programming was essentially specific to each application and, therefore, took time to implement and verify.

CyberLab Products

The CyberLab 800 System was a robot, although it certainly did not have the futuristic appearance of the more publicized of its kind (see Exhibit 1). Simply put, the CyberLab 800 was a liquid transfer or pipetting device. It was capable of performing any repetitive laboratory liquid-preparation procedure currently done by hand. The system consisted of three separate components and a computer to execute the functions.

The main component was a pipette transport device that worked in three dimensions using eight independent probes for transferring liquid into or out of the test tubes. It was extremely accurate, operating within 1 percent with volumes as low as 10 microliters (a microliter is one millionth of a liter).

The second component was a precision syringe pump with three channels that delivered the liquid to the pipetting system. A typical setup had two of these units.

The third component was a reversible pump. It could draw out samples that were complete from the test tubes and transfer them to other analytical equipment for further testing.

Exhibit 1   The CyberLab 800

At the end of the summer of 1987, one complete CyberLab system was at work in the New York Psychiatric Institute. Dr. Meltzer used federal grant money to pay for the machine. It replaced two lab technicians who were doing sample preparation, saving over $70,000 the first year. Dr. Meltzer's review of the new system's performance showed that less enzyme was being wasted and that the samples being prepared were more accurate.

News of the system spread within the psychiatric community, as well as without, because of the system's accuracy, associated savings in wasted material, and relatively low cost. By the end of July 1988, CyberLab had sold 4 units, and had interested buyers for 25 more.

Competition in the Laboratory Robotics Industry

An estimated 18,000 sites in the United States could use the CyberLab system. In addition, Zymark had indicated that the worldwide market was around 30,000 to 50,000 units. At the end of the second quarter of 1988, only 3,050 of those potential sites had lab robots installed. Zymark, the first entrant in the lab robot industry in 1982, had 42 percent of the installations to date. Two other competitors, Cetus and Micromedic, entered in 1983 and had 15 percent and 17 percent of installations, respectively. Cetus was acquired in 1986 by Perkin-Elmer, a large corporation in the analytical instruments field with $1.3 billion in sales for fiscal year 1987. Three more players entered in 1985, one of which was Beckman Instruments, a subsidiary of SmithKline Beckman, a very large corporation in the health care and life-sciences industry with $4.3 billion in sales in fiscal year 1987. In 1987, Hewlett-Packard and Dynatech entered the market. See Exhibit 2 for a more complete description of the major competitors.

In spite of the eight other companies manufacturing lab robots, CyberLab believed its presence was needed because none of the existing players offered a machine similar to the "800" system for a similar cost. A CyberLab system cost $32,470 and would replace one chemist (average salary of $41,800 in 1987). Thus CyberLab had a payback of 0.78 years.

The Current Negotiations

To obtain necessary financing, Tom Friedlander, CEO of CyberLab, had hired a full-time consultant from a large venture-capital firm. This consultant had brought the CyberLab proposal to PRICO. Earlier this consultant had helped in a deal for PRICO, and so James Campbell was interested in studying the proposal. In presenting CyberLab's proposal, the consultant acknowledged reluctantly that he had already approached Dean Witter and Salomon Brothers for financing, but with no success. CyberLab's proposal to PRICO was to give them 30 percent of their equity and the rights to market CyberLab products through PRICO's distribution system in exchange for $1 million in capital. Under this agreement, PRICO would become the sole wholesale purchaser and marketer of the Cyber-Lab systems produced. CyberLab would manufacture the machines and sell them at a prearranged transfer price to PRICO. Exhibit 3 shows the pro forma spreadsheet provided by CyberLab of the manufacturing-only venture. Campbell was concerned about the value this business would have, given PRICO would own 30 percent of it if he took the current offer. He saw a number of potential measures of performance in the spreadsheet that could be useful to him and assumptions that he would need to evaluate. This would be part of considering whether the entire package of the marketing opportunity and the equity investment was attractive. If not, he might think about a counteroffer to CyberLab with different terms for the equity percentage, transfer price, or amount of investment. Unfortunately, it appeared that CyberLab did need the entire $1 million to make a viable start, and, of course, a different transfer price would both help and hurt CyberLab, given their participation on both the marketing and manufacturing sides of the business.

As to the marketing issue, PRICO would provide its established name, sales force, and advertising in exchange for a 23 percent margin. The company had been in the laboratory-equipment business for over 50 years and currently had 100 sales and service offices in the United States and 220 such offices in 60 countries throughout the world. Campbell was effectively paying $700,000 for the CyberLab patent and the business idea as it stood, since he would retain 30 percent ownership of anything purchased with the $1 million investment. It certainly seemed reasonable to Campbell that if CyberLab's patent and manufacturing

EXHIBIT 2   Major Competitors

Company Name	Yrs. in Bsns.	No. Instld. to Date	Percent Instld. to Date	Genl. Description of Company	Sales of Company ($MM)	Sales of Lab Instr. Div. ($MM)	Competing Product Description
Zymark	6	1,000	42.0%	First one to market, privately held	$ 15	$ 15	Slow, cost 50K to 70K
Micromedic	5	400	17.0	Subsidiary of ICN Biomedicals, govt. contract, intl. sales	43	17	Only dilutes and dispenses, cost 5K
Perkin-Elmer/Cetus	5	350	15.0	Design and mfg. of hi-tech analytic equip., intl. sales	1,334	416	No computer, robot arm, cost 50K
Tecan	3	300	13.0	Subsidiary of Swiss corp., been in US 4 yrs	?	?	Limited use and warranty, cost 20K
Beckman	2.5	175	7.0	Technology intensive health care/life science company, intl. sales	4,329	693	Moves sample to probe, cost 26K
Hamilton	3	100	4.0	Been in lab equip. bsns. 30 yrs, intl. sales	25	25	One probe w/ steel tip, cost 20K
HP/GenenChem	1	50	2.0	Established force in computers, starting in scientific equipment	8,090	405	Slow w/ genl. purpose, only works w/HP computers cost 40–55K
Dynatech	1	4	0.2	Plan to go national	305	13	Cost 6K

Sources: Annual reports, S&P OTC reports, *Million Dollar Directory.*

EXHIBIT 3   CyberLab's Pro Forma Income Statement: Manufacturing Only

Year	1	2	3
Selling price/unit	$25,000	$25,000	$25,000
Matrl. & labor/unit	$8,651	$8,651	$8,651
Units sold	29	47	51
Sales revenue	$725,000	$1,175,000	$1,275,000
Material, dir. labor	250,879	406,597	441,201
Overhead	138,000	196,430	207,641
Cost of goods sold	$388,879	$603,027	$648,842
Gross margin	$336,121	$571,973	$626,158
Selling, gen. & adm.	$258,044	$343,047	$344,908
Depreciation	16,000	9,600	5,760
Profit before tax	$62,077	$219,326	$275,490
Taxes	$24,831	$87,730	$110,196
Profit after tax	$37,246	$131,596	$165,294
Return on sales	5.14%	11.20%	12.96%
Equity at beginning of year . .	$1,000,000	$1,037,246	$1,168,842
Return on equity	3.72%	12.69%	14.14%

Year	1	2	3	Term Value
Pat	37,246	131,596	165,294	
Dep'n add-back	16,000	9,600	5,760	
Change in work cap.	(47,176)	(58,841)	(72,912)	
Cash flow fr. opns	6,070	82,355	98,142	1,750,199
Cash flow (1,000,000)	6,070	82,355	1,848,341	
NPV opns	$1,350,861			
IRR	25.17%			

Assumptions:

Total market size—yr. 1	595
CyberLab mkt. share—yr. 1	5.00%
Total mkt. growth—yr. 2+	7.00%
Cyber mkt. share—yr. 2+	7.50%
Discount rate	13.00%
Tax rate	40.00%
Material and labor/unit	$8,651

EXHIBIT 4   PRICO's Pro Forma Income Statement: Marketing Only

Year	1	2	3	
Selling price/unit	$32,470	$32,470	$32,470	
Transfer price/unit	$25,000	$25,000	$25,000	
Margin/unit	$7,470	$7,470	$7,470	
PRICO margin (%)	23.0%	23.0%	23.0%	
Units sold	29	47	51	
Sales revenue	$941,630	$1,526,090	$1,655,970	
Cost of goods sold	725,000	1,175,000	1,275,000	
Gross margin	$216,630	$351,090	$380,970	
Advertising	$51,000	$60,000	$60,000	
Sales expense	$137,400	$208,200	$210,600	
Total sell., gen. & admin	$188,400	$268,200	$270,600	
Profit before tax	$28,230	$82,890	$110,370	
Taxes	$11,292	$33,156	$44,148	
Profit after tax	$16,938	$49,734	$66,222	
Return on sales	1.80%	3.26%	4.00%	
Return on investment	11.29%	33.16%	44.15%	

Year	1	2	3	Term Value
Pat	16,938	49,734	66,222	
Change in work cap.	(28,249)	(45,783)	(49,679)	
Cash flow fr. opns.	(11,311)	3,951	16,543	295,015
Cash flow . . . . . . (150,000)	(11,311)	3,951	311,558	
NPV	$59,010			
IRR	25.80%			

Assumptions:

Total market size—yr. 1	595
CyberLab mkt. Share—yr. 1	5.00%
Total mkt. growth—yr. 2+	7.00%
Cyber mkt. share—yr. 2+	7.50%
Discount rate	13.00%
Tax rate	40.00%
Initial investment	$150,000

business as it stood was worth the $700,000 up front, then his company's marketing clout should be worth at least the $59,010 he had calculated as the net present value (NPV) of the marketing agreement (see Exhibit 4).

To establish the marketing of CyberLab products, PRICO would actually incur initial expenses of $150,000, for a one-time seminar and new brochures to train all the sales force on the new product, as well as ongoing expenses of $51,000 the first year and approximately $60,000 per year for the second and third years for advertising. Additional expenses included a commission of $600 per CyberLab system sold.

Another possible expense was the sales force. Frank Adams, the vice president of sales, argued there was an "opportunity" cost associated with using the sales force. He estimated the new product would take about 1.0 percent of each salesperson's schedule the first year and 1.5 percent for years two and three. The total sales expense the previous year for PRICO was $12 million, which made the opportunity cost equal $120,000 (0.01 × 12,000,000). Because the average salary for one salesman was $24,000 a year in addition to expenses of $36,000 a year, this "cost" was the equivalent of two full-time salespeople the first year and three in years two and three.

PRICO would not actually have to hire any new salespeople, but adding CyberLab products would take away some of the sales force's time spent on existing products. In a "typical" sales call to a lab director, part of the time was spent ordering routine supplies (beakers, cylinders, test tubes, pipettes, and the like), while the remainder was spent talking about new and existing nonroutine products. Campbell believed there would be some erosion of the standard-supply selling, and Adams and his staff concurred. Even if there were some erosion, it would probably be made up by the increase in disposable pipette tip sales that would certainly accompany sales of the CyberLab system. Vince Pauli, the financial analyst for new ventures at PRICO, had argued that competing effects were a wash and that the sales force's time should not be included as an expense in the analysis.

The projected cash flows from PRICO's perspective, for the marketing aspect only, are shown in Exhibit 4 (*Note:* this exhibit includes the opportunity cost for the sales force's time in the "sales expense" line). The lab-instrument manufacturing industry average for return on sales (based on profit after tax) was 3.1 percent. Other major corporations in this industry had values for return on equity of 12 to 13 percent. Overall, for the million dollar investment, PRICO would get 30 percent of the value of CyberLab or $405,258 (0.3 × $1,350,861) plus the value of the marketing agreement, $59,010 for a net of –$535,732.

Campbell thought he had some negotiating room, even though CyberLab had made it clear that it wanted both the marketing arrangement and an investment. Friedlander had just called to say that he had received an offer from a privately held company, Sperling Equipment Company, to buy a fixed number of units per year for the first three years and market them in exchange for a 30 percent discount from retail price. This raised questions about the desirability of the exclusive marketing proposal. However, the immediate task was to evaluate the offer on the table.

CASE 11
CYBERLAB: SUPPLEMENT

Lab-Robot Market Growth

Lab robots were highly suited for any area that required repetitive testing and sample preparation on a large scale. These areas included such biotechnology industries as pharmaceuticals, agricultural products, genetic engineering, and medical technology, in addition to the research and development division of almost any company. The biotechnology market anticipated sales of $1.2 billion in 1988 and was expecting to grow to $25 billion by 2000, which would represent 28.8 percent annual growth. R&D expenditures were forecast by *Predicasts* to grow at 7 to 9 percent annually in the near future. Lab and analytical equipment sales were forecast to grow from $1.65 billion in 1985 to $2.35 billion in 1990— an annual growth rate of 7.3 percent. In the past two years, sales had grown 5 to 9 percent. Experts believed that the annual growth would be between 5 and 9 percent more often than not, but growth rates as high as 10 percent and as low as 0 were possible over several years. The rates generally centered around 7 percent. Retention of the 20 percent R&D tax credit would provide continued investment incentives.

Market Size for Current Year

Based on Zymark's actual 1987 sales of $15 million and the cost of its systems of $50,000 to $70,000, Zymark sold approximately 250 units (15,000,000/$60,000) in 1987. When CyberLab combined this estimate with Zymark's estimated 42 percent share of installations to date, the result was an estimate of the annual market of 595 units (250/0.42).

A high-side estimate of the market was made using Zymark's average cost as $50,000 and assuming that its market share had dropped to about 35 percent in 1987 from the 42 percent share of total installations from 1982 to 1987. This approach gave an estimated market size of 809 units. Similarly, a low-side estimate was calculated of 510 units using an average cost of $70,000 and assuming that current-year market share equaled cumulative market share.

CyberLab Market Share

Tom Friedlander estimated that first-year market share could be as low as 0 if the product completely bombed and as high as 7 percent, with a median value of 5 percent. In his mind, he believed that market share was more likely to fall near the 5 percent level than near the 0 percent extreme based on observations of

This case was prepared in conjunction with Research Assistant Larry Weatherford (Darden).

other new product situations. He gauged that it would be equally likely to fall in the 0 to 4 percent market share interval as to fall between 4 and 5 percent. His impressions were similar about the side above the median: The 6 percent level would split the 5 to 7 percent interval into equally likely intervals. He had thus defined four quartile intervals. Rather than push further, he was willing to assume that the likelihood was spread evenly over each of those intervals. In the second and successive years, he figured CyberLab would achieve an extra 2.5 percent of the market over the first-year share.

Cost of Materials and Labor

Walter Meltzer, the CyberLab-system inventor, had kept track of how long it took him to machine the 80 parts he bought and then machined, as well as what it cost to buy the other 75 parts he used unchanged in creating the system. To estimate the total cost, he added up the cost of the 75 purchased parts and his estimate of the labor and material cost for the 80 machined parts. The labor portion of the machined parts' cost was calculated by multiplying the time he took by the labor rate charged by local machine shops in New England ($100/hour). His conservative estimate of the total cost came out to be $8,651.

Both the time to do the machining and the rate charged for machined parts could vary from previous estimates. Because Meltzer was conservative when assigning the overall costs, he expected that they might tend to be a little high already. After reviewing the components of cost, he could not see how they could vary by more than 9 percent below his estimate. They might, on the other hand, be as much as 5 percent higher than his estimate.

Tax Rate

A 40 percent tax rate was used as an estimate (the top federal rate was 38 percent; the top Connecticut rate 10 percent), but if the company did not do well, the tax rate would be much lower. Another factor that could change the tax rate was the presidential election coming in November of 1988.

CASE 12
CYBERLAB: A NEW BUSINESS OPPORTUNITY FOR PRICO (B)

James Campbell, president of Precision Instrument Corporation (PRICO), had come to work early to finish up his evaluation of the CyberLab proposal. Vince Pauli, financial analyst for new ventures, had just worked out the numbers for what he thought represented the best estimate of CyberLab's future. Pauli had taken his estimate from a combination of the business plan he'd received from Tom Friedlander, chief executive officer of CyberLab, and a separate estimate from a consultant for the venture-capital firm with which PRICO worked.

Pauli found that Friedlander and the consultant had made different estimates for just about every variable from total market size to the cost of the CyberLab 800 system. He thus decided to sketch out the major uncertainties for each variable and identify the range of possible values along with their appropriate probabilities. Of all the variables that had to be estimated, he selected the three that he believed would have the most impact on the bottom line and spent the remainder of his time with them.

The first quantity Pauli wrestled with was CyberLab's *first-year market share*. Friedlander's best guess was that CyberLab could achieve 5 percent; whereas the consultant's estimate was 4 percent. Pauli decided the market share could be as low as 0 percent and as high as 7 percent, with it being equally likely to be greater than or less than 5 percent. He further felt that it was as likely as not that the actual market share would be within 1 percent of Tom's estimate. For a graph of the cumulative probability distribution function, see Exhibit 1.

The next quantity Vince looked at was the *cost of materials and direct labor for the system*. He figured the total cost could vary as much as 9 percent below the engineer's prediction of \$8,651 to 5 percent above the prediction and that any percentage in this interval was possible. The following risk table was developed:

Cost Variance (percent)	Probability of Value or Less
–9%	0.00%
–4	0.25
–2	0.50
0	0.75
+5	1.00

This case was prepared in conjunction with Research Assistant Larry Weatherford (Darden).

Exhibit 1

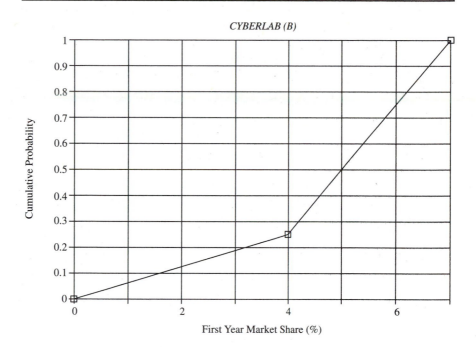

The last quantity was *total market growth*. Pauli figured that the fastest the lab-robot market would grow was 10 percent and the slowest it would grow was 0 percent. His best guess was that market growth would be 7 percent. In fact, it seemed to him that the chances were about the same that actual growth would be above or below 7 percent. It also seemed to him that the growth wouldn't be too far away from the 7 percent. Half the time it should come out between 6 and 8 percent, he thought.

Now that his financial analyst had hammered out these new ranges for each quantity and the associated probabilities, Campbell wanted to see what they implied for the evaluation of CyberLab. Pauli had offered to run for him worst- and best-case scenarios to complement the existing "most likely" scenario. Campbell told him it was fine to look at these scenarios, but "Who's to say these extreme scenarios will ever happen?"

Campbell asked Pauli to choose realistic scenarios based on the assessments of what really could happen with each of the three uncertain quantities. For each scenario Pauli was to calculate the financial impact on PRICO using the spreadsheet. "Then create a detailed picture of the financial risk from these scenarios," Campbell directed.

"And what about all the other scenarios that could happen? No matter how many we do, there are still other scenarios possible," Pauli responded.

"Just run enough to get a complete picture so we can decide if we want to take this opportunity."

CASE 13
DHAHRAN ROADS (A)

Hassan Malik, the financial manager of SADE, a Bahrain-based civil engineering company, reread the recently received fax. He was delighted that the nearly endless conversations with the Transportation Ministry of the municipality of Dhahran in eastern Saudi Arabia were finally coming to a close.

SADE had been selected as the prime contractor for a 168 million Saudi riyal (SR) project that involved the reconstruction and upgrading of the highway network linking the several terminals of the Dhahran airport and connecting the entire complex with the city. The Dhahran Roads project was indicative of projects on which SADE had established its international reputation for being a leading construction contractor. The total cost of the project was estimated to be SR 146 million, so the SR 168 million value provided only a 15 percent return, which was, unfortunately, below the 18 percent hurdle rate required by SADE for projects of this nature. On the other hand, the slightly less-than-desired return seemed a small cost to pay to maintain a steady flow of new projects during these slow economic times.

The fax requested that Malik respond to the project proposal within a week. The wording of the contract would then be finalized in the subsequent weeks and the contract signed by mid-January 1993.

The Project

The terms of the proposed contract contained several provisions:

- At the signing of the contract, the ministry would advance to SADE 15 percent of the contract's total value.
- If work progressed on schedule, SADE could bill the ministry as milestones were reached in accordance with the following schedule:

1993	SR 11,000,000
1994	SR 36,000,000
1995	SR 45,000,000
1996	SR 43,000,000
1997	SR 33,000,000

- The ministry would pay 80 percent of each bill received. Payment would, of course, be subject to a satisfactory inspection of the site by the ministry.

This case was prepared in conjunction with Professor Michel Schlosser (the Swedish Management Institute, IFL). Copyright © by the University of Virginia Darden School Foundation, Charlottesville, Virginia. All rights reserved.

The 20 percent deduction would be withheld for (1) the recovery of the advance payment (15 percent) and (2) the accumulation of a retention fund (5 percent).

- Half of the retention would be reimbursed at the time of completion (end of 1997). The second half would be repaid at the end of 1998, provided the roads did not show any flaws in their first year of use.

During the past several months, the SADE engineering department had inspected the site, confirmed the surveys, and reviewed the drawings that had been provided by the ministry. In the opinion of the vice president of engineering, the project presented "no unusual challenges." It was similar to several SADE projects in other countries that were now nearly complete and that had moved ahead without difficulty.

For SADE to proceed, equipment would have to be ordered immediately so it would be available in the fourth quarter of 1993 when earth moving would commence. The cost of the equipment would be SR 38 million. Seventy-five percent of the cost would have to be paid upon placement of the order; the balance was due on delivery. At the end of the project, the equipment would have no salvage value. The engineering department estimated that the cost of completing the project (not including the equipment) would be SR 108 million. SR 7 million would be expended in 1993 for preliminary site work. The project would then proceed with estimated costs of SR 25 million, SR 29 million, SR 27 million, and SR 20 million for the subsequent years.

Preliminary discussions with several banks indicated that SADE would be able to raise SR 4 million in loans to help finance the project. The loans would carry a 12 percent annual interest (2 percent above prime, 5 percent above government securities) and would have to be repaid in full at the end of 1997.

The project would be managed by one of SADE's experienced project managers, Harold Smithers. Smithers had just completed a major waterworks project in East Africa and was noted for strong engineering skills and tight fiscal control.

Although the contract would be denominated in Saudi riyals, the foreign exchange exposure would be minimal since the Bahraini dinar was pegged to the Saudi riyal. In addition, Saudi Arabian and Bahraini tax laws would not require SADE to pay taxes on the profits of this contract.

CASE 14
DHAHRAN ROADS (B)

Although the base-case analysis indicated that the Dhahran Roads contract would generate substantial value to SADE, Hassan Malik recognized that such a favorable result would require all facets of the project to proceed smoothly. Even though the task was unpleasant, he turned his thoughts to those aspects of the project that could go wrong.

As he thought about the risks associated with the Dhahran Roads project, he decided that there were two key areas in which former projects of a similar nature had run into trouble.

Delayed Payments by the Client

SADE had occasionally experienced problems with a client failing to pay in accordance with an agreed billing schedule. SADE was not the only contractor that faced these problems; in fact, several informal discussions had taken place among contractors to share their experiences in this area. During these conversations, a pattern of customer behavior seemed to emerge. If problems in honoring the billing schedule occurred, the delay usually appeared in the third year of long-term contracts, but occasionally in the second year. A delay usually lasted a year and pushed back all subsequent payments by a year. Many contractors believed that clients purposely delayed payments at a point when the project had gone so far that the contractor could not afford to abandon it. Delays had occurred in about 30 percent of the recent projects, and they were often justified by the client on the basis of the slightest of deviations from the performance specifications or the invoicing procedures of the contract. About 80 percent of the delays began in the third year of the project and 20 percent in the second year.

Cost Overruns

Even though SADE prided itself on its ability to control costs, it occasionally experienced overruns—sometimes substantial ones. Malik reviewed the files of the following 10 completed projects, each of which was the size of the Dhahran Roads project (see Exhibit 1).

Malik was not surprised with these results, because the numbers were consistent with his informal assessment of SADE's cost-control performance. A subsequent examination of the progress of each of the projects showed that there was no pattern in when the cost deviations began to arise, and he concluded that the deviations were spread rather evenly over the lives of the contracts.

This case was prepared in conjunction with Professor Michel Schlosser (the Swedish Management Institute, IFL). Copyright © by the University of Virginia Darden School Foundation, Charlottesville, Virginia. All rights reserved.

EXHIBIT 1   Historical Accuracy of Estimated Costs

Project	Estimated Cost (in millions)	Actual Cost (in millions)	Actual as Percent of Estimated
India-2	620 rupees	633 rupees	102.1
India-13B	790 rupees	789 rupees	99.9
India-15	640 rupees	650 rupees	101.6
Kuwait-4	11.3 dinars	12.6 dinars	111.5
Kuwait-5A	5.9 dinars	5.65 dinars	95.8
UAE-1	117 dirhams	118 dirhams	100.9
UAE-3	106 dirhams	129 dirhams	121.7
UAE-4C	128 dirhams	128 dirhams	100.0
UAE-5	143 dirhams	142 dirhams	99.3
Pakistan-3	780 rupees	832 rupees	106.7

CASE 15
DISCOUNTED CASH FLOW EXERCISES

1. In each of the following situations, which alternative is the better, assuming that you would put whatever money you receive in a secure investment that returns 10 percent annually?

   a. $100 now, or $130 three years from now.

   b. $250 now, or $350 five years from now.

   c. $500 two years from now, or $675 five years from now.

2. The Financially Astute Company (FAC) is considering two different options for repayment of a loan. The first option requires payments of $40,000 at the end of each of the next four years. The second option requires $20,000 at the end of the first year, $30,000 at the end of the second, $50,000 at the end of the third, and $70,000 at the end of the fourth. Thus the second option requires the payment of an extra $10,000 in all, but it allows FAC to make smaller payments in the first two years. Which option should the company choose if its hurdle rate is 12 percent? 16 percent?

3. The Quick Response Company is considering the purchase of a piece of labor-saving machinery. The machine has a useful life of five years. It would result in a net cash outflow (after consideration of tax effects) of $100,000, immediately followed by net cash inflows (after tax) from increased sales of $28,000 in each of the next five years. Is the equipment attractive if the company has adopted a hurdle rate of 10 percent? 12 percent? 14 percent? What is the internal rate of return?

4. In advertising its five-year guaranteed certificate of deposit, the Neighbor's Bank states: 12.50 percent per annum compounded quarterly (13.10 percent effective annual yield).

   a. What does this mean and how are these numbers related?

   b. To strengthen the appeal of their certificates, the bank is considering a change to compounding monthly. How much would it cost them? How much would it cost them to change to daily compounding?

5. The Information Technology Company (ITC) is considering the purchase of a new minicomputer for data processing. The purchase price is $150,000 delivered and installed. It has been estimated that the new computer will produce annual savings of $50,000 in enhanced productivity as compared with the current computer. ITC assumes the new computer will have an economic life of five years, at which time it will be essentially obsolete and have zero salvage value over the costs of

removal. The present computer, which is fully depreciated, is in good working order and could conceivably be used for at least five more years, but its present salvage value is zero, net of all costs of removal. The company has adopted a hurdle rate of 12 percent. For ease in calculation, assume that the marginal tax rate is 50 percent, that the new computer will be straight-line depreciated over no less than five years, and that the cash flows occur in a lump sum at year's end.

a. Show that the company cannot justify the computer on purely economic grounds. What happens if the flows are assumed to occur quarterly?

b. What would the salvage value of the present computer have to be to make the new computer attractive? Assume that the salvage income is subject to the 50 percent tax rate. Why does the old computer's salvage value influence the new computer's attractiveness?

c. Suppose again that the present computer has zero salvage value. What would the salvage value of the new computer at the end of its five-year life have to be to make the new computer attractive? Assume that the book value of the computer at the end of year five is zero.

CASE 16
EDGCOMB METALS (A)

The Troy Plant

Alex Tereszcuk, plant manager of Edgcomb Metals' Troy, Virginia, facility, had a problem. Frank Spencer, considered to be the best and most conscientious of the seven Troy truck drivers, had complained at the July 1983 drivers' meeting that some drivers were not working as hard as others. Spencer when on to point out that a driver who took 10 hours to complete a run that could actually be done in 8 was *rewarded* with "time-and-a-half" for the 2 overtime hours. To investigate these claims, Alex had compiled data on total hours, total miles, and number of delivery stops for each of several delivery runs made from his facility in recent months. He was now faced with the tasks of analyzing these data and preparing an appropriate response. Alex wanted to respond to the issue as soon as possible—perhaps at the August meeting.

Company Background

Founded in Philadelphia in 1923, Edgcomb Metals had expanded to 21 service centers serving 37 eastern, midwestern, and southern states, with total sales of over $500 million a year by 1983. These service centers acted as middlemen between the large metal manufacturers, such as U.S. Steel, and the myriad of diverse companies using metal products in their operations.

The service centers stored and distributed thousands of standard metal products (steel bars, sheets, and rods) and also provided specialized cutting and shaping services to customer specification. In total, Edgcomb offered some 15,000 products to 35,000 different customers. The company had a reputation for providing a high-quality product coupled with excellent service and delivery standards.

The Troy plant, constructed in 1976, was Edgcomb's most modern facility. It covered 72,000 square feet and housed a full line of metal processing equipment. The Troy plant serviced the entire state of Virginia with the exception of a small area bordering Washington, D.C.

The Distribution System

The state was divided into seven distribution sectors, as shown in Exhibit 1. Deliveries were made five days a week, with the busier sectors receiving one or

This case was based on the Supervised Business Study of Glenn A. Ferguson (Darden Class of 1985).
Copyright © by the University of Virginia Darden School Foundation, Charlottesville, Virginia. All rights reserved.

EXHIBIT 1   Distribution Sectors

Sector Number	General Location	Days Delivered per Week
1	Virginia Beach/Norfolk	5
2	Richmond	5
3	Charlottesville	5
4	Harrisonburg	3
5	Roanoke	5
6	Lynchburg	5
7	Southwest Virginia	2

---

more deliveries daily. Each afternoon the plant scheduler determined which orders would be delivered the following day, grouped the orders into runs within each sector, and carefully sequenced the orders within each run. This sequencing attempted to minimize the amount of time and distance for the run, while at the same time accommodating special customer delivery requests. Trailers were loaded during the night according to this schedule (the last order to be delivered was loaded first into the trailer). The customers took responsibility for unloading their particular orders. The scheduler also assigned drivers to runs, trying to achieve an equitable pattern of assignments so each driver had the same percentage of long (or short) runs.

Because Edgcomb's drivers and tractor/trailers were the primary representatives of Edgcomb Metals (few customers had ever seen the Troy facility), the company took special pride in their image and appearance. The drivers wore customized uniforms, complete with epaulets and an American flag. The tractor/trailers were brightly painted with the Edgcomb logo and were replaced every four years. Traffic violations were rare, and the drivers paid their own traffic fines.

Drivers were paid well ($9.50 an hour with a 50 percent premium for overtime) with an extensive benefit package. The standard day was eight hours with a half-hour for lunch (unpaid) and two paid 10-minute breaks. The eight-hour day was guaranteed, so a driver finishing early had the option of working in the plant or taking the time off without pay. Approximately one half-hour per day was allocated for paperwork, consisting primarily of a daily log listing customers delivered, miles driven, and hours spent. Overtime was accumulated any time more than eight hours were worked in a given day. The nonunion Troy drivers accumulated 1,950 overtime hours in the first half of 1983. Exhibit 2 gives recent monthly data for total driver hours, overtime, miles, and number of deliveries.

Edgcomb leased seven trucks and eight trailers at a cost of $1,600 per month for a tractor/trailer combination. The company estimated variable costs (excluding driver wages) to be 27 cents per mile. The fleet covered 207,293 miles during the first six months of 1983, delivering a total of 15,806 tons of metal and making 4,227 stops.

EXHIBIT 2   Monthly Data for the Troy Facility

Month	Tons	Miles	Stops	Regular Hours	Overtime
1983:					
June	3,043	34,907	719	1,182	362
May	2,889	38,799	728	1,259	360
Apr.	2,384	33,367	695	1,230	382
Mar.	2,500	35,288	763	1,345	283
Feb.	2,312	29,876	613	1,205	257
Jan.	2,678	35,056	709	1,253	306
1982:					
Dec.	1,678	27,171	568	962	187
Nov.	2,209	29,917	624	915	276
Oct.	2,382	30,143	713	962	239
Sept.	2,315	34,771	617	1,091	272
Aug.	2,624	36,523	724	1,108	283
Jul.	1,745	34,693	640	1,030	249

Drivers' Meeting, August 1983

Shortly after assuming the job of plant manager in July of 1982, Alex Tereszcuk initiated a regularly scheduled series of drivers' meetings. He hoped these meetings would facilitate communication between him and the drivers and give the drivers an opportunity to air their gripes and make suggestions.

The first few meetings produced a small number of minor complaints and suggestions, and Alex made several small changes in response. It was not until the July meeting, however, that the first significant problem was brought up. Frank Spencer, one of the more experienced drivers, stood up during that meeting to speak his mind:

> First, I'd like to say that I think these drivers' meetings are a real good thing. It's always nice to know that management is willing to listen.
>
> I want to bring up something that bothers me and I know bothers some of the rest of you. Quite simply, I don't think we're all pulling our weight. I work hard and conscientiously and get done in 8 hours what takes others 10. We all enjoy our freedom out there on the road, and we also know that the harder we work, the more we deliver and the faster we finish. And we also know that this freedom brings plenty of opportunity to goof off.
>
> What's doubly bad about the situation is that the best drivers, those who finish in 8 hours, don't get paid as well as those who take 10 and get overtime. It's discouraging to see that I'm penalized for doing a good job.
>
> I enjoy my work and I think we've got real good jobs, but I think there's something wrong and unfair with this system that pays you more if you're not doing your job.

Frank's comments were seconded by a couple of other drivers, and Alex got the sense that it was one newer driver in particular, John Williams, who was the target of these criticisms. The meeting ended with a promise from Alex that he would look into the matter.

Alex believed that Spencer was probably the best and most conscientious driver in the plant, and he also believed that Williams was as poor as Spencer was good. But Alex did not believe that Williams was intentionally goofing off. He thought it was more a matter of Williams' being less energetic and skillful than the others—and just plain slower in general. He could see that Williams was being paid slightly more; Williams had made close to $30,000 a year in 1982 because of overtime. Exhibit 3 gives the 1983 overtime accumulations of the seven full-time delivery drivers.

Data Analysis

Alex decided to see what he could learn from the daily logs of the two drivers, Spencer and Williams. The total accumulated overtime had to be judged relative to the number of days worked, the number of miles traveled, and the number of stops made. To do this, Alex compiled data on hours worked outside the plant (excluding any explainable nonproductive hours, such as tire changes, breakdowns, and so on) versus miles driven and stops made over a four-month period (April to July of 1983) for both Spencer and Williams. These data are in Exhibit 4. Several days' were found to be unusable because of the presence of extenuating circumstances (poor weather, malfunctioning truck, and the like) and were not included.

In the period covered by the daily log data, Spencer averaged 10.6 hours per run while Williams averaged only 9.72, which conflicted with the contention that Williams tended to be slower than Spencer. Alex wondered whether the four-month period considered might not be representative or whether Spencer's higher time per run might be explained by his larger average number of miles and stops.

To check his belief that sectors made a difference in the number of hours to expect for a given run, Alex compiled daily data on two sectors. The Virginia Beach/Norfolk sector and the local Charlottesville sectors were picked to represent extremes. A delivery run to the Charlottesville sector was one of

---

EXHIBIT 3   Overtime by Driver in First Six Months of 1983

Driver	Regular Hours	Overtime Hours
1	960	320
2	924	291
3	969	325
4	896	199
5	928	277
Williams	907	215
Spencer	931	284
Total*	6,515	1,911

* The hours of one other back-up driver are not included in this total.

Exhibit 4   Daily Data for Williams and Spencer

Williams Data

Miles	Stops	Hours		Miles	Stops	Hours
331 3		10.17		176	5	7.75
206 2		8.00		147	7	9.10
221 4		8.25		536	2	13.32
193 4		10.00		55	4	7.50
129 4		7.50		191	6	11.00
208 5		9.33		237	7	10.33
368 3		11.50		258	6	12.17
163 6		8.50		276	1	9.67
264 1		8.00		130	3	9.25
238 3		9.00		241	5	10.00
193 5		9.00		364	8	13.00
145 6		8.00		207	3	7.25
331 5		12.50		251	8	9.75
427 5		14.00		157	5	7.83
204 6		9.00		179	3	7.75
298 4		7.75		335	12	10.67
225 12		13.17		179	2	8.67
203 8		13.08		398	1	10.33
253 6		10.67		147	3	5.42
279 9		12.00		132	4	9.00
193 4		8.00		378	2	10.50
182 8		10.00		218	4	10.00
279 6		10.50		401	4	13.25
177 5		7.50		275	1	9.33
195 5		9.75		123	5	7.67
171 4		9.17		174	8	9.50
223 5		10.00		119	3	8.00
320 4		11.33		261	7	11.40
226 4		8.00		292	3	10.75
193 4		7.75		200	7	10.50
				292	4	11.33

	Miles	Stops	Hours
Average . . .	235.52	4.80	9.72
St. dev	87.48	2.34	1.84
Count	61	61	61

Exhibit 4 *(Continued)*

Spencer Data

Miles	Stops	Hours		Miles	Stops	Hours
182	3	8.25		189	8	8.25
364	9	12.50		326	6	11.00
227	9	10.50		176	7	8.00
188	4	6.50		352	7	11.50
275	6	9.50		197	5	8.00
440	4	11.50		312	10	12.00
214	6	8.50		110	6	6.00
265	4	8.00		334	5	10.50
352	6	10.50		339	9	12.00
321	4	9.00		201	11	9.50
174	8	9.75		340	7	12.00
372	11	13.50		382	4	9.83
188	6	8.00		189	8	8.50
249	2	9.00		262	6	9.50
386	5	14.00		290	2	7.75
112	3	6.00		350	6	10.50
164	6	7.67		286	6	10.00
338	2	10.50		178	3	7.10
522	8	15.75		286	2	9.50
262	6	10.00		292	5	10.00
333	3	9.25		392	5	12.85
321	6	10.50		379	5	11.50
240	3	8.67		199	8	9.50
345	2	8.75		226	9	10.00
262	8	9.25		176	6	8.50
254	3	9.00		379	8	11.00
310	6	10.83		225	4	8.00
203	11	11.50		311	8	11.75
540	11	16.00		186	9	9.00
216	9	9.50		228	10	9.00
415	3	11.75		205	2	8.42
375	2	10.00		346	9	10.00
306	11	11.75		320	9	11.50
341	10	11.50		181	9	9.50
311	9	13.25		369	7	11.75

	Miles	Stops	Hours
Average	284.00	6.29	10.06
St. dev.	88.63	2.69	1.99
Count	70	70	70

the shortest, while a delivery run to the Virginia Beach sector was one of the longest and most difficult. A comparison of the averages for these two sectors (shown in Exhibit 5) confirmed that Virginia Beach runs were indeed longer (both in miles and hours) and required more stops.

If the analysis of these data confirmed Frank Spencer's contentions, Alex had several options.

- One of the more extreme alternatives was to remove John Williams from his position as driver. Alex wondered whether the data provided enough evidence to support such a decision.

- A second, and less drastic, alternative was to set up some sort of monitoring system that would track the drivers' performances. Alex envisioned a system that would periodically compare the performance of each driver with a standard. The standard would be based on the miles driven and stops made and might also consider the particular sectors in which the driver's runs were made.

- A third alternative was to equip the trucks with tachographs, machines that kept a record of miles per hour over the course of a run. Such a record would provide almost complete information about the speed and activities of the drivers; but several other plants in the Edgcomb Metals Company had used tachographs with mixed success. After several phone calls to these plants, Alex learned that drivers universally disliked the little machines. The idea of being "watched" and recorded did not sit well with the drivers, individuals who generally enjoyed the freedom of being alone on the road. There was also some question about whether overall performance would improve because of the tachographs. From a purely economic standpoint, Alex wondered if the $75-per-month lease cost of a tachograph could be justified by improved performance. If the installation of tachographs changed Williams' performance to, for example, a level equal to that of Spencer's, would the tachograph be attractive?

- One final alternative that had several attractive features was to change the basis on which drivers were paid. Rather than pay by the hour and reward the poorer performers, Edgcomb might pay instead by the mile and number of deliveries. Paying drivers only for the amount of work accomplished would remove any incentive to stretch out a run to incur overtime.

EXHIBIT 5   Daily Data by Sector

Sector 1—Virginia Beach/Norfolk

Miles	Stops	Hours	Miles	Stops	Hours
331 3		10.17	366	11	12.50
364 9		12.50	329	4	11.42
304 4		10.00	348	9	11.75
419 7		12.25	368	10	13.00
341 5		9.92	372	9	12.67
349 6		12.25	373	11	13.00
340 7		11.00	416	3	11.75
334 2		9.50	320	4	11.33
368 3		11.50	367	5	12.00
280 3		9.25	399	12	13.83
352 6		10.50	328	1	8.75
339 7		12.00	341	10	11.50
264 1		8.00	353	7	12.00
326 5		11.00	366	9	12.25
420 3		11.67	337	5	12.25
372 11		13.50	288	4	10.00
335 4		9.50	352	7	11.50
273 2		8.00	363	9	11.25
331 6		10.50	373	8	12.75
328 9		13.00	278	4	10.00
331 5		12.50	339	3	11.25
311 4		10.00	312	5	10.75
322 4		9.25	327	5	10.42
338 2		10.50	334	5	10.50
368 4		10.75	360	8	11.75
347 7		12.50	272	4	10.00
347 4		10.00	310	3	11.50
333 3		9.25	276	1	9.67
321 6		10.50	340	7	12.00
335 5		12.00	354	11	15.00
370 10		12.80	276	2	8.25
343 7		12.00	364	8	13.00
353 9		11.75	354	7	13.00
279 9		12.00	343	6	11.00
333 7		12.00	350	6	10.50

	Miles	Stops	Hours
Average	339.27	5.89	11.26
St. dev.	33.62	2.80	1.41
Count	70	70	70

EXHIBIT 5 *(Continued)*

Sector 3—Charlottesville

Miles	Stops	Hours	Miles	Stops	Hours
182	3	8.25	179	4	7.50
131	4	6.75	125	6	6.00
136	4	8.00	149	5	6.50
193	4	10.00	108	5	6.00
129	4	7.50	152	3	6.00
214	6	8.50	55	4	7.50
162	6	8.50	165	4	8.75
227	4	8.75	197	5	8.00
226	5	8.00	131	4	8.50
215	4	8.50	110	6	6.00
197	2	7.50	191	5	8.25
112	3	6.00	105	7	8.00
156	5	7.50	240	3	8.00
204	6	9.00	130	3	9.25
298	4	7.75	265	4	10.60
109	6	7.50	207	3	7.25
231	8	11.08	88	3	5.00
127	5	7.25	178	3	7.08
184	3	7.50	158	5	9.67
89	5	8.00	188	6	8.25
93	3	6.67	151	6	8.75
176	4	7.33	132	4	9.00
131	6	8.50	142	2	6.67
177	5	7.50	204	5	8.50
171	4	9.17	205	6	8.50
223	5	10.00	123	5	7.67
193	4	7.75	180	7	8.25
			62	4	8.00

	Miles	Stops	Hours
Average	163.75	4.53	7.93
St. dev.	50.11	1.29	1.10
Count	55	55	55

CASE 17
FLORIDA GLASS COMPANY (A)

As Oscar Paik, materials manager of the Florida Glass Company, reviewed his day planner, he noted that the monthly run of the Energy Planning Model was scheduled for today. This model calculated the optimal mix of products for the coming month, October 1982, and the quantities of energy (electricity and distillate-fuel oil) required. In the past, when Paik received the results of the model, he simply placed an order for the recommended quantity of distillate-fuel oil. On this particular occasion, however, he decided to take the time to question his perfunctory monthly ordering of distillate.

The model made calculations on a monthly basis, and, as a result, it ignored the opportunity to purchase more than one month's supply of distillate, even though ample storage capacity was available. During the past few years of oil price volatility, Paik had never taken advantage of a relatively low price, even when he firmly believed that prices would rise in the subsequent month. The current situation was another of these opportunities. Paik was convinced that the price he now faced at the end of September (93.66 cents per gallon) marked a temporary low in distillate prices. He believed that the price at the end of October (the next time he would normally purchase distillate) would be 94.5 or even 98.0 cents. This seemed an ideal time to address the policy of single-month purchases.

The Flat-Glass Industry

The major products of the flat-glass industry (Standard Industrial Classification [SIC] 3211) included float, plate, tempered, and laminated glass. Float glass was formed by cooling a layer of molten glass on a bed of molten tin. Plate glass was formed by a rolling process and then ground and polished on both sides. Tempered glass was flat glass that had been toughened by being heated above its strain point, then quickly cooled. Laminated glass consisted of plates of glass bonded to a sheet of plastic that provided protection against shattering.

In 1981, the industry shipped only $1.657 billion of product, approximately the same level at which it had been stagnating for the past four years. Forecasts for 1982 were no brighter, still at the $1.6 billion level. In fact, ever since World War II, depressed growth had plagued the industry. During this period, the industry had grown more slowly than the economy as a whole and more slowly than the two major industries that it supplied, building construction and automobile production. This performance reflected the loss of market to two types of competitors: foreign producers of glass and domestic producers of substitute materials. The outlook for the next five years was closely tied to the expansion of the economy. Forecasts were hopeful. It was anticipated that 1983 would present a welcome upturn. Shipments to the automobile industry would lead the way as a result of lower interest rates, increased consumer confidence, and pent-up demand. The construction industry was expected to rebound in 1984 as the current vacancy rates were reduced.

The flat-glass industry was dominated by four major corporations, Libby-Owens-Ford, PPG Industries, Corning Glass Works, and Guardian Industries. These firms accounted for 90 percent of the industry shipments. According to the *1977 Census of Manufacturers,* the remaining 10 percent was shared by 58 firms.

The glass industry was a major energy consumer. Among industries with two-digit SIC codes, Stone, Clay, and Glass (SIC 32) had the fourth-largest gross energy consumption (1,864 trillion Btus,[1] or 8 percent of the total manufacturing consumption), and glass accounted for 20 percent of this amount. The sources of the glass industry's energy had been shifting over the past decade. There had been a sharp increase in the relative use of oil (from 6.1 percent in 1971 to 29.7 percent in 1980), a sharp drop in the relative consumption of gas (from 72.4 percent to 40.2 percent), and a moderate rise in the use of electricity (from 20.4 percent to 27.0 percent).

Over the last two decades, however, aggregate energy use by the glass industry had increased more slowly than output, despite increases in energy consumption by pollution-control equipment. A number of technological developments were credited for these gains in efficiency, including the use of larger furnaces, the reuse of waste heat, the introduction of an auxiliary heating unit inside the body of the molten glass in the furnace, and the widespread adoption of the "float" process of making plate glass, which eliminated grinding and polishing of the flat surfaces.

Glass Manufacturing

The hard, brittle substance that is known as glass is actually a liquid. It is one of a number of substances that are formed from chemical compositions that have the property of cooling below their freezing point without crystallizing, thus becoming liquids of increasingly high viscosity until eventually they are so stiff that, to all ordinary appearances, they are solids. Scientifically, glass is classified as a "supercooled" liquid. Toffee is another such substance—a supercooled sugar solution.

Glass is made from three primary raw materials: sand (silicon dioxide), limestone (calcium carbonate), and soda ash (sodium carbonate). The ideal composition is approximately 75 percent silica, 10 percent lime, and 15 percent soda. In

---

[1]One Btu (British thermal unit) is the amount of heat required to raise one pound of water by one degree Fahrenheit. One gallon of fuel-oil distillate produces on average 105,000 Btus, one kilowatt-hour (kWh) of electricity 3,400 Btus, and one cubic foot of natural gas 1,000 Btus.

the actual manufacturing of glass, crushed waste glass (cullet) is added to the batch of materials in an effort to speed the melting process, because glass melts at a lower temperature than any of its separate ingredients.

The production of glass involves (1) mixing the ingredients; (2) heating the mixture in a furnace to 850 degrees Celsius until the ingredients combine and melt; (3) forming the product by one or more means, such as drawing, molding, pressing, and floating; (4) annealing, or reheating and slowly cooling the products to relieve stresses caused by the uncontrolled and unavoidable cooling that takes place during the forming process; (5) cutting, inspecting, and packaging. (See the flowchart in Exhibit 1.) Flat glass is made in such volumes that manufacturing is a continuous process from melting to packing. The melting operation accounts for more than half of the process's energy requirements.

In the past decade, considerable attention had been devoted to energy conservation in the melting operation. Improved refractory materials had lengthened furnace campaign lives and thus reduced the number of energy-consuming start-ups. Electric "boosters" had been added to the fuel-fired furnaces. By passing current between electrodes placed near the bottom of the furnace, these boosters had introduced more heat and created a stirring action that had improved furnace output by more than the relative amount of additional energy.

The widespread adoption during the late 1960s and early 1970s of the "float" process of making plate glass had been an important energy-conservation development in the flat-glass industry. Previously, the production of flat, distortion-free glass had involved extensive grinding and polishing, which consumed 10 to 20 percent of the glass. In the float process, the molten glass left the furnace in a

---

EXHIBIT 1   Process Flowchart

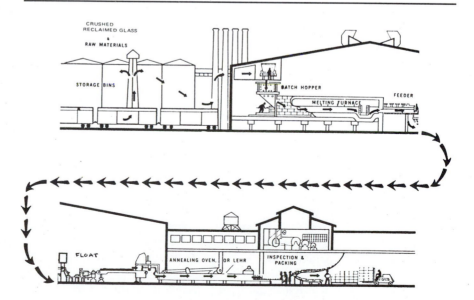

continuous strip and floated directly on the surface of an enclosed pool of molten tin. By surrounding the glass with a controlled atmosphere and sufficient heat, irregularities on both surfaces of the glass flowed out, yielding flat, smooth, and parallel surfaces. Elimination of the grinding and polishing of the flat surfaces saved both the direct energy of grinding and the indirect energy of making the glass that had been ground into waste.

Finished flat glass could be processed further to improve its safety characteristics. There were two principal methods. The first consisted of laminating a sheet of plastic between two sheets of glass; the second of heat-treating a single layer of glass. In laminated glass, splinters firmly adhered to the plastic layer when a fracture occurred. In heat-treated (or tempered) glass, a fracture resulted in cracks throughout the entire body of the glass, and the glass broke into a large number of comparatively small, harmless pieces. This unusual property was the result of heating finished glass sheets to just below their softening point, then uniformly and rapidly cooling them with a blast of air. This rapid cooling placed the outside surfaces of the glass under compressional strain. If the glass fractured, this strain was catastrophically relieved throughout the piece of glass.

Florida Glass Company

The Florida Glass Company, located in Seffner, Florida, produced float, laminated, and tempered glass in its 37,500 square feet per month plant. It employed the float process for manufacturing its glass and fueled its furnaces by oil with electric boosters.

Even though it was not located in the primary glass-producing states of Ohio, Tennessee, Illinois, and Pennsylvania, where raw materials were readily accessible and less expensive, Florida Glass was more profitable than the rest of the industry. In 1981, it posted over a 4 percent return on sales, compared with a 2 percent return for the rest of the industry. Exhibit 2 was the 1981 operating statement. This performance was attributed to Florida Glass's having developed a strong position in an attractive market niche as well as having paid careful attention to manufacturing efficiencies, particularly with regard to energy.

Although the flat-glass industry as a whole had been weak for the past five years, the Florida market had been moderately strong. The architectural designs in Florida continued to be heavily glass oriented, and residential and commercial construction had persisted despite national economic conditions, so demand remained strong for glass products. Since its founding in 1951, the Florida Glass Company had promoted itself in this regional market and had established itself as a leading supplier to the market.

For the past five years, sales had been sufficient to keep the plant operating at or near full capacity. The 1982 aggregate production plan is shown in Exhibit 3. This plan allowed ranges on certain products when market conditions permitted. These ranges in turn gave flexibility in production planning so the product mix could be altered in an effort to optimize profitability. This flexibility was a key to the operational efficiencies at Florida Glass. When energy costs severely affected the industry, Florida Glass adjusted its mix to control energy expense.

EXHIBIT 2   1981 Operating Statement (in thousands of dollars)

	Float	Tempered	Laminated	Total
Shipments ('000 sq. ft.) . . .	217.8	78.6	85.2	211.1
Revenue	$272.2	$255.4	$238.6	$766.2
CGS (excluding energy) . . .	63.1	48.7	96.3	208.1
Energy—electricity*	88.5	98.9	69.0	256.4
Energy—distillate†	62.7	93.5	38.9	195.1
Selling, admin., R&D	32.2	16.6	12.6	61.4
Total cost	246.5	257.7	216.8	721.0
Income before taxes	25.7	(2.3)	21.8	45.2
Income after taxes				33.3

*At an average cost of $0.0351 per kWh.

†At an average cost of $0.9926 per gallon.

EXHIBIT 3   1982 Aggregate Market Plan (square feet of finished output)

	Float		Tempered		Laminated	
	Min.	Max.	Min.	Max.	Min.	Max.
January	—	14,000	6,500	12,000	—	14,000
February . . .	—	14,000	6,500	12,000	—	14,000
March	10,500	15,500	5,000	12,000	—	15,000
April	12,000	16,500	5,000	12,000	4,000	16,500
May	12,000	18,500	—	9,000	4,000	16,500
June	12,000	19,500	—	9,000	7,000	17,500
July	14,500	20,000	—	9,000	7,000	17,500
August	14,500	20,000	—	9,000	7,000	17,500
September . . .	16,000	21,000	—	8,500	—	15,000
October	16,000	21,000	—	8,500	—	15,000
November . . .	16,000	21,000	—	8,500	—	15,000
December . .	—	17,000	4,500	7,500	—	16,500

Note: All figures are for nominal ¼-inch product. Because laminated glass requires two sheets of ⅛-inch float, a planning factor of 1.75 must be applied to the output when computing capacity requirements. This factor is less than two because the process time is slightly reduced for the thinner glass.

Energy Planning

For the past several years, the strong market position of Florida Glass had helped to keep its cost per square foot of finished product significantly below the industry average. Because the plant operated at full capacity, costs were spread over as wide a base as possible. More important, Florida Glass was able to address its energy expense through adjustments in its product mix. At the end of each month, on the basis of the current price for distillate fuel and the contract price for electricity, the product mix was set for next month's manufacturing.

EXHIBIT 4   Distillate Fuel Price History (end-of-month prices in cents per gallon)

Month	1980	1981	1982
January	75.02	94.86	99.11
February	77.77	102.51	94.68
March	78.84	102.83	87.42
April	78.85	100.86	86.00
May	79.38	100.69	91.16
June	80.28	99.30	95.45
July	79.14	98.51	93.81
August	79.28	98.16	92.51
September	79.25	97.84	93.66
October	80.74	98.00	
November	83.99	100.02	
December	88.60	100.56	

Electricity and distillate fuel were the two sources of energy in the Florida Glass manufacturing process. The distillate fired the melting furnaces, the annealing kilns, and the tempering furnaces. Electricity powered the process flow, the boosters in the melting furnaces, and the cutting and grinding wheels in the finishing area.

Distillate was purchased at the end of each month in sufficient quantity to fuel just the next month's operations, even though there was sufficient storage capacity (32,000 gallons) for two months of normal operations. The one-month purchase policy was adopted for a variety of reasons: (1) there had never been a disruption in operations due to fuel shortages; (2) working-capital needs were reduced and short-term money, which currently cost 18 percent, was kept to a minimum; and (3) the savings due to avoiding the delivery charge of $150 were minimal. The end-of-month prices that Florida Glass paid for distillate fuel over the past three years are shown in Exhibit 4.

Electricity was supplied by the local utility and was billed on the basis of both peak demand and usage. Demand was measured in terms of the peak kilowatts demanded in any 30-minute interval during the billing month. This charge was directly related to the amount of production capacity brought on line. Because Florida Glass had operated at capacity for some time, the peak demand was virtually unchanged from month to month and the charge was treated as a fixed cost.[2] The usage charge was based on the kilowatt-hours consumed and was billed at a progressive rate, according to the following schedule:

---

[2]Approximately $6,500 per month, which was allocated one-sixth to float, one-half to tempered, and one-third to laminated.

- First 72,000 kWh at $0.0331 per kWh.
- Next 462,000 kWh at $0.0348 per kWh.
- Additional kWh at $0.0396 per kWh.

The usage charge varied from month to month depending on the production mix.

For several years, Florida Glass had been using its Energy Planning Model on a monthly basis to establish the monthly production schedule. The model was a linear program that determined the product mix that maximized total contribution for a given distillate price and appropriate aggregate market-planning ranges.

CASE 18
FLORIDA GLASS COMPANY (A) SUPPLEMENT

The results of the monthly run of the Energy Planning Model had just been received by Oscar Paik, materials manager of the Florida Glass Company. Exhibit 1 presents those results. The model's relationships with the October 1982 inputs are shown in Exhibit 2.

Paik noted that for the current market price of 93.66 cents per gallon, the optimal October production schedule called for 13,425 gallons of distillate-fuel oil. Before placing the order, however, Paik decided to explore the possibility of ordering at this time a two-month supply that would last through both October and November. He reasoned that the current 93.66 cents per gallon price was too good an opportunity to miss, that the company's storage capacity was large enough to handle delivery of a double order, and that next month's ordering and delivery charges ($150) would be avoided.

To see exactly how much distillate would be needed in November, Paik knew he would have to rerun the Energy Planning Model using November's data. This run required a price for distillate, and Paik thought that 94.5 was a reasonable guess for the distillate price at the end of October. Alternatively, Paik thought a higher price of 98 cents was quite possible (especially in light of the recent history of volatile distillate prices) and would serve as a best case for the "savings" associated with the option of buying a two-month supply now.

EXHIBIT 1   Model Results for October

Total Contribution $10,290

Production	Square feet	Price per square ft. ($)	Contribution (excl. energy) ($)	Oil Required (gallons)	Electricity Required (kWh)
Float	21,000	$0.96	$20,160	6,090	243,180
Tempered . . .	3,234	2.63	8,505	3,848	115,935
Laminated . . .	7,581	1.67	12,660	3,487	174,885
Total			$41,325	13,425	534,000

Production Capacity	Used		Avail.	Slack	Shadow Price ($)	Allowable Decrease	Increase
	37,500	<	37,500	0	$0.24	8,388	5,560

Market Constraints	Actual		Limit	Slack or Surplus	Shadow Price ($)	Allowable Decrease	Increase
Float:							
Minimum	21,000	>	16,000	5,000	$0.00	—	5,000
Maximum	21,000	<	21,000	0	0.04	5,000	12,390
Tempered:							
Maximum	3,234	<	8,500	5,266	0.00	5,266	—
Laminated:							
Maximum	7,581	<	15,000	7,419	0.00	7,419	—

Energy Requirements	Used		Required	Slack or Surplus	Shadow Price ($)	Allowable Decrease	Increase
Oil	13,425	>	13,425	0	$0.9366	13,425	—
Electricity:							
Step 1	72,000	<	72,000	0	0.0025	72,000	119,369
Step 2	462,000	<	462,000	0	0.0008	73,303	119,368
Step 3	0						
Total electricity	534,000	>	534,000	0	0.0356	119,369	73,303

Energy Costs	Cost per Unit ($)	Use	Total Cost ($)
Oil	$0.9366	13,425	$12,574
Electricity:			
Step 1	0.0331	72,000	2,383
Step 2	0.0348	462,000	16,078
Step 3	0.0396	0	0
Total			$31,035

EXHIBIT 2   Energy Planning Model—October 1982 Inputs

Variables

FLOAT . . . . .   production of float glass (square feet)
TEMPD . . . . .   production of tempered glass (square feet)
LAMIN . . . . .   production of laminated glass (square feet)
OIL . . . .   amount of oil purchased (gallons)
E1 . . . .   amount of electricity purchased—step 1 (kilowatt-hours)
E2 . . . .   amount of electricity purchased—step 2 (kilowatt-hours)
E3 . . . .   amount of electricity purchased—step 3 (kilowatt-hours)
ETOTAL . . . .   total amount of electricity purchased (kilowatt-hours)

Objective

$$\text{Maximum contribution} = 0.96 \times \text{FLOAT} + 2.63 \times \text{TEMPD} - 1.67 \times \text{LAMIN} -$$
$$0.9366 \times \text{OIL} - 0.0331 \times \text{E1} - 0.0348 \times \text{E2} - 0.0396 \times \text{E3}$$

Constraints

Energy:

    Capacity: $\text{FLOAT} + \text{TEMPD} + 1.75 \times \text{LAMIN} \leq 37{,}500$

    Oil purchase: $0.29 \times \text{FLOAT} + 1.19 \times \text{TEMPD} + 0.46 \times \text{LAMIN} - \text{OIL} = 0$

    Electricity requirement: $11.58 \times \text{FLOAT} + 35.85 \times \text{TEMPD} + 23.07 \times \text{LAMIN} -$
                                      $\text{ETOTAL} = 0$

    Electricity purchase: $-\text{E1} - \text{E2} - \text{E3} + \text{ETOTAL} = 0$

    Electricity 1st step: $\text{E1} \leq 72{,}000$

    Electricity 2nd step: $\text{E2} \leq 462{,}000$

Market:

    Float minimum: $\text{FLOAT} \geq 16{,}000$
    Float maximum: $\text{FLOAT} \leq 21{,}000$
    Tempered maximum: $\text{TEMPD} \leq 8{,}500$
    Laminated maximum: $\text{LAMIN} \leq 15{,}000$

CASE 19
FOULKE CONSUMER PRODUCTS, INC.
The Southeast Region

In 1977 Foulke Consumer Products, Inc., was a small manufacturer and distributor of Brand A of a durable consumer product, with $42 million in sales and less than 5 percent of the market. Ten years later, Foulke had almost $600 million in sales and over 25 percent of the market. This tremendous growth, achieved primarily through acquisitions, caused a strain on the organization, particularly the manufacturing side. The company had grown from 4 plants serving five states to over 40 plants serving the entire country. Many of the acquired plants had formerly competed within the same regions; hence, some redundancies existed. Foulke faced the task of dealing with these regional capacity/profitability problems.

The Industry

The industry in 1987 was composed of a diverse group of manufacturers serving a $1.9 billion wholesale market. Over 800 firms, ranging from small local producers to industry giants, each typically aligned with a particular brand, competed in this brand-sensitive market. Nine brands controlled 67 percent of the market; the four top brands and their respective market shares were:

Brand A	25%
Brand B	11%
Brand C	10%
Brand D	7%

The business was highly competitive at the retail and wholesale levels. Industry growth was low and not expected to pick up in the near future. The product was sold primarily through manufacturers' sales forces directly to retailers.

The Company

Foulke Consumer Products, Inc., founded in 1907, became one of eight Brand A licensees in 1924, with exclusive manufacturing and distribution rights in Massachusetts. Foulke began acquiring other Brand A licensees in 1956, and, by the time the company went public in 1970, it had four plants from which it distributed Brand A in five states and Puerto Rico.

This case was based on a Supervised Business Study prepared by William Hosler (Darden, Class of 1989).

EXHIBIT 1   The Southeast Region

Average Plant Income Statement

Net sales	100.0%
Material	45.8
Labor	7.0
Overhead:	
Variable	7.5
Fixed	4.0
Cost of sales	64.3
Gross margin	35.7%
Delivery:	
Variable	2.7%
Fixed	1.0
Selling and advertising:	
Variable	12.0
Fixed	4.0
Plant administration	3.9
Operating expense	23.6
Operating margin	12.1
Corporate charge	5.8
Income before tax	6.3
Taxes	2.8
Net income	3.5%

Brand A and the other licensees, not pleased with Foulke's success, tried to stall further expansion by the company. In response, Foulke filed an antitrust suit against Brand A in 1971. While the suit stalled in court, Foulke continued to expand by acquiring Brand A's Dallas licensee in 1976 and Brand E, a competitor, in 1983. The company began to market and sell aggressively nationwide—in the process competing directly with other Brand A licensees in their own backyards. Prices and margins in the industry fell, and product historically shipped no farther than 200 miles was routinely transported over 1,000 miles.

In 1986, a jury ruled in favor of Foulke over Brand A and its main licensees. As settlement of the $77 million judgment, Foulke acquired Brand A and all but one of its licensees, thereby doubling its sales and assets and increasing its number of manufacturing facilities to 42.

Although the company now had nationwide rights to Brand A, the earlier competition meant that some markets were being served by as many as four different Foulke plants. These plants operated completely autonomously, with responsibility for both sales and production in their territories. As profit centers, plants were provided with all the functions of small companies (see Exhibit 1 for an average plant income statement). Although sales territories had been redrawn after the acquisition to improve delivery efficiency, problems remained. Some plants lacked capacity, while others had excess. Not all plants had the same

EXHIBIT 2   The Southeast Region
Brand A Product Demand (pieces/year)

Brand A	
Markets	*Demand*
Atlanta	89,179
Birmingham	17,750
Charleston	8,093
Columbia	24,604
Columbus	5,339
Greensboro/W.S.	77,640
Knoxville	19,316
Miami	109,902
Orlando	29,173
Raleigh/Durham	37,900
Savannah	6,493
Tampa	86,799

profitability, and some suffered from severe operating problems. Traditionally, these types of problems had been addressed plant by plant; no effort was made to examine them on a national, or even regional, basis.

The Southeast Region

The Southeast region was one of Foulke's most profitable, with operating margins of 12.5 percent (Exhibit 2 presents annual Brand A demand in the Southeast region by market). The company had three plants in the region (see Exhibit 3). Exhibit 4 gives profit-and-loss statements for the first seven months of 1988 for each plant. Prior to the acquisition, these plants had competed for sales in the region. Sales territories within the region had been reorganized to minimize delivery expense, but no attempt had been made to balance capacity and service with long-term profitability.

Following is a brief description of each plant.

Orlando, Florida, Plant (225,000 units capacity). The Orlando plant was the largest in the region but the least profitable in terms of operating margin. Little could be done to improve margins. Delivery costs were high because most of Orlando's product was shipped south to the Miami area. The plant had a worsening workforce situation because of the area's recent urbanization and rapid growth of high-paying service industries. On the other hand, Orlando's growth also had caused the value of the plant and land on which it was located to skyrocket, to approximately $3.25 million. The plant could be expanded by an additional 75,000 units at a cost of $900,000. With an expansion, however, would come an estimated increase in variable manufacturing costs of approximately $2 per unit for all units, and fixed costs would increase by about $400,000 per year.

EXHIBIT 3   The Southeast Region

The Southeast Region

○   Existing plant site

●   Potential plant site

□   Center of market area

Atlanta, Georgia, Plant (175,000 units capacity).   In contrast to Orlando, the Atlanta plant had a good work force with high stability. Also unlike Orlando, the facility was short on space and had no room to expand. Like Orlando, however, the market value of the plant and the land on which it was situated had increased rapidly, to about $4 million.

Lexington, North Carolina, Plant (187,500 units capacity).   The Lexington plant, the most profitable brand-label plant in the entire company, was ideal in almost every way. It had an excellent work force and was close to its suppliers. The plant and property itself was not as valuable as the other plants (market price of around $2 million). The plant could be expanded by an additional 50,000 units at a cost of $600,000. The estimate was that expansion would increase variable manufacturing costs by $1 per unit for all units and fixed costs by $250,000 per year.

EXHIBIT 4 **The Southeast Region**
Southeast Region Income Statements (7 months ending June 30, 1988)

	Orlando	Atlanta	Lexington
Net sales ($000)	$ 11,788	$ 8,075	$ 7,444
Total pieces	125,952	84,177	78,677
Net sales	100.0%	100.0%	100.0%
Material	46.5	45.4	43.9
Labor	7.1	6.2	6.1
Overhead	9.1	10.2	7.4
Cost of goods	62.7%	61.8%	57.4%
Gross margin	37.3%	38.2%	42.6%
Delivery	4.6	4.1	3.2
Sell. & adv.	18.6	17.8	15.4
Administration	3.5	3.4	3.8
Operating expense	26.7%	25.3%	22.3%
Operating margin	10.6%	13.0%	20.3%

In addition to these three plants, the company was considering two potential new plant sites: Lake City and Ft. Myers, Florida. The Lake City site was attractive primarily because of its rural location, which was similar to that of the Lexington plant. A recent study of Foulke's plants had shown that rural locations tended to be more efficient and profitable than urban ones. The hope was that a plant in Lake City could emulate the production performance of the Lexington plant.

Ft. Myers, on the other hand, was attractive because of its proximity to the Miami-area market. Such a location would significantly reduce the company's overall delivery costs (see Exhibit 5 for per-unit delivery costs from each plant to each major market area). Unfortunately, the company was not optimistic about the possibility of achieving a Lexington-like production record at Ft. Myers, because of the surrounding demographics. More likely, a plant in the Ft. Myers area would resemble Orlando's less-efficient operation. In addition, building a plant of any size in Ft. Myers would cost a base amount of $4.0 million plus $4 per unit of capacity, compared with a $3.5 million base with the same $4 per unit of capacity at Lake City. At either location, the capacity of the new plant would have to be between 62,500 and 250,000 units.

EXHIBIT 5   **The Southeast Region**
Per-Unit Transportation Cost

	Plants				
Markets	*Orlando*	*Atlanta*	*Lexington*	*Ft. Myers*	*Lake City*
Atlanta	$ 5.72	$ 0.66	$ 4.61	$ 8.62	$ 3.36
Birmingham	6.45	1.97	6.58	9.34	4.08
Charleston	5.53	3.80	3.62	8.42	3.16
Columbia	6.18	2.63	2.63	9.08	3.82
Columbus	56.85	14.62	74.71	92.58	27.61
Greens./W.S.	7.89	4.61	0.66	10.79	5.53
Knoxville	8.29	2.54	2.89	11.18	5.92
Miami	4.34	8.62	12.24	1.97	6.71
Orlando	0.66	5.72	7.89	2.89	2.37
Ral./Durham	8.82	4.89	1.97	11.71	6.45
Savannah	20.21	15.16	28.87	36.09	7.22
Tampa	1.38	5.92	9.47	1.58	3.09

CASE 20

FOULKE CONSUMER PRODUCTS, INC., SUPPLEMENT

Memorandum

To: Leander Green, VP–Operations, Southeast Region
From: Paul Jenkins, Senior Analyst
Re: Distribution Issues in the Southeast Region

As per your request, I have analyzed the impact on sourcing of the proposed new plant in Lake City, assuming the closing of the Atlanta plant.

First, it was necessary to estimate the variable production costs of each of our existing plants. These data, along with each plant's annual fixed operating expenses, can be found in Exhibit S1. I derived these figures from the information in case Exhibits 1 and 4 (see Case 19).

I then constructed a linear programming (LP) model using the variable production costs and the per-unit transportation costs provided in case Exhibit 5. The LP model is designed to minimize the Southeast Region's total annual transportation and variable production costs; Exhibit S2 contains an annotated version of the spreadsheet. The resulting sourcing plan for the base case (existing plants and capacities) can be found in Exhibit S3. These results seem to suggest that Lake City is indeed a more promising site than Ft. Myers for a new plant. Exhibit S4 shows the new sourcing plan given a large new plant in Lake City (capacity of 250,000), assuming that we close down the Atlanta facility and that the new plant emulates the cost performance of the Lexington facility. As you can see, the annual savings are dramatic.

I am sending you this report today because you indicated time was of the essence. Though generally pleased with the model and convinced that the Lake City plant does in fact reduce our annual distribution costs, I must qualify my recommendation for the following reason. After building the original model, it occurred to me that, for the sake of presentation and to accentuate the positive, maybe we should be *maximizing* contribution, rather than *minimizing* cost. I thought the two approaches would yield the same result and was surprised when—in the case of the new Lake City plant—they did not (see Exhibits S5 and S6). Admittedly, the difference is not great, but it is still somewhat disconcerting. I will get back to you as soon as I have resolved the matter.

Exhibit S1   Per-Unit Variable Cost of Production

	Orlando	Atlanta	Lexington
Net sales (000)	$11,788	$8,075	$7,444
Total pieces	125,952	84,177	78,677
Price per unit	$93.59	$95.93	$94.61
Variable costs per unit:			
Material	$43.52	$43.55	$41.54
Labor	6.64	5.95	5.77
Variable overhead*	5.55	6.38	4.57
Variable selling/admin.†	13.06	12.81	10.93
Total variable cost per unit . . .	$68.78	$68.69	$62.80

*Variable overhead calculated as 7.5%/(7.5% + 4.0%) of total.

†Variable selling/admin. calculated as 12.0%/(12.0% + 4.0%) of total.

EXHIBIT S2 Annotated *What's Best!* Linear Programming Spreadsheet

	A	B	C	D	E	F	G
3	COST SUMMARY						
4							
5			Per-Unit				
6			Variable	Variable			
7		Production	Production	Distribution			
8	Plant	Volume	Cost	Cost	Cost	Total	
9							
10	Orlando	+C37	$68.78	+B10*C10		+D10+E10	
11	Atlanta	+D37	$68.69	+B11*C11		+D11+E11	
12	Lexington	+E37	$62.80	+B12*C12		+D12+E12	
13	Ft. Myers	+F37	$0.00	+B13*C13		+D13+E13	
14	Lake City	+G37	$0.00	+B14*C14		+D14+E14	
15							
16	TOTAL ANNUAL VARIABLE OPERATING COST		=		@SUM(COL)	(MINIMIZE)	

19 DISTRIBUTION SCHEDULE AND COST

		----Plants----							Brand		Shadow	-----Range-----	
22	Markets	Orlando	Atlanta	Lexington	Ft. Myers	Lake City	Total		Demand	Surplus	Price	Decrease	Increase
24	Atlanta	0	0	0	0	0	@SUM(ROW)	>	89,179	+H24-I24	$0.00	0	0
25	Birmingham	0	0	0	0	0	@SUM(ROW)	>	17,750	+H25-I25	$0.00	0	0
26	Charleston	0	0	0	0	0	@SUM(ROW)	>	8,093	+H26-I26	$0.00	0	0
27	Columbia	0	0	0	0	0	@SUM(ROW)	>	24,604	+H27-I27	$0.00	0	0
28	Columbus	0	0	0	0	0	@SUM(ROW)	>	5,339	+H28-I28	$0.00	0	0
29	Greens./W.S.	0	0	0	0	0	@SUM(ROW)	>	77,640	+H29-I29	$0.00	0	0
30	Knoxville	0	0	0	0	0	@SUM(ROW)	>	19,316	+H30-I30	$0.00	0	0
31	Miami	0	0	0	0	0	@SUM(ROW)	>	109,902	+H31-I31	$0.00	0	0
32	Orlando	0	0	0	0	0	@SUM(ROW)	>	29,173	+H32-I32	$0.00	0	0
33	Ral./Durham	0	0	0	0	0	@SUM(ROW)	>	37,900	+H33-I33	$0.00	0	0
34	Savannah	0	0	0	0	0	@SUM(ROW)	>	6,493	+H34-I34	$0.00	0	0
35	Tampa	0	0	0	0	0	@SUM(ROW)	>	86,799	+H35-I35	$0.00	0	0
37	Production volume	@SUM(COL)	@SUM(COL)	@SUM(COL)	@SUM(COL)	@SUM(COL)							
39	Distribution cost	TOTAL*	TOTAL	TOTAL	TOTAL	TOTAL							

* +C24*C60+C25*C61+C26*C62+C27*C63+C28*C64+C29*C65+C30*C66+C31*C67+C32*C68+C33*C69+C34*C70+C35*C71

	A	B	C	D	E	F	G	H	I	J	K	L	M	N
41														
42														
43	PRODUCTION SCHEDULE/COST													
44	--													
45						Shadow		Range						
46		Produced		Capacity	Slack	Price	Decrease	Increase						
47		--------		--------	--------	--------	--------	--------						
48	Orlando	+C37	<	225,000	+D48-B48	$0.00	0	0						
49	Atlanta	+D37	<	175,000	+D49-B49	$0.00	0	0						
50	Lexington	+E37	<	187,500	+D50-B50	$0.00	0	0						
51	Ft. Myers	+F37	<	0	+D51-B51	$0.00	0	0						
52	Lake City	+G37	<	0	+D52-B52	$0.00	0	0						
53														
54														
55	PER-UNIT DISTRIBUTION COSTS													
56	--													
57					--------------Plants-------------									
58	MARKETS			Orlando	Atlanta	Lexington	Ft. Myers	Lake City						
59	-------			-------	-------	---------	---------	---------						
60	Atlanta			$5.72	$0.66	$4.61	$8.62	$3.36						
61	Birmingham			$6.45	$1.97	$6.58	$9.34	$4.08						
62	Charleston			$5.53	$3.80	$3.62	$8.42	$3.16						
63	Columbia			$6.18	$2.63	$2.63	$9.08	$3.82						
64	Columbus			$56.85	$14.62	$74.71	$92.58	$27.61						
65	Greensboro/W.S.			$7.89	$4.61	$0.66	$10.79	$5.53						
66	Knoxville			$8.29	$2.54	$2.89	$11.18	$5.92						
67	Miami			$4.34	$8.62	$12.24	$1.97	$6.71						
68	Orlando			$0.66	$5.72	$7.89	$2.89	$2.37						
69	Raleigh/Durham			$8.82	$4.89	$1.97	$11.71	$6.45						
70	Savannah			$20.21	$15.16	$28.87	$36.09	$7.22						
71	Tampa			$1.38	$5.92	$9.47	$1.58	$3.09						

Exhibit S3 Cost-Minimization Solution for Base Case

COST SUMMARY

Plant	Production Volume	Per-Unit Variable Production Cost	Variable Production Cost	Variable Distribution Cost	Total
Orlando	225,000	$68.78	$15,475,500	$615,435	$16,090,935
Atlanta	99,688	$68.69	$6,847,569	$257,728	$7,105,296
Lexington	187,500	$62.80	$11,775,000	$370,556	$12,145,556
Ft. Myers	0	$68.78	$0	$0	$0
Lake City	0	$62.80	$0	$0	$0

TOTAL ANNUAL VARIABLE OPERATING COST = $35,341,787

DISTRIBUTION SCHEDULE AND COST

Markets	Orlando	Atlanta	Lexington	Ft. Myers	Lake City	Total		Brand Demand	Surplus	Shadow Price	Range Decrease	Range Increase
Atlanta	0	70,106	19,073	0	0	89,179	>	89,179	0	$69.35	70,106	75,312
Birmingham	0	17,750	0	0	0	17,750	>	17,750	0	$70.66	17,750	75,312
Charleston	0	0	8,093	0	0	8,093	>	8,093	0	$68.36	8,093	19,073
Columbia	0	0	24,604	0	0	24,604	>	24,604	0	$67.37	24,604	19,073
Columbus	0	5,339	0	0	0	5,339	>	5,339	0	$83.31	5,339	75,312
Greens./W.S.	0	0	77,640	0	0	77,640	>	77,640	0	$65.40	70,106	19,073
Knoxville	0	0	19,316	0	0	19,316	>	19,316	0	$67.63	70,106	19,073
Miami	109,902	0	0	0	0	109,902	>	109,902	0	$76.31	874	19,073
Orlando	28,299	0	874	0	0	29,173	>	29,173	0	$72.63	874	19,073
Ral./Durham	0	0	37,900	0	0	37,900	>	37,900	0	$66.71	37,900	19,073
Savannah	0	6,493	0	0	0	6,493	>	6,493	0	$83.85	6,493	75,312
Tampa	86,799	0	0	0	0	86,799	>	86,799	0	$73.35	874	19,073
Total production volume	225,000	99,688	187,500	0	0							
Distribution cost	$615,435	$257,728	$370,556	$0	$0							

EXHIBIT S3 *Concluded*

PRODUCTION SCHEDULE/COST

		Produced	Capacity	Slack	Shadow Price	Range Decrease	Increase
Orlando	<	225,000	225,000	0	$3.19	19,073	874
Atlanta	<	99,688	175,000	75,312	$0.00	75,312	*********
Lexington	<	187,500	187,500	0	$1.94	19,073	70,106
Ft. Myers	<	0	0	0	$5.56	0	874
Lake City	<	0	0	0	$13.83	0	6,493

COST SUMMARY

Plant	Production Volume	Per-Unit Variable Production Cost	Variable Production Cost	Distribution Cost	Total
Orlando	74,688	$68.78	$5,137,041	$324,146	$5,461,187
Atlanta	0	$68.69	$0	$0	$0
Lexington	187,500	$62.80	$11,775,000	$367,689	$12,142,689
Ft. Myers	0	$68.78	$0	$0	$0
Lake City	250,000	$62.80	$15,700,000	$1,072,964	$16,772,964

TOTAL ANNUAL VARIABLE OPERATING COST = $34,376,840

DISTRIBUTION SCHEDULE AND COST

Markets	Orlando	Atlanta	Lexington	Ft. Myers	Lake City	Total	Brand Demand	Surplus	Shadow Price	Range Decrease	Increase
Atlanta	0	0	19,974	0	69,232	89,179	89,179 >	0	$69.77	69,232	35,214
Birmingham	0	0	0	0	17,750	17,750	17,750 >	0	$70.49	17,750	35,214
Charleston	0	0	8,093	0	0	8,093	8,093 >	0	$68.78	8,093	19,947
Columbia	0	0	24,604	0	0	24,604	24,604 >	0	$67.79	24,604	19,947
Columbus	0	0	0	0	5,339	5,339	5,339 >	0	$94.02	5,339	35,214
Greens./W.S.	0	0	77,640	0	0	77,640	77,640 >	0	$65.82	69,232	19,947
Knoxville	0	0	19,316	0	0	19,316	19,316 >	0	$68.05	19,316	19,947
Miami	74,688	0	0	0	35,214	109,902	109,902 >	0	$73.12	74,688	150,312
Orlando	0	0	0	0	29,173	29,173	29,173 >	0	$68.78	29,173	35,214
Ral./Durham	0	0	37,900	0	0	37,900	37,900 >	0	$67.13	37,900	19,947
Savannah	0	0	0	0	6,493	6,493	6,493 >	0	$73.63	6,493	35,214
Tampa	0	0	0	0	86,799	86,799	86,799 >	0	$69.50	74,688	35,214
Total production volume	74,688	0	187,500	0	250,000						
Distribution cost	$324,146	$0	$367,689	$0	$1,072,964						

109

Exhibit S4 *Concluded*

PRODUCTION SCHEDULE/COST

	Produced		Capacity	Slack	Shadow Price	Range Decrease	Range Increase
Orlando	74,688	<	225,000	150,312	$0.00	150,312	*********
Atlanta	0	<	0	0	$10.71	0	5,339
Lexington	187,500	<	187,500	0	$2.36	19,974	69,232
Ft. Myers	0	<	0	0	$3.89	0	0
Lake City	250,000	<	250,000	0	$3.61	35,214	74,688

EXHIBIT S5   Annotated *What's Best!* Linear Programming Spreadsheet with Maximize Contribution Objective

	A	B	C	D	E	F	G	H
3	COST SUMMARY							
4	---							
5								
6				Per-Unit				
7		Production	Per-Unit Selling	Variable Production	Per-Unit	Total	Distrib.	
8	Plant	Volume	Price	Cost	Contrib.	Contrib.	Cost	Total
9	---							
10	Orlando	+C37	$93.59	$68.78	+C10-D10	+B10*E10	+C39	+F10-G10
11	Atlanta	+D37	$95.93	$68.69	+C11-D11	+B11*E11	+D39	+F11-G11
12	Lexington	+E37	$94.61	$62.80	+C12-D12	+B12*E12	+E39	+F12-G12
13	Ft. Myers	+F37	$94.71	$68.78	+C13-D13	+B13*E13	+F39	+F13-G13
14	Lake City	+G37	$94.71	$62.80	+C14-D14	+B14*E14	+G39	+F14-G14
15								
16					TOTAL ANNUAL CONTRIBUTION	=	@SUM(COL)	

	A	B	C	D	E	F	G	H	I	J	K	L	M	N
19	DISTRIBUTION SCHEDULE AND COST													
20														
21				---Plants---							Shadow	-----Range-----		
22	Markets	Orlando	Atlanta	Lexington	Ft. Myers	Lake City	Total		Brand Demand	Surplus	Price	Decrease	Increase	
23	---													
24	Atlanta	0	0	0	0	0	@SUM(ROW)	<	89,179	+J24-H24	$0.00	0	0	0
25	Birmingham	0	0	0	0	0	@SUM(ROW)	<	17,750	+J25-H25	$0.00	0	0	0
26	Charleston	0	0	0	0	0	@SUM(ROW)	<	8,093	+J26-H26	$0.00	0	0	0
27	Columbia	0	0	0	0	0	@SUM(ROW)	<	24,604	+J27-H27	$0.00	0	0	0
28	Columbus	0	0	0	0	0	@SUM(ROW)	<	5,339	+J28-H28	$0.00	0	0	0
29	Greens./W.S.	0	0	0	0	0	@SUM(ROW)	<	77,640	+J29-H29	$0.00	0	0	0
30	Knoxville	0	0	0	0	0	@SUM(ROW)	<	19,316	+J30-H30	$0.00	0	0	0
31	Miami	0	0	0	0	0	@SUM(ROW)	<	109,902	+J31-H31	$0.00	0	0	0
32	Orlando	0	0	0	0	0	@SUM(ROW)	<	29,173	+J32-H32	$0.00	0	0	0
33	Ral./Durham	0	0	0	0	0	@SUM(ROW)	<	37,900	+J33-H33	$0.00	0	0	0
34	Savannah	0	0	0	0	0	@SUM(ROW)	<	6,493	+J34-H34	$0.00	0	0	0
35	Tampa	0	0	0	0	0	@SUM(ROW)	<	86,799	+J35-H35	$0.00	0	0	0
36														
37	Production volume	@SUM(COL)	@SUM(COL)	@SUM(COL)	@SUM(COL)	@SUM(COL)								
38	---													
39	Distribution cost	TOTAL*	TOTAL	TOTAL	TOTAL	TOTAL								
40														

* +C24*C60+C25*C61+C26*C62+C27*C63+C28*C64+C29*C65+C30*C66+C31*C67+C32*C68+C33*C69+C34*C70+C35*C71

EXHIBIT S5 *Concluded*

	A	B	C	D	E	F	G	H	I	J	K	L	M	N
41.														
42.														
43	PRODUCTION SCHEDULE/COST													
44														
45						Shadow		Range						
46		Produced	Capacity		Slack	Price	Decrease	Increase						
47														
48	Orlando	+C37	225,000	<	+D48-B48	$0.00	0	0						
49	Atlanta	+D37	0	<	+D49-B49	$0.00	0	0						
50	Lexington	+E37	187,500	<	+D50-B50	$0.00	0	0						
51	Ft. Myers	+F37	0	<	+D51-B51	$0.00	0	0						
52	Lake City	+G37	250,000	<	+D52-B52	$0.00	0	0						
53														
54														
55	PER-UNIT DISTRIBUTION COSTS													
56														
57				-------Plants-------										
58	MARKETS	Orlando	Atlanta	Lexington	Ft. Myers	Lake City								
59														
60	Atlanta	$5.72	$0.66	$4.61	$8.62	$3.36								
61	Birmingham	$6.45	$1.97	$6.58	$9.34	$4.08								
62	Charleston	$5.53	$3.80	$3.62	$8.42	$3.16								
63	Columbia	$6.18	$2.63	$2.63	$9.08	$3.82								
64	Columbus	$56.85	$14.62	$74.71	$92.58	$27.61								
65	Greensboro/W.S.	$7.89	$4.61	$0.66	$10.79	$5.53								
66	Knoxville	$8.29	$2.54	$2.89	$11.18	$5.92								
67	Miami	$4.34	$8.62	$12.24	$1.97	$6.71								
68	Orlando	$0.66	$5.72	$7.89	$2.89	$2.37								
69	Raleigh/Durham	$8.82	$4.89	$1.97	$11.71	$6.45								
70	Savannah	$20.21	$15.16	$28.87	$36.09	$7.22								
71	Tampa	$1.38	$5.92	$9.47	$1.58	$3.09								

112

EXHIBIT S6 Contribution-Maximizing Solution for Case of 250,000-Volume Plane in Lake City; No Plant in Atlanta

COST SUMMARY

Plant	Production Volume	Per-Unit Selling Price	Per-Unit Variable Production Cost	Per-Unit Contrib.	Total Contrib.	Distrib. Cost	Total
Orlando	69,349	$93.59	$68.78	$24.81	$1,720,549	$300,975	$1,419,574
Atlanta	0	$95.93	$68.69	$27.24	$0	$0	$0
Lexington	187,500	$94.61	$62.80	$31.81	$5,964,375	$367,689	$5,596,686
Ft. Myers	0	$94.71	$68.78	$25.93	$0	$0	$0
Lake City	250,000	$94.71	$62.80	$31.91	$7,977,500	$961,379	$7,016,121

TOTAL ANNUAL CONTRIBUTION = $14,032,381

DISTRIBUTION SCHEDULE AND COST

Markets	Orlando	Atlanta	Lexington	Ft. Myers	Lake City	Total		Brand Demand	Surplus	Shadow Price	Range Decrease	Range Increase
Atlanta	0	0	19,947	0	69,232	89,179	<	89,179	0	$23.82	69,232	40,553
Birmingham	0	0	0	0	17,750	17,750	<	17,750	0	$23.10	17,750	40,553
Charleston	0	0	8,093	0	0	8,093	<	8,093	0	$24.81	8,093	19,947
Columbia	0	0	24,604	0	0	24,604	<	24,604	0	$25.80	24,604	19,947
Columbus	0	0	0	0	0	0	<	5,339	5,339	$0.00	5,339	********
Greens./W.S.	0	0	77,640	0	0	77,640	<	77,640	0	$27.77	69,232	19,947
Knoxville	0	0	19,316	0	0	19,316	<	19,316	0	$25.54	19,316	19,947
Miami	69,349	0	0	0	40,553	109,902	<	109,902	0	$20.47	64,349	155,651
Orlando	0	0	0	0	29,173	29,173	<	29,173	0	$24.81	29,173	40,553
Ral./Durham	0	0	37,900	0	0	37,900	<	37,900	0	$26.46	37,900	19,947
Savannah	0	0	0	0	6,493	6,493	<	6,493	0	$19.96	6,493	40,553
Tampa	0	0	0	0	86,799	86,799	<	86,799	0	$24.09	69,349	40,553
Total production volume	69,349	0	187,500	0	250,000							
Distribution cost	$300,975	$0	$367,689	$0	$961,379							

Exhibit S6 *Concluded*

PRODUCTION SCHEDULE/COST

	Produced		Capacity	Slack	Shadow Price	Range Decrease	Range Increase
Orlando	69,349	<	225,000	155,651	$0.00	155,651	********
Atlanta	0	<	0	0	$21.53	0	0
Lexington	187,500	<	187,500	0	$3.38	19,947	69,232
Ft. Myers	0	<	0	0	$5.01	0	0
Lake City	250,000	<	250,000	0	$4.73	40,553	69,349

FREEMARK ABBEY WINERY

In September 1976, William Jaeger, a member of the partnership that owned Freemark Abbey Winery, had to make a decision: should he harvest the Riesling grapes immediately or leave them on the vines despite the approaching storm? A storm just before the harvest is usually detrimental, often ruining the crop. A warm, light rain, however, will sometimes cause a beneficial mold, *botrytis cinerea,* to form on the grape skins. The result is a luscious, complex sweet wine, highly valued by connoisseurs.

The Winery

Freemark Abbey was located in St. Helena, California, in the northern Napa Valley. The winery produced only premium wines from the best grape varieties. Of the 25,000 cases of wine bottled each year (about the same as Chateau Lafite-Rothschild), most were Cabernet Sauvignon and Chardonnay. About 1,000 cases of Riesling and 500 cases of Petite Syrah were also bottled. (A case contains 12 bottles of wine.)

The Napa Valley extends for 30 miles, from Calistoga in the north to Napa in the south. The average temperature decreases as one moves south, closer to San Francisco Bay and the cold ocean waters. Freemark Abbey's grapes came from an ideal climate in the central and southern parts of the valley.

Winemaking

Wine is produced when the fruit sugar, which is naturally present in the juice of grapes, is converted by yeast, through fermentation, into approximately equal molecular quantities of alcohol and carbon dioxide. Sparkling wines excepted, the carbon dioxide is allowed to bubble up and dissipate. The wine then ages in barrels for one or more years until it is ready for bottling.

By various decisions during vinification—for example, the type of wooden barrel used for aging—the winemaker influences the style of wine produced. The style adopted by a particular winery depends mainly on the owners' preferences, though it is influenced by marketing considerations. Usually, as the grapes ripen, the sugar levels increase and the acidity levels decrease. The winemaker tries to harvest the grapes when they have achieved the proper

Copyright © 1980 by the President and Fellows of Harvard College.
Harvard Business School case 181-027
This case was prepared by William S. Krasker as the basis for class discussion rather than to illustrate either effective or ineffective handling of an administrative situation. Reprinted by permission of the Harvard Business School.

balance of sugar and acidity for the style of wine sought. The ripening process is variable, however, and, if the weather is not favorable, the proper balance might never occur.

Several different styles of Riesling (more accurately, Johannisberg Riesling) are on the market. If the grapes are harvested at 20 percent sugar, the wine is fermented "dry" (all the sugar is converted to alcohol and carbon dioxide) or "near dry." The resulting wine, at about 10 percent alcohol, is light bodied. If the grapes are harvested at 25 percent sugar, the winemaker can produce a wine with the same 10 percent alcohol but with 5 percent residual sugar; this wine is sweet and relatively full bodied.

A third and rare style results when almost-ripe Riesling grapes are attacked by the *botrytis* mold. The skins of the grapes become porous, allowing water to evaporate while the sugar remains. Thus, the sugar concentration increases greatly, sometimes to 35 percent or more. The resulting wine, with about 11 percent alcohol and 13 percent residual sugar, has extraordinary concentration, and the *botrytis* itself adds to the wine's complexity. Freemark Abbey had already produced a *botrytised* Riesling from its 1973 vintage.

Jaeger's Decision Problem

From the weather reports, Jaeger concluded that there was a 50-50 chance that the rainstorm would hit the Napa Valley. Since the storm had originated over the warm waters off Mexico, he thought there was a 40 percent chance that, if the storm did strike, it would lead to the development of the *botrytis* mold. If the *botrytis* did not form, however, the rainwater, which would be absorbed into the grapes through the roots of the vines, would merely swell the berries by 5–10 percent, decreasing their concentration. This would yield a thin wine that would sell wholesale for only about $2.00 per bottle, about $0.85 less than Jaeger could obtain by harvesting the not-quite-ripe grapes immediately and eliminating the risk. Freemark Abbey always had the option of not bottling a wine that was not up to standards. It could sell the wine in bulk, or it could sell the grapes directly. These options would bring only half as much revenue, but would at least avoid damaging the winery's reputation, which would be risked by bottling an inferior product.

If Jaeger decided not to harvest the grapes immediately in anticipation of the storm, and the storm did not strike, Jaeger would probably leave the grapes to ripen more fully. With luck, the grapes would reach 25 percent sugar, resulting in a wine selling for around $3.50 wholesale. Even with less-favorable weather, the sugar levels would probably top 20 percent, yielding a lighter wine selling at around $3. Jaeger thought these possibilities were equally likely. In the past, sugar levels occasionally failed to rise above 19 percent. Moreover, while waiting for sugar levels to rise, the acidity levels must also be monitored. When the acidity drops below about 0.7 percent, the grapes must be harvested whatever the sugar level. If this happened, the wine would be priced at only about $2.50. Jaeger felt that this event had only about 0.2 probability.

EXHIBIT 1

FREEMARK ABBEY

1973
NAPA VALLEY
Sweet Johannisberg Riesling

Edelwein

Produced and Bottled by
FREEMARK ABBEY WINERY, ST. HELENA, CALIFORNIA
Alcohol 11.4% by volume
Residual Sugar 10% by weight

Winery label.

The wholesale price for a *botrytised* Riesling would be about $8 per bottle. Unfortunately, the same process that resulted in increased sugar concentration also caused a 30 percent reduction in the total juice. The higher price was, therefore, partly offset by a reduction in quantity. Although fewer bottles would be produced, there would be essentially no savings in vinification costs. The costs to the winery were about the same for each of the possible styles of wine and were small relative to the wholesale price.

CASE 22
GALAXY MICRO SYSTEMS

For the past three months, Taylor Jansen of Galaxy Micro Systems had been discussing with a national computer sales-and-service franchiser the subcontracting of the warranty contract for the new Galaxy work station, the GMS-II. In addition to featuring an advanced technology chip and a state-of-the-art processor, the GMS-II would be sold with a three-year warranty that included parts and labor. Galaxy had decided to subcontract the service support for the warranty, rather than expand its regional offices to include a technical support staff. As the GMS-II project manager, Jansen had moved contract discussions to a point where the specification of the terms and conditions of the warranty contract were acceptable to both parties, but the pricing of the contract was undecided.

At a recent meeting, the franchiser's negotiating team had proposed to Jansen the choice of two pricing schemes for the warranty of those units installed during the introductory year. The first approach was a fixed-price contract with a lump-sum payment of $770,000 due on May 1, 1993, the planned date for the introduction of the GMS-II. Alternatively, the price could be a function of the number of units installed during the introductory year, and payments would be spread over three years. The specific terms would be $70,000 payable on May 1, 1993, plus three annual installments of $80 per unit for those units installed during the introductory year, May 1, 1993, to April 30, 1994. The annual installments were subject to a minimum of $250,000 and were payable on the first of May of 1994, 1995, and 1996. For either alternative, a new contract would be negotiated for sales occurring after the introductory year.

For the services to be rendered by the franchiser, both proposals seemed reasonable to Jansen and compatible with the negotiating limits specified by Galaxy senior management. The choice between the alternatives, however, was difficult. The deferred-payment schedule of the installment contract was a real advantage in light of Galaxy's hurdle rate of 18 percent. Offsetting that advantage, however, was the sense that the installment contract was riskier than the fixed-price contract, because first-year sales of the GMS-II were very uncertain.

During the introductory year, GMS-II sales would come from two sources: (1) the successful closure by senior management of an extraordinarily large purchase by a single customer and (2) the efforts of the Galaxy regional offices. Unfortunately, Jansen was uncertain about the final results of both sources.

The potentially large purchase would be from a long-standing customer that had been provided, as part of the development effort, a prototype version of the GMS-II. The initial feedback from this firm had been quite positive, and a purchase of 1,500 units was mentioned. Galaxy senior management had aggressively pursued this opportunity. They had confirmed the size of the potential order but believed that the firm was still months away from a final commitment, even though the prototype had already been under evaluation for six months. The delay in the decision made the Galaxy management nervous; current sentiment put the chances of closing the deal at about 60 percent. This major purchase was pivotal to the successful launch of GMS-II. Not only was it a significant order, but it could also be used by the sales force in discussions with smaller clients as testimony to the "recognized advantages of the GMS-II work station."

In addition to the potential 1,500-unit purchase by the long-standing client, Jansen estimated that first-year sales of the GMS-II from the efforts of the regional offices would be 3,000 units. She recognized that this figure was only a "best guess" and that actual sales would be in a range around this figure. If the major purchase were landed, she believed that the range would be skewed to the high side. She feared that, without the big purchase, not only would the range be skewed to the low side, but also her best guess would also have to be revised downward. In a rough-cut fashion, the following outcomes and their respective probabilities captured Jansen's assessment of sales from the regional offices during the introductory year of the GMS-II.

Sales by Regional Offices			
If Major Purchase		**If No Major Purchase**	
Sales	*Probability*	*Sales*	*Probability*
2,000	0.2	1,000	0.4
3,000	0.4	2,500	0.4
4,500	0.4	4,000	0.2

The pricing issue had to be resolved expeditiously, because deadlines were approaching. The final text of the promotional literature was due at the printers in a week, and the public introduction of the GMS-II was only two months away.

CASE 23
GALAXY MICRO SYSTEMS SUPPLEMENT

Taylor Jansen, after reviewing her assessment of GMS-II sales from the regional offices, felt uneasy about the forecast's simplicity. Focusing on three possible outcomes did not seem to capture adequately the possibility that sales could be anywhere within a range of values and that the extremes of the range could be beyond the high and low figures of her forecasts. In addition, the three outcomes were given extraordinary weight in the decision, even though they were just a few among many possible outcomes.

The Galaxy planning system required that sales forecasts be made in the form of cumulative distribution functions, using the terminology below to describe the 0.05, 0.25, 0.50, 0.75, and 0.95 fractiles. Jansen saw this forecasting format as a means to address her concerns with her rough-cut forecast. The resulting forecasts were:

Sales by Regional Offices

	If Major Purchase	*If No Major Purchase*
1 in 20 low	1,900	500
1 in 4 low	2,500	1,500
Midrange	3,000	2,300
1 in 4 high	4,000	3,000
1 in 20 high	5,500	4,000

CASE 24
GEORGE'S T-SHIRTS

For the last six years, George Lassiter, a project engineer for a major defense contractor, had enjoyed an interesting and lucrative side business—designing, manufacturing, and hawking "special event" T-shirts. He had created shirts for a variety of rock concerts, major sporting events, and special fund-raising events. Although his T-shirts were not endorsed by the event sponsors and were not allowed to be sold within the arenas at which the events were held, they were cleverly designed, well produced, and reasonably priced (relative to the official shirts). They were sold in the streets surrounding the arenas and in the nearby parking lots, always with the appropriate licenses from the local authorities. Lassiter had a regular crew of vendors to whom he sold the shirts on consignment for $100 per dozen. These vendors then offered the shirts to the public at $10 apiece.

A steady stream of T-shirt business came to Lassiter, and he was generally working on several designs in various stages of development. His current problem centered around the number of shirts he should have stenciled for a rock concert that was scheduled to be staged in two months.

This concert was almost certain to be a huge success. Lassiter had no doubt that the 20,000 tickets for the standing area around the stage would be instantly bought by the group's devoted fans. The major unknown was the number of grandstand seats that would be sold. It could be anywhere from a few thousand to more than double the number of standing tickets. Given the popularity of the performing group and the intensity of the advance hype, Lassiter believed the grandstand sales were more likely to be at the high, rather than the low, end of the spectrum. He decided to think in terms of three possibilities (a high, a medium, and a low value), specifically, 80,000, 50,000, and 20,000 grandstand seats. Despite his optimism, he believed that 50,000 was as likely as either of the other two possibilities combined. The two extreme numbers were about equally likely; maybe 80,000 was a little more likely than 20,000.

A second unknown was the percentage of the attendees who would buy one of his shirts. To the credit of his designs and the quality of the shirts, the number generally (about 6 times out of 10) ran about 10 percent of the attendance, but sometimes it was in the range of 5 percent. On a rare occasion, sales would be in the vicinity of 15 percent (maybe 1 time out of 10, if Lassiter's memory served him right).

Several weeks ago, Lassiter had requested a cost estimate for this concert's design from the silk screener/shirt supply house with which he had been working for several years. He used this particular firm almost exclusively because he had found it to be reliable in both quality and schedule and to have reasonable prices. The estimate had arrived yesterday. It was presented in the usual batches of 2,500 shirts with the usual volume discounts:

Order Size	Cost
10,000	$32,125
7,500	$25,250
5,000	$17,750

The order had to be one of the quoted multiples of 2,500 shirts.

On the basis of his volume estimates, Lassiter was prepared to place an order for 5,000 shirts. With his sales generally about 10 percent of attendance, he didn't believe he could justify an order for 7,500 shirts. Such an order would require the concert's attendance to be 75,000, and while he was optimistic about the popularity of the event, he wasn't quite that optimistic. Also, in the past, he had taken the conservative route and it had served him well. He had never had an appreciable number of shirts left over, but those that were left were sold to a discount clothing chain for $1.50 per shirt.

CASE 25
HARIMANN INTERNATIONAL

My first impression was that the Pioneer order would be a very attractive opportunity so late in the season. Not only would I be supporting an old and established customer, but the order would be profitable and the unexpected business would permit me to keep some of my workers on the payroll during the early portion of the off-season. These small gestures often pay handsome rewards in future years. But that April 6 deadline to ship the goods seems terribly close. If I accept the order and miss the date, I could be left with a substantial amount of finished goods that would be impossible to move at this time of the year. I have squeezed the production schedule as far as possible, and I don't know what else I can do. Do you think I should turn down the order?

> Vikram Dhawan
> President, Harimann International
> March 2, 1992

Harimann International was a Delhi-based manufacturer and exporter of finished textiles (primarily table linens and women's clothing) with sales in excess of 10 million Indian new rupees (INR). The company was launched in May 1990 by Vikram Dhawan after his graduation with a bachelor of arts degree in mathematics from St. Stephen's College. In addition to providing a livelihood in the short term, the business was to be a stepping stone to an MBA in the United States. Dhawan believed that the experience of managing a small company would be of invaluable assistance during the MBA program and hoped that the profits from a successful business would provide the necessary funds to finance the education.

Dhawan's decision to be an exporter of finished goods was influenced by the variety of incentives the Indian government offered in an effort to reduce the country's international trade deficit. Whenever goods were exported to one of several targeted countries, any profits from the sale were accorded tax-exempt status. In addition, if the order resulted in payments in excess of 150,000 INR, several other attractive incentives applied, including a partial rebate of duties paid for imported raw materials used in the manufacture of exported goods (duty drawback), a cash incentive designed to improve the competitiveness of Indian products in world markets (cash compensatory support), and the granting of licenses to replenish domestic raw materials used in the production of exported goods (replenishment licenses).

During the first year of operations, Dhawan limited his business to brokering linen household goods. He bought finished linens from a supplier, labeled and packaged them according to customer specifications, and shipped the packaged

This case was prepared in conjunction with Professor Dana R. Clyman (Darden) and Research Assistant Hasmeeth S. Uppal (Darden).

goods to the customer. The first nine months were slow: Customers were few and orders were small. Toward the end of the year, however, a particular style of hand-embroidered table linen became very popular and sales were excellent. On the strength of this product, it appeared that the goal for first-year sales would be achieved. Unfortunately, Dhawan's sources could not keep up with demand, and sales were lost. The frustration of being unable to satisfy customer demand led Dhawan to enlarge the scope of his business and to become directly involved in manufacturing.

In May 1991, Dhawan added women's blouses and skirts to his product line in response to requests by satisfied customers. Thereafter, the business grew quickly. Over the remaining months of 1991, shipments were made to Canada, France, Great Britain, Italy, Japan, and the United States. Over the final few months of the year—Harimann's peak season—internal production had averaged 1,000 garments per day. The company had recently acquired a second manufacturing facility and now employed over 100 people.

Pioneer Trading Company, Ltd.

The Pioneer Trading Company was one of Dhawan's first customers and had been a regular customer ever since. Pioneer was a large importer with over 20 retail outlets in Japan. It sourced many of its goods from India and Hong Kong to spread political risks and to encourage competitive pricing.

Over the years, Mori Fuji, the founder and president of Pioneer, had emphasized that his interests were "quality goods delivered on time at reasonable prices." Dhawan believed that Fuji had been fair in all of their previous transactions. Although Fuji looked after himself, he never did so at the expense of his suppliers, and he made special efforts to help his suppliers meet his expectations. For example, instructions for the labels and hang tags that were to be attached to the garments were not only detailed, they were pictographic. This practice greatly reduced the chance of error in printing the labels in Japanese and in meeting the specifications of the applicable laws. This attention to detail not only benefited Pioneer and its suppliers but was appreciated as well.

The Pioneer Order

Discussions regarding the most recent order from Pioneer began at the end of January 1992, when Dhawan received Pioneer's request for samples of six styles of garments along with a preliminary order should the samples and prices prove satisfactory. The samples were prepared within a week and sent by courier, with their respective prices. Because the cloth vendors were moving into their off-season, to be sure of the availability of material, Dhawan ordered all of the necessary fabric, lining, and zippers for Pioneer's order at this time. He reasoned that the investment of 188,400 INR was not really significant because, even though embroidered cloth could only be sold for about 65 percent of cost, unembroidered cloth and the other materials could always be resold for 90 percent of their respective costs.

EXHIBIT 1   Pioneer Profit Analysis (figures in INR)

	Style E 1756	Style E 1757	Style E 1758	Style E 1759	Style E 1760	Style E 1761	Total
Unit costs							
Materials:							
Grey cloth	18.75	22.50	14.25	36.00	17.00	21.00	
Lining cloth	6.75			11.25			
Zipper	7.00			7.00			
Processing:							
Bleaching	4.75	5.00	4.50	5.75	4.00	5.00	
Embroidery	19.50			50.00	22.00		
Cutting/sewing	9.00	5.25	5.50	13.00	8.00	7.50	
Washing/packing . . .	5.00	5.00	5.00	5.00	5.00	5.00	
Other direct costs	7.00	5.00	5.00	12.00	5.00	6.00	
Total unit cost	77.75	42.75	34.25	140.00	61.00	44.50	
Contract							
Quantity	1,000	1,400	1,400	1,000	1,100	1,500	
Selling price (per unit) . .	82.75	47.75	38.25	146.00	65.00	48.50	
Revenue	82,750	66,850	53,550	146,000	71,500	72,750	493,400
Materials cost	32,500	31,500	19,950	54,250	18,700	31,500	188,400
Processing cost	38,250	21,350	21,000	73,750	42,900	26,250	223,500
Other direct costs	7,000	7,000	7,000	12,000	5,500	9,000	47,500
Total cost	77,750	59,850	47,950	140,000	67,100	66,750	459,400
Contribution*	5,000	7,000	5,600	6,000	4,400	6,000	34,000
Government Incentives†							281,238
Total value							315,238

* Because Japan was one of the qualifying countries, no taxes were assessed.

† Because Japan was one of the qualifying countries and because the revenues received would exceed 150,000 INR, the order qualified for the government incentives (duty drawback 10 percent, cash compensatory support 15 percent, and replenishment licenses with a 40 percent face value, which Dhawan valued at 80 percent of face value). In total, these incentives were valued at 57 percent of revenues received.

Several weeks later, Dhawan received the order from Pioneer for all six styles, conditional on Harimann's ability to make minor changes to three of the styles and to meet a shipping date of April 6.

Although he was somewhat concerned about meeting the April 6 shipping date, Dhawan thought that the order was an attractive opportunity. The Indian government was encouraging exports to Japan, and, as a result, the profits from the Pioneer contract would be tax-free. (See Exhibit 1 for Dhawan's profit analysis of the contract.) More important, however, because receipts would exceed the qualifying minimum of 150,000 INR, the contract would also qualify for the other government incentives. Thus, Dhawan would be able to claim 10 percent of the actual receipts in duty drawback and 15 percent in cash compensatory support. Each of these incentives would be paid in cash by the Indian government. In addition, Dhawan would also qualify for a replenishment license with a face value of 40 percent of actual receipts. Although replenishment licenses were not cash instruments, they were very liquid assets due to an informal yet well-established market. Prices for these licenses were relatively stable at 80 percent of face value. Because Dhawan had no direct need for the licenses, he routinely sold any he received in this market. As a result, Dhawan valued the total package of government incentives at 57 percent of revenue, which in this case amounted to 281,238 INR, as shown in Exhibit 1.

Dhawan was inclined to accept the order, not only because it was profitable but also because it would allow him to keep many of his employees on the payroll longer than he had anticipated. Since the Pioneer order was being placed late in the manufacturing season, Dhawan would be able to delay the planned furlough of many of his manufacturing-plant workers. An extra week or two of work would be greatly appreciated by most of them.

The Schedule

Dhawan was nervous about the production schedule, however, particularly because the first step of the process—embroidery—would be contracted out to a third-party vendor. (The rest of the production process would be carried out in-house.) If production began on the morning of March 3, the date on which the embroiderer said that he could begin work, Harimann would have to complete the order within 35 days to meet Pioneer's April 6 shipment deadline. Dhawan estimated that, with considerable personal attention, the order could be completed and shipped within 27 days (by the end of the day, March 29). This estimate allowed the eight days required by the embroider, two days for cutting, eight days for sewing, eight days for washing and packing, and one day for final shipping activities. Although the cloth that was not to be embroidered would have to be bleached, this process would not influence the schedule, because bleaching (which would take five days) would be done in parallel with embroidery. Exhibit 2 presents Dhawan's proposed schedule pictorially.

EXHIBIT 2   Proposed Schedule

	March													April		
	3	5	7	9	11	13	15	17	19	21	23	25	27	29	31	2	4	6

In all, the benefits of accepting the order seemed to outweigh the difficulties of meeting the schedule. Nevertheless, Dhawan, hoping to arrange for extra time in case any unanticipated problems arose, faxed Pioneer a confirmation of the order on the condition that the shipment date be postponed to April 17. Pioneer's response was immediate: April 6 was preferred, and would Dhawan please confirm that it would indeed be possible for him to meet that date.

Pioneer's response prompted Dhawan to look again at the schedule. Although he was fairly confident that he would be able to ship the order by April 6, he admitted to himself that there was a possibility of missing that date. In fact, he knew that unanticipated problems arose fairly regularly in this business, and in this case he estimated there was a 20 percent chance some problem would arise that caused him to miss the date. In the event that the shipping date was missed, Pioneer would probably still accept the order but—in keeping with industry practice—only at a greatly reduced price. Generally, a buyer would pay 30 to 50 percent of the contract price for a late shipment, though in some circumstances payment had been as little as 20 percent. Even though the relationship with Pioneer was a good one, it was late in Pioneer's season and, as a result, a 20 percent payment was a definite possibility. In this particular case, Dhawan believed there was a 40 percent chance that Pioneer would pay 50 percent of the contracted price, a 40 percent chance it would pay only 30 percent, and a 20 percent chance it would pay as little as 20 percent. What's more, Dhawan knew that once he accepted the order, he would have to deliver the goods to protect his future business relationship with Pioneer, even if that meant incurring a loss.

Before deciding whether to accept the order, Dhawan explicitly considered the possibility of a late delivery and each of the possible percentages that might be applied to the contracted price to reduce the payment should the order be late. After weighing all of these possibilities and their chances of occurring, Dhawan concluded that the order would still be profitable, on average. On the basis of this analysis, which is presented in Exhibit 3, Dhawan was inclined to accept the order.

The Embroiderer

Prior to faxing back his confirmation of the order, Dhawan called the embroiderer to confirm the schedule. To his dismay, the embroiderer was no longer willing to confirm the schedule he had originally proposed. The original commitment had been made on the basis of starting the Harimann job on March 3, just as soon as the embroiderer's current job was completed; this start date would have permitted completion of embroidery on March 10. Unfortunately, since they had last spoken, the embroiderer had accepted several other important jobs, and the Harimann order would have to take its place behind them. The embroiderer was apologetic, but he would only commit to completing the order by March 27.

Dhawan was outraged by the change and argued strongly for the original timetable. Because the embroiderer agreed that he would reexamine his

---

EXHIBIT 3   Dhawan's Analysis (figures in INR)

On-Time Delivery
(chance of occurring, 80%)

Receipts	493,400
Costs	459,400
Contribution	34,000
Government incentives*	281,238
Total value	315,238

Late Delivery
(chance of occurring, 20%)

Average percent payment[†]	36%
Average receipts[‡]	177,624
Costs	459,400
Contribution	(281,776)
Government incentives*	101,246
Total value	(180,530)

Average Value

$$315{,}238 \times 0.80 + (180{,}530) \times 0.20 = 216{,}084$$

---

* When receipts exceed 150,000 INR, government incentives apply and Dhawan values them at 57 percent of receipts.

[†] Average percent payment: 50 percent × 0.40 + 30 percent × 0.40 + 20 percent × 0.20 = 36 percent.

[‡] Average receipts: 493,000 × 36 percent = 177,624.

---

schedule, Dhawan believed that he had made some progress, but he remained pessimistic. By the end of the conversation, Dhawan believed there was about a one in eight chance that the embroiderer would adjust his schedule and complete the Harimann order by the original date of March 10. The discussions, however, had also enabled Dhawan to piece together the vendor's production schedule and discover that it would be possible for the embroiderer to complete the Harimann job on March 20. When Dhawan raised this possibility, the vendor agreed that this was possible and that he would try to make it happen, but he did not commit. Based on this part of the conversation, Dhawan believed that he was four times as likely to receive the goods on March 20 as on March 10.

Although Dhawan made clear to the embroidery vendor that he was infuriated by the vendor's behavior, he had no other choices. Only 8 to 10 firms in all of India embroidered cloth. This oligopolistic condition encouraged exploitation by vendors, who made production decisions on the basis of the profitability of the order and the extent to which the customer could be delayed before the order would be canceled. The current situation was even worse than usual because it was near the end of the season and all of the other embroiderers' schedules were full. Dhawan would have to live with the possibility of a March 27 completion date.

EXHIBIT 4   **Revised Schedule (assuming a March 20 embroidery delivery date)**

	March			April
	3 5 7 9 11 13 15 17 19 21 23 25 27 29 31		2 4 6	

Activity

Embroidery

Bleaching

Cutting

Sewing

Washing & packing

Shipping

The Schedule Revisited

The potential delay in embroidery prompted Dhawan to look even more closely at his own operations for ways to reduce his production schedule. His initial thinking had been very sequential—cut, then sew, then wash and pack, and finally ship. This sequence allowed the batches to remain intact and, as a result, required far less management attention to control than a schedule that broke up the batches. In light of the schedule demands, however, the Pioneer order would have to be treated differently. Even though two days would be needed to complete the cutting, sewing could begin after the first day's cutting. Similarly, washing and packing could begin before all of the sewing was completed, thereby saving an additional three, or possibly even five, days.

Dhawan was encouraged. At no extra cost, the parallel processing of the Pioneer order could reduce production time from 19 days to 15 or maybe even 13 days, if everything went smoothly. These time savings would allow him to ship the order just before the April 6 deadline, even if he did not receive the embroidered cloth until the evening of March 20, as shown by the revised schedule in Exhibit 4.

If a problem arose during parallel processing, however, the usual control systems might not identify it. Dhawan believed that, if such a problem arose, by the time it was all sorted out, his in-house production time for cutting, sewing, washing and packing, and shipping could take anywhere from 20 to 22 days to complete. Furthermore, because he had never before attempted to control such a complicated operating process, Dhawan believed that the chance of such a problem arising had to be about 40 percent, twice the rate at which problems normally arose when processing was sequential.

CASE 26
HIGHTOWER DEPARTMENT STORES: IMPORTED STUFFED ANIMALS

On the morning of January 17, 1993, Julia Brown gathered together the past sales data on stuffed animals. As toy buyer for the chain of Hightower Department Stores, she knew that a careful review of the performance of the various models of stuffed animals sold during 1992 was necessary prior to her annual round-the-world buying trip in late January.

During this trip she would be buying all the imported toys that the Hightower chain would carry during the 1993 Christmas season. In particular, she would choose approximately 15 different types of bears, raccoons, elephants, and so on from the stuffed animals offered by various manufacturers in West Germany. These choices would be made after viewing what each manufacturer had to offer and then considering the overall attractiveness of this menagerie. She often made the decisions fairly quickly, using the sound judgment she had gained through her many years of buying experience.

Julia knew that her major purchase would be Steiff stuffed teddy bears, which Hightower had carried almost every year since they were first manufactured in Germany in 1903. She also had had experience with other stuffed-animal manufacturers and planned to reorder with them. But in choosing the last few animals for her assortment, Julia sometimes hedged her bets by ordering a minimum quantity of new models to test their sales potential. These test models were sold in only one store within the chain, and the results of the sales were then used to decide the fate of each animal for the succeeding year.

Julia was preparing to go over the test sales data for the three models tested in 1992: a bear, a pig, and a raccoon. A description of these models and the sales results are given in Exhibit 1. At first glance, the raccoon results looked very promising. Julia tentatively decided she would go with it for 1993 but knew she still needed to determine what quantity to order. In contrast, the pig had turned out to be a real "dog," and Julia was ready to admit that her attraction to this model on last year's trip may have been a mistake. Last, deciding whether to order the bear was one of those tough choices Julia had to make quite often. Although the test market had indeed succeeded in separating the raccoon from the pig, it had done nothing to help determine the future success of the bear.

Hightower Department Stores

The Hightower chain was a small but profitable company operating 16 full-line department stores in six major metropolitan areas in the eastern United States. The Hightower name was associated with quality, large selection, and good

---

EXHIBIT 1   1992 Test Animals

Animal	Description	Landed Cost*	Retail Price	Sales Proj.†	Purchases	Sales	Closeout Inventory
Bear	Dark brown, long nose, 12 inches, handmade, plush	$5.43	$12.95	150	50	10	40
Pig	Cartoon-like, pink, 10 inches, soft plastic handmade	$6.23	$13.95	180	50	4	46
Raccoon	Grey/black, 14 inches, plush, realistic, handmade	$6.42	$13.95	170	50	32	18

---

* Total cost per unit; includes manufacturer's cost, shipping, import duties, and insurance.

† During her January 1992 buying trip, Julia Brown projected these holiday-season unit sales volumes based on all stores.

value. The company envisioned itself as a fashion leader; it took special pride in its ability to respond quickly to changes in fashion and style. Management also emphasized that TV and newspaper advertising, point-of-sale presentations, and knowledgeable and friendly sales personnel had been important to the success of the chain.

For the fiscal year ending January 31, 1992, the Hightower chain had reported $371 million in sales and $17.5 million net profit after taxes (see Exhibit 2). The expectations for the 1993 fiscal year were for small increases over 1992, but, as in previous years, these increases would not keep up with the general inflation rate.

Toy Department

Buying toys that could be sold at a profit had been an increasingly difficult challenge for Julia Brown and department stores in general. Toy departments were typically not so profitable as other store departments. Competition from general merchandise chains, mass merchandisers, variety stores, toy supermarkets, and toy specialty stores had lowered conventional department store toy sales to about 9 percent of the total market. The department stores' need for high margins made it difficult for them to compete in the toy business. Whereas the Hightower chain looked for margins of 40 to 50 percent, specialty toy chains such as Toys R Us operated with only 30 percent margins for most merchandise.

EXHIBIT 2   Store Sizes and Sales Volume (year ending January 31, 1992)

Store	Size (thousand square feet)	Sales Volume ($ millions)
Washington, D.C.		
Downtown	370	$ 36.7
Prince George's Plaza, Md.	182	22.2
Columbia Md.	150	19.7
Tysons Corner, Va.	205	26.8
Boston		
Downtown	361	34.0
Burlington Mall	104	14.4
South Side Plaza	139	18.3
Philadelphia		
Downtown	369	32.8
King of Prussia	145	17.7
Cherry Hill, N.J.	105	12.3
Baltimore		
Downtown	320	27.4
Towson	139	17.0
Golden Ring	107	12.4
Pittsburgh		
Downtown	420	39.2
Monroeville	150	18.3
Westmoreland Mall	171	21.6
Total	3,437	$370.8

Julia Brown had developed the following strategies to help cope with the increasing competition:

1. Deemphasizing TV-promoted toys—the high-demand, lower-margin toy category.
2. Excelling in areas that mass merchants could not, such as special events, displays, and demonstrations.
3. Emphasizing imported items and exclusive items not available elsewhere.
4. Varying the amount of floor space devoted to toys; in many department stores, toy floor space tripled during the Christmas season.
5. Developing the "grandmother" business—that is, stocking toys often purchased by grandmothers, who tended to shop in department stores and usually were not as concerned about price as other toy buyers.

As a consequence of these strategies, about one-half of Hightower's toy business was imports, compared with probably less than 20 percent for the mass merchandisers and toy supermarkets.

EXHIBIT 3   Stuffed-Animal Performance History: Christmas-Season Sales

Year	1988	1989	1990	1991	1992*
Unit sales	5,932	5,837	5,879	6,025	5,983
Dollar sales (thousands)	52.7	58.0	63.9	66.8	68.5
Gross margin† (thousands)	25.0	26.2	26.8	31.0	31.5

*Preliminary figures.

†Retail sales plus end-of-year closeout minus landed cost.

EXHIBIT 4   Performance Statistics (year ending January 31, 1992)

	Toy Departments	Total Stores
Net sales percentage change from last year	2.8%	4.7%
Cumulative mark-on	41.3%	47.5%
Mark-downs (total price reductions from original retail—as a percentage of net overall sales)	13.3%	11.6%
Stock shortage (lost merchandise from theft, unrecorded mark-downs, and so on—as a percentage of sales)	2.2%	2.6%
Gross margin	30.8%	43.4%
Gross margin return on inventory cost (gross margin/ average inventory)	$1.40	$2.60
Stock turns	3.2×	3.4×
Sales per square foot	$86.00	$108.00

In almost all types of stores, nearly 50 percent of the toy sales occurred in November and December each year. Data on sales and gross margins for November and December of the last five years for Hightower's stuffed animals are given in Exhibit 3. Although the margin figures appeared considerably higher than those for the toy department in general, Julia knew that, when the total year was considered, stuffed animals performed only slightly better than average.

Figures for 1991 (see Exhibit 4) showed that the Hightower toy department's performance was like other department stores. The two figures Brown paid particular attention to were gross margin return on investment (inventory) and sales per square foot. Gross margin return on investment was calculated as the ratio of gross margin (sales minus cost of goods sold) to average inventory at cost. Sales per square foot was relevant, because it specifically considered the amount of selling space consumed to produce a given dollar of sales volume.

Stuffed animals occupied about 20 square feet of display space in each store during the Christmas season, compared with 5 square feet at all other times. The nature of the display varied somewhat from one year to the next, but the animals were always exhibited together in a single display. Anywhere from 15 to 20 different animals were available in a given year.

Imported stuffed animals were items consistent with Brown's merchandising strategy. They carried relatively high margins, responded well to creative display efforts and to advertising, and appealed to the grandmother business. If carefully chosen, they could be distinctive Hightower department store items; in most cases a particular imported animal would be exclusive to the Hightower chain.

Imported stuffed animals were carried only through the Christmas season. In January unsold inventory was unloaded at 80 cents on the dollar[1] to Fernstone's, a job-lot retailer. This policy had been instituted to clear out year-end inventories in preparation for the cut-back in display space allocated to toys. Brown felt this alternative was preferable either to marking the merchandise down for the year-end sale or storing unsold animals until the next season. Marking down items hurt the Hightower image, and carrying inventory until the next year was costly and greatly interfered with the selection of new animals for the succeeding year. The higher-valued imports were thus always sold before fiscal year-end, and the small selection carried in the off-season consisted entirely of domestic products.

Imported Toy Buying

Each January a number of buyers from the Hightower Department Stores chain went on round-the-world buying trips to select and order merchandise Hightower would offer during the fall and Christmas seasons. Since most foreign manufacturers operated on a make-to-order basis, lead times ranged from six to eight months. Hence, a January trip was necessary to ensure deliveries in time for the next Christmas selling season.

Julia Brown had bought toys for 15 years and had been on 10 previous Hightower foreign buying trips. This large base of experience served her well when evaluating new items. Her usual procedure was to decide a retail price and project a sales volume for each item of interest. If these projections were particularly encouraging, Julia would then place an order on the spot, using a very rough rule of thumb to determine exactly how many to order.

For the riskier items, she would try to buy test models for possible inclusion in the succeeding year's line of toys. Specific offerings changed greatly from one year to the next; but Julia was often able to persuade some of the smaller manufacturers to provide a small lot in one year, with a promise that the same item would be manufactured the next.

---

[1]Sold at 80 percent of the landed cost. *Landed cost* included all costs associated with buying an imported item: manufacturer's cost, freight, import duties, and so on.

Terms for the purchase of European-manufactured toys were delivery net 30. Payment was due within 30 days of delivery, and the purchaser was responsible for import duties, freight, insurance, and so forth.

The buying procedure for stuffed animals differed slightly from that used with other toy merchandise. Because the stuffed-animal manufacturers were concentrated in West Germany, Julia was able to visit each in turn before placing any orders. At the end of these visits, Julia determined her desired stuffed-animal merchandise assortment for the following season. In this manner she was able to judge each item relative to the others available that year.

This buying strategy necessitated a careful system of note-taking and evaluation. For each animal of interest, Julia filled out a form she had personally developed. The completed form contained a description of the animal, information on the manufacturer, the manufacturer's price (in U.S. dollars), and estimated landed costs. In addition, Julia usually jotted down her evaluation of the salability of the animal, the features that differentiated this item, and any other information that might make her order-writing easier.

Two quantitative judgments also included were the retail price Julia thought the animal should carry and a projected sales potential at that price. Mark-ups on stuffed animals were customarily at least 50 percent over landed cost, and Julia set the retail price based on her feel for the appeal and price sensitivity of a particular animal. To round out her notes, Julia would then estimate the unit sales to expect if this animal was placed in the Hightower chain for the Christmas season.

Test Market

Each year Julia selected up to three imported animals as test models, which she bought in small lots of 50 units, the customary minimum order accepted by the German manufacturers. They were then sold exclusively in the Tysons Corner, Virginia, store (chosen as a representative Hightower store because of its size, sales volume, and consumer profile).

Once purchased, the test animals were treated like the other imported items. To avoid complications associated with the test, each test animal replaced a similar nontest animal. Thus the total number of animals was the same at the test store as at all other stores. Likewise, the display space per animal was not affected by the test.

Over the past 10 years, 20 different animals had been tested. Eighteen of these had been adopted for the succeeding year, and data were available on resulting total sales. The two animals not chosen were a rabbit in 1984 and a skunk in 1988, because both had very poor sales during their test years. Exhibit 5 contains the relevant information on these 20 test animals, including the projected sales volume Julia had estimated on her first exposure to each item. When a test animal was adopted as a regular the next year, it was offered at all 16 stores (the Tysons Corner store included) at the same retail price used in the test.

EXHIBIT 5   **Past Test Results**

Test Year	Animal	Landed Cost (dollars)	Retail Price (dollars)	Sales* Projection (units)	Test Sales (units)	Realized Sales (units)
1981 .... Ape		$2.33	$4.95	260	27	304
1982 .... Bear		3.15	5.95	280	19	374
1982 .... Dragon		2.52	4.95	230	14	234
1983 .... Bird		2.63	5.95	170	7	144
1984 .... Rabbit		2.85	5.95	180	6	ANA+
1984 .... Bear		3.18	6.95	140	8	133
1985 .... Dog		2.99	5.95	260	12	209
1986 .... Elephant		2.74	6.95	250	11	140
1986 .... Cat		3.20	6.95	270	30	458
1987 .... Bear		3.91	8.95	160	13	245
1987 .... Monkey		4.39	9.95	210	10	208
1987 .... Dinosaur		2.70	5.95	150	14	308
1988 .... Skunk		3.14	5.95	190	4	ANA+
1988 .... Mouse		4.91	10.95	150	7	47
1989 .... Raccoon		4.29	8.95	200	16	244
1990 .... Bear		4.34	9.95	220	23	385
1990 .... Alligator		5.88	11.95	250	8	269
1990 .... Dog		5.04	10.95	270	15	243
1991 .... Monkey		5.88	12.95	270	8	146
1991 .... Bear		5.19	11.95	170	10	259

*Made prior to the test market.

+ANA means animal not adopted.

Brown's Analysis

Julia Brown called up her Lotus spreadsheet file that contained historical test sale data. Her first step in analyzing test animals was to update her plot of the first full year's unit sales versus the previous year's test sales. This year she had two points to add, one for a monkey that sold 8 during its 1991 test and 146 when adopted for 1992 and the other for a bear that tested at 10 units and sold 259 last year. This scatter plot is given in Exhibit 6.

The general shape of this cloud of points convinced Julia that test results were a good indicator of eventual sales volume. It appeared to her that the better the animal did during the test market, the better it would generally do when offered in all stores the succeeding year.

Turning to the three items tested in 1992, Julia made some mental notes about the sales potential of each. The pig, tested at four units, was in uncharted territory. Julia guessed that, if she did adopt it for 1993, sales would run about 100 units. Julia figured that the bear, with a test of 10 units, ought to sell about 200 units. Last, the raccoon looked like the leading seller of the season. Test sales of 32 projected to a total sales volume of 500 for the coming year.

EXHIBIT 6   Scatter Plot of Realized versus Test Sales

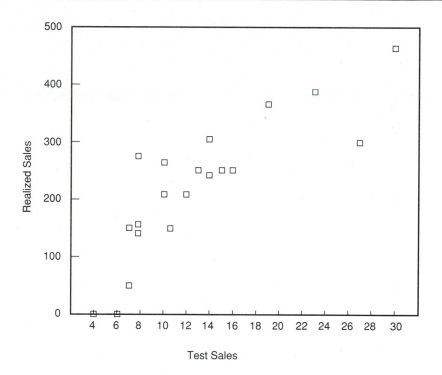

Next, Julia ran some numbers to decide the fate of the three animals. Exhibit 7 shows the calculated gross margin of each animal at its projected sales volume. The figures for the raccoon and bear looked promising, but Julia felt the pig was not worthy of adoption. She reasoned that Hightower was better off using the display space for another animal. She could certainly find a domestic animal that would still bring in at least $1,150 contribution during the Christmas season. In addition, the domestic animals could be ordered as needed, avoiding the inevitable mark-down and closeout to Fernstone's.

Julia then turned to work out order quantities for the two adopted animals. Her 150 percent rule of thumb implied ordering 300 bears and 750 raccoons. This rule had worked well in the past—she had almost never stocked-out of an imported stuffed animal. She had always felt that the only way to turn a profit was to make sure her inventories lasted through the Christmas season. In her mind a stock-out would be deadly to profits. Not only would Hightower lose the foregone contribution of the stocked-out item, but it might also lose some amount of future sales to those customers upset because a particular item was not available. On the other hand, Julia could also see that, since stock-outs would probably occur at the very end of the year, panicky last-minute buyers might easily switch to another animal. In this situation, the consequences of

---
EXHIBIT 7   Calculated Gross Margins of Each Animal

Animal	Projected Unit Sales	Gross Margin per Unit	Estimated Total Gross Margin
Bear	200	$7.52	$1,504
Pig	100	7.72	772
Raccoon	500	7.53	3,765

---

stocking-out of any one item were not that damaging. Julia figured that upset customers and switchable customers might cancel each other out, so the net effect of a stock-out was probably just the lost contribution of that item. Julia promised herself she would think more about lowering the order quantities.

CASE 27
INTERNATIONAL GUIDANCE AND CONTROLS

Time was running out on the $20 million CARV (Confined Aquatic Recovery Vehicle) project, and project manager Thomas Stearns was concerned about meeting schedule. With 10 months left, considerable portions of the software remained to be developed, and he was by no means certain that all necessary development work would be completed on time.

Software Development

Stearns had had his project team working all out in recent months on the software development for CARV's command and guidance system. His headcount (the number of full-time-equivalent workers assigned to the project) had been increased recently, so total development costs were running at $300,000 per month, 25 percent over budget. Stearns believed there was but an 80 percent chance that the necessary software would be completed in the remaining 10 months. Despite this risk of not meeting schedule, he could not increase the headcount on the project or increase the rate of software development in any way.

If the software were not completed on time, Stearns was fairly certain that one or two extra months of work would suffice to complete the project. Unfortunately, each month's delay in project completion meant a 2.5 percent ($500,000) reduction in the price of the contract. In addition to this precisely defined cost of not meeting schedule, a hard-to-quantify but no less significant cost of lost reputation was associated with not completing a project as scheduled.

Hardware Expansion

Part of the difficulty in developing the software for CARV was a result of the original design for the hardware. This somewhat underdesigned hardware was making the software development much more difficult and time-consuming than originally planned.

One remedy that would virtually eliminate schedule risk would be to immediately begin an expansion of the hardware portion of the system. This expansion would require five months of effort at a total cost to the project of $1.5 million. In addition, this action would significantly reduce the software-development effort, to a point where software-development costs would decrease to $200,000 per month for the remaining 10 months of the project.

Delaying the Hardware Expansion

Because the hardware expansion could be completed in five months, Stearns thought continuing with the all-out development of the software for the next five months would be prudent before committing to the hardware expansion. The software progress of the next five months would certainly give him a better idea of the chances of completing the project on schedule. If the five-month progress were favorable, then Stearns reasoned that the chances of completing the project on time would rise to 90 percent. If the progress were unfavorable, the chances would decrease to something like 40 percent. However, the distinct possibility also existed that the progress over the next five months would leave him in the same position in which he now found himself, with an 80 percent probability of completing the project as scheduled. Stearns believed that this latter event (not learning anything new in the next five months) had a probability of about 30 percent. He thought carefully about how to distribute the remaining 70 percent probability between the "favorable progress" and "unfavorable progress" events and soon realized that, in order to remain consistent with all of his earlier assessments, the probability of "favorable progress" had to be 56 percent and the probability of "unfavorable progress" had to be 14 percent.

If he decided to expand the hardware at the end of five months, he would again eliminate all the risk of not meeting the schedule and would also alleviate much of the software-development burden. He reasoned that the remaining five months of software development would cost only $150,000 per month because much of the previous five months of developed software would be usable.

CASE 28
JADE SHAMPOO (A)

Debbie Kennedy, assistant product manager for Jade Shampoo, was delighted with the results of the just-completed test market of her proposed change to the Jade bottle cap. From the beginning of the 18-month project, she had been convinced that replacing Jade's traditional twist-off cap with a more convenient flip-top-dispenser cap would more than pay for itself in increased sales and profits. The test results confirmed her position—sales in the test market exceeded the break-even level.

The only remaining hurdle was to convince the product manager to endorse the national introduction of the change.

Shampoo Market

The shampoo market was one of the most competitive, highly fragmented markets in the health-and-beauty-aids (HBA) business. With retail sales exceeding $1.8 billion in 1986, it was the largest HBA category after analgesics. The category was very profitable, with high margins and simple technology, and it was fashion driven, with different additives and scents appealing to different consumers. As a result, there were over 200 national shampoo brands, most of them commanding less than 1 percent of the market.

Jade Shampoo was a relatively large, stable player in this volatile market. It was positioned as a basic, all-family shampoo and avoided the frequent formulation and fragrance changes of its more trendy competitors. The strategy had been successful: Jade commanded a steady 5 percent share of the market and was usually in the top five shampoo brands in sales.

Kennedy was forecasting 1987 sales to be $91,500,000 retail, $58,560,000 factory. At Jade's average factory price of $1.28 per unit, the sales forecast translated into a projected volume of 45,750,000 units. The current contribution of 36 cents per unit was not expected to change in the coming year.

The Dispenser-Cap Project

The dispenser-cap project had special significance for Kennedy; it was the first project that she had begun as a recently hired MBA, almost 18 months ago. She had come up with the idea while reviewing the results of the brand's biannual usage and attitude survey, in which consumers had been questioned as to their likes and dislikes about various shampoo brands. Kennedy noticed that several

This case was based on a Supervised Business Study prepared by Donna M. Packard (Darden, Class of 1987).

brands had improved their overall preference ratings since the previous study, with the strongest gains in the area of convenience. When she investigated any changes that these brands may have made in the past two years, she discovered that all of them had introduced flip-top-dispenser caps to replace their old-fashioned twist-off caps.

Although management had historically been reluctant to change Jade in response to market trends, Kennedy believed that this was one trend she could not afford to overlook. The study showed that convenient dispensing was especially important to Jade's primary target markets, children and over-40 adults. A dispenser cap might help attract consumers in these groups who were now using another family shampoo. The product manager of Jade Shampoo, Marion Hoffman, to whom Kennedy reported, agreed with the assessment and suggested that Kennedy form a Dispenser-Cap-Project team. In addition to Kennedy, this task force included representatives of the departments in the company that would be involved in developing, testing, producing, and selling the new dispenser cap. After several meetings, the group agreed on a plan for testing and implementing the proposed Jade dispenser cap.

The cap would be the same color as the current Jade cap and, to minimize costs, would be of a standard flip-top design, rather than a custom design. It would require the purchase of a new molding machine and a set of molds at a cost of $1 million. The new cap would use a different kind of plastic and would cost 1.5 cents more than the old cap. The team did not expect any other costs to increase with the new cap, nor did the team expect the price to change in response to this product improvement.

There was general enthusiasm among the members of the project team for the new cap. The "product news" would help obtain better advertising and display support from retailers. The brand's advertising agency was looking forward to incorporating the dispenser cap into a new "all-family-convenience" campaign. Both the sales department and the ad agency expressed confidence that the dispenser cap would increase sales for Jade. The only notes of caution came from the brand's research and development technician, who suggested that the smaller aperture in the dispenser cap might lead to the use of less product on each application as well as a reduction in spillage, an often overlooked source of sales. Kennedy noted both points but was not overly disturbed by them. She believed that users would continue to dispense the amount of product they felt appropriate, regardless of the size of the opening, and that spillage could not be a significant portion of sales.

In a memorandum to Hoffman (Exhibit 1), Kennedy expressed her confidence that the dispenser cap would result in a sales increase substantially above her calculated break-even increase of 7.8 percent. She also argued that the downside risk of moving ahead with the new cap was outweighed by the upside potential.

The Test Plan

The first step in testing the new cap was a product-use test, which was intended to determine if current Jade users would like the new dispenser at least as well as the current cap. It was a blind, paired comparison in which 100 current Jade users were given two bottles of Jade, one with the dispenser cap and one with the current cap. The bottles were not labeled, and the subjects were not told what product they had or if there were any differences between the actual products (there were not). The subjects were instructed to use one bottle for one week and the other bottle for the next week. At the end of the second week they were telephoned and asked which of the shampoos they preferred overall and how the shampoos compared on specific attributes such as convenience, cleaning, and manageability.

The results (Exhibit 2) were very encouraging to Kennedy. Consumers preferred the dispenser-cap product over the current-cap product for convenience. They also preferred the dispenser-cap product overall, even though there was no other difference between the two products than the cap.

With these successful results in hand, Kennedy obtained permission to proceed to a full-market test of the dispenser cap—a much more comprehensive test than the product-use test. The national plan for introducing the new cap would

---

EXHIBIT 1   Break-Even Volume for Dispenser Cap

To: Marion Hoffman, Product Manager, Jade Shampoo

From: Debbie Kennedy, Asst. Product Manager, Jade Shampoo

Subject: Jade Dispenser-Cap Economics

The following calculations are based on the recently promulgated guidelines for capital-expenditure analysis: three-year horizon, 18 percent hurdle rate, straight-line depreciation, and a 40 percent tax rate.

On the basis of our detailed cost estimates for the special tooling investment associated with the proposed dispense cap ($1.0 million) and the incremental cost of the new caps themselves ($0.015 per unit), the break-even volume is 49.316 million units per year. See the attachment for the spreadsheets that detail this calculation.

A volume of 49.316 million units represents a 7.8 percent increase over current volume. This increase is well within my most likely estimate of a 10 to 12 percent increase.

On the downside exposure, let us take a pessimistic view of the cap's success and suppose that volume in the first year increases by only half of the amount required for break-even (3.9 percent). Profitability with the dispenser cap ($9.640) would then be below the forecasted level with the current cap ($9.882). Under these conditions, company policy would require that we drop the dispenser cap and return to the old cap. The net present value of this scenario is $20.755 million, $0.731 million less than staying with the current cap. See attached spreadsheet for details.

On the other hand, if the volume were to be double the break-even increase (15.6 percent—less than 4 percentage points above my most likely range), the net present value would be $23.093 million. See the attachment for details. This is $1.607 million more than staying with the current cap. The downside exposure seems small relative to this potential!

Attachment

EXHIBIT 1   *Concluded*

Calculation of the break-even-sales level

NPV without the dispenser cap

Unit volume		45.750	45.750	45.750
BT contribution		16.470	16.470	16.470
AT profits		9.882	9.882	9.882
Cash flow		9.882	9.882	9.882
NPV @ 18%	21.486			

NPV with the dispenser cap

Initial investment	1.000			
Unit volume		49.316	49.316	49.316
BT contribution		17.014	17.014	17.014
Depreciation		0.333	0.333	0.333
AT profit		10.008	10.008	10.008
Cash flow	(1.000)	10.342	10.342	10.342
NPV @ 18%	21.486			

Pessimistic scenario (3.9% increase—50% of break-even increase)

Initial investment	1.000			
Unit volume		47.534	45.750	45.750
BT contribution		16.399	16.470	16.470
Depreciation		0.333	0.667	0.000
AT profit		9.640	9.482	9.882
Cash flow	(1.000)	9.973	10.149	9.882
NPV @ 18%	20.755			

Optimistic scenario (15.6% increase—200% of break-even increase)

Initial investment 1.000				
Unit volume		52.887	52.887	52.887
BT contribution		18.246	18.246	18.246
Depreciation		0.333	0.333	0.333
AT profit		10.748	10.748	10.748
Cash flow	(1.000)	11.081	11.081	11.081
NPV @ 18%	23.093			

---

be replicated in a small portion of the country to measure the new cap's effect on volume. The market research department recommended that the test be conducted in Phoenix, Arizona, and offered a long list of reasons. Phoenix contained almost exactly 1 percent of the U.S. population and represented about 1 percent of Jade sales. The size was large enough to yield statistically significant results but small enough to minimize test costs and the risk of disrupting brand sales should the cap prove to have problems. Phoenix was indicative of the U.S. market for Jade in both demographics and share trends. The managers of the 94 grocery stores were accustomed to test markets and were known to be

EXHIBIT 2   Results of Product-Use Test

	Percentage of Respondents Preferring		
Attribute	*Dispenser Cap*	*Current Cap*	*No Preference*
Overall 55%	37%	8%
Convenience 76	19	5
Cleaning 21	19	60
Manageability 23	25	52

Note: results based on 100 respondents.

cooperative. From an advertising point of view, the Phoenix market was well contained, in that advertisements for the dispenser cap would not be picked up on TVs in other areas where the new cap was not available. The market test began on June 1, 1986, at a budgeted cost of $500,000.

Thirteen months later, Kennedy received a phone call from a friend in the market research department. The test results had just come in and average volume was 5,341 units per store with a standard deviation of 2,131 units. Kennedy was delighted with the news—the test-market performance would amount to 50,205,400 units ($5,341 \times 94 \times 100$) on a national basis. This was almost a million units above the break-even volume of 49,316,000 units. She could now push ahead with the national introduction of the change.

Hoffman, however, was less enthusiastic. In a brief hallway conversation, Hoffman had focused more on the standard deviation than on the average and had expressed concern that, with such a large standard deviation, the introduction could in fact result in a loss.

CASE 29
JADE SHAMPOO (B)

The good news of the morning was shattered in the afternoon when Warren Jenkins, the director of market research, walked into Debbie Kennedy's office and glumly announced:

> You heard, the test results are in. Unfortunately, they aren't what we had hoped for. Even though average store sales for the year were 5,341 units and this is above our break-even, the individual-store data had a standard deviation of 2,132 units. Our standard hypothesis test cannot reject at the 0.05 level the null hypothesis that the new cap generates sales at or below break-even. In fact, there is a 33 percent chance that we could have a test result of at least 5,341 even if the true sales were at the break-even. Here's a copy of the memo [Exhibit 1] that I just received from my staff statistician. I'm sorry, Debbie, but the way we look at things, these results don't support the national introduction of the dispenser cap.

It had been a long time since Kennedy had thought about hypothesis tests, and the language seemed rather remote. That evening, she reviewed her notes from a statistics course (Exhibit 2) and began to think about why the hypothesis-test approach did not seem right.

She knew that she would have to get her thoughts straightened out quickly. The next morning there was to be a meeting with Marion Hoffman, the Jade product manager, and Carol Williams, the director of marketing. At that meeting, she would have to take a position on the future of the dispenser cap. On the one hand, the easy position would be to go along with company procedure and let the hypothesis test make the decision. On the other hand, she was committed to the project. The cap had been her idea, and she had directed the study team since its inception. If it increased sales as she expected, the new cap would generate additional profits for her brand. But then again, she was not anxious to be the one responsible for reducing profits if sales proved to be below the break-even level, particularly if she had gone against company guidelines to continue the product. Regardless, it just did not seem right that a simple statistical test could so easily kill an 18-month project to which she was firmly committed.

This case was based on a Supervised Business Study prepared by Donna M. Packard (Darden, Class of 1987).

EXHIBIT 1   Analysis of the Test-Market Results

To: Warren Jenkins, Director of Market Research
From: Susan Hauser, Statistician
Subject: Jade Dispenser Cap Test Market—Final Results

The year-long (June 1, 1986–May 31, 1987) market test of the proposed Jade dispenser cap in our 94 retail markets in Phoenix has resulted in an average volume of 5,341 units per store with a standard deviation of 2,132 units.

The 49.316 million break-even volume that was provided by Product Management translates into 5,246 (49.316 × 0.01 / 94) units per store.

With this figure in mind, I performed our usual hypothesis test by taking as the null hypothesis the statement that the "average annual sales of Jade with the dispenser cap will be less than or equal to the break-even level of 5,246 units per store." Assuming that this hypothesis is true, and making the conservative assumption that the average annual sales will be equal to the break-even figure, there is a 33 percent probability that we could have observed a test result at least as large as the one we did. More specifically, the t-statistic is

$$0.432 = [5341 - 5246] / [2132 / \sqrt{94}]$$

with 93 degrees of freedom. The chances of an outcome being greater than 0.432 are 33 percent. As a result, there is a high probability that our test result could have occurred with an average annual sales equal to break-even. Consequently, this test result does not provide sufficient evidence to change our assumption that the average annual sales will be at or below break-even.

In traditional statistical parlance, we cannot reject the null hypothesis at the 0.05 level of significance.

EXHIBIT 2   Class Notes on Hypothesis Testing

Hypothesis testing

- Decision-making tool.
- Assesses evidence provided by data in an effort to select between two hypotheses (claims) concerning an unknown population parameter.
- Each hypothesis has a different action associated with it.

The two hypotheses

- The null hypothesis (H_0, H-nought)—a claim of disbelief, of no change, of no effect. "Despite what you say, I don't believe your claim." Generally, the associated action is to do nothing.
- The alternative hypothesis (H_1)—the claim that there is a difference and that action is warranted.
- Both hypotheses make claims about an unknown population parameter;   hypotheses must be mutually exclusive and exhaustive.

Exhibit 2   *Concluded*

- Generally the null hypothesis refers to parameter values on one side of a cut-off value (CO); the alternative hypothesis refers to values on the other side of CO.

Types of errors

- Because you must choose either H_0 or H_1, two types of errors possible:
  - —Type 1 error: accept the alternative hypothesis when the null hypothesis is correct.
  - —Type 2 error: accept the null hypothesis when the alternative hypothesis is correct.
- Generally we want to have the chances of making a Type 1 error to be no more than 0.05 (0.01, if more conservative); don't want to make a change when it is unjustified; the 0.05 (or 0.01) is called the "level of significance" of the test.

Interpreting sample data

- The n observations, sample average (x-bar), sample standard deviation (s).
- Assume the null hypothesis to be true, but be as generous for H_1 as possible by assuming that the mean of the distribution of sample averages is CO, the cut-off value between H_0 and H_1 (closest value to H_1 range that is still in H_0).
- The standard deviation of the distribution of sample averages is $s/\sqrt{n}$.
- The distribution of sample averages is the normal distribution (*t* if *s* is based on less than 30 observations—not a big difference, though, between normal and *t*).
- Find the region of rejection—the tail of the distribution that has probability 0.05, equal to CO $+ 1.645 \times s/\sqrt{n}$.
- If x-bar falls in the region of rejection, then either H_0 is true and we got an unusual result (probability is at most 0.05), or the null hypothesis is false; the second explanation is the more reasonable.
- If x-bar is not in the region of rejection, we cannot reject H_0 without increasing the probability of making a Type 1 error.

CASE 30
JAIKUMAR TEXTILES, LTD.: THE NYLON DIVISION (A)

In early April, N. S. Kadiyala, deputy general manager of the Nylon Division of Jaikumar Textiles, Ltd. (JTL), had two days in which to make a decision that would have a major impact on May's production schedule. A proposal from one of JTL's major customers for the purchase of 5,000 kilograms (kgs) of denier 15/1g nylon (see Nylon Production section) had just crossed Kadiyala's desk. The offering price was 182 rupees (Rs) per kg. Kadiyala knew that, if he accepted the order, it would have to be filled entirely from May's production of that denier, which would require a major commitment of production resources.

Prior to the mid-1980s, such considerations as future business potential and goodwill had dwarfed the immediate economic impact of decisions of this type, but intense competition, much of it stemming from the introduction of new fiber technology by competitors, had changed all that. Kadiyala was sure that JTL now needed to squeeze every potential rupee of contribution from its production facilities.

Nylon Production at JTL

The production of nylon yarn in JTL's main nylon-production facility took place in four basic areas: polymerization, spinning, drawtwisting, and packing and testing.

In the polymerization area, the raw material *caprolactum powder* was first washed in large vats and reshaped into small pellets. These pellets were then channeled into heating tanks, where they were transformed, through the addition of various acids and chemicals, into three basic types of nylon—glittering, semidull, and full dull. The resulting chips were melted down and sent to the spinning area.

In spinning, nylon yarn was formed by forcing the melted caprolactum chips (now about the consistency of honey) through the tiny holes of a device called a *spinneret.* Unlike natural fibers, nylon yarn could be extruded into different thicknesses. The spinneret, used in the production of all man-made fibers, was similar in design to a shower head, with anywhere from one to literally thousands of tiny holes. Melted chips were forced through these holes, the size and number of which determined the weight and thickness of the resulting nylon. The thickness and weight of a particular yarn was called its *denier.* The 15/1g denier was a monofilament (single strand) of glittering nylon weighing 15 kgs per 9,000 meters, for example, while a 84/21fd denier was a multifilament (in this case, 21 strands) of full dull nylon weighing 84 kgs per 9,000 meters.

As the filaments, still in a semiliquid state, emerged from the holes in the spinneret, cold air was forced across them, causing them to solidify. The filaments were spun onto spools using one of two types of spinning machine groups: an old grid system or a more modern and efficient extruder system. After the filaments hardened, the spools were taken to the drawtwisting area.

In drawtwisting, the spools were stretched on special machines, causing a reduction in the diameter of the filaments. This reduction was accomplished by a rearrangement of the molecules in the fiber into a more orderly pattern. This new pattern strengthened the filaments, making the fiber more resistant to breaking.

After drawtwisting, spools were systematically tested to assure quality. Once a batch of spools was approved, it was moved to the packing area, where each type of denier was packed by hand into a special container. The packing process was expected to be automated in the near future. Currently, there was ample, albeit expensive, capacity in the packing and testing area to handle all denier production.

Production Planning

Kadiyala and his staff were responsible for the monthly decision of how much of each denier to produce during the upcoming month. The resulting production plan was required to conform to the broad guidelines of an annual master plan, the purpose of which was to ensure the efficient use of production facilities and to smooth the production of individual deniers throughout the year, thus controlling inventory cost. For example, the master plan for this year specified that deniers 15/1g and 84/21fd be produced exclusively on extruder spinning machine group #5. A maximum of 300 hours of spinning time on this machine group was allocated each month, to be divided between production of these two deniers. Furthermore, it was specified that deniers 15/1g and 84/21fd require no more than 1,600 hours of drawtwisting time between them each month. (See Exhibit 1 for spinning-machine and drawtwisting utilization rates for deniers 15/1g and 84/21fd.) In addition, the annual plan specified that no fewer than 3,000 nor more than 10,000 kgs of denier 15/1g, and no fewer than 6,000 nor more than 15,000 kgs of denier 84/21fd, could be produced in a given month. (Because both polymerization and packing and testing capacities were plentiful, no constraints were placed on use of either area.)

Kadiyala met with his staff on the first of each month to determine the production plan for that month. Thus, the final production plan for May would be determined on May 1. By waiting until the first of the month to make this decision, Kadiyala and his staff retained maximum flexibility to respond to changes in the market price of each denier. Based on the prevailing prices at that time, the production plan would be set and the month's planned output would be presold to vendors at the current market prices for delivery at the end of the month.

While Kadiyala was quite comfortable using the prevailing market prices on the first of the month to set and presell the month's production, he had some concerns about the ad hoc way he and his staff used the prevailing prices to

EXHIBIT 1   Resource Use by Deniers 15/1g and 84/21fd

Extruder Spinning Group #5

	Denier	
	15/1g	*84/21fd*
Average number of kgs that could be processed in an hour of machine time	30 kgs	60 kgs

Drawtwisting

	Denier	
	15/lg	*84/21fd*
Average number of kgs that could be processed in an hour of drawtwisting time	15 kgs	12 kgs

Raw material cost

	Denier	
	15/1g	*84/21fd*
Variable cost of producing 1 kg	Rs 88	Rs 74

arrive at production levels. In April, for example, the decision had been made to produce 4,200 kgs of denier 15/1g and 9,600 kgs of denier 84/21fd. At market prices of Rs 178 and Rs 124 per kg, respectively, this plan had resulted in a contribution of Rs 858,000 from April's production. Kadiyala wondered if a more profitable production plan might not have existed.

The Proposal

At first glance, the proposed purchase of 5,000 kgs of May's production of denier 15/1g appeared to be attractive. The Rs 182 per kg offer was not only above the current market price of Rs 178 but also above the marketing department's May 1 forecasted price of Rs 179. (Each month, for planning purposes, the marketing department made a forecast of the price of each denier on the first of the following month; see Exhibit 2 for a recent history of marketing department forecasts for 15/1g.) Yet, the price of denier 15/1g (also in Exhibit 2) had fluctuated widely over the past couple of years. If prices were to rise unexpectedly, Kadiyala might regret being locked into the contract. On the other hand, the 5,000 kgs specified by the contract would count toward the required minimum May production level of 3,000 kgs of denier 15/1g. Hence, if prices were to drop, Kadiyala would avoid having to sell 3,000 kgs at the reduced price. Whether or not to accept the proposal thus appeared to depend on the expected market price in May for denier 15/1g.

EXHIBIT 2 **Recent History of Actual Market Prices of Deniers 15/1g and 84/21fd and Marketing Department Forecasts of 15/1g (in rupees)**

Month	Actual 15/1g	Actual 84/21 fd	Forecast 15/1g
Jan	158	123	146
Feb	171	123	161
Mar	231	124	165
Apr	223	125	210
May	237	124	225
Jun	203	123	215
Jul	180	123	190
Aug	192	124	175
Sep	174	124	185
Oct	162	124	165
Nov	162	126	170
Dec	155	125	165
Jan	154	124	156
Feb	158	123	160
Mar	157	124	158
Apr	178	124	160
May	—	—	179

CASE 31
JAIKUMAR TEXTILES, LTD.: THE NYLON DIVISION (B)

On May 1, N. S. Kadiyala and his staff met to determine the production plan for May. The market price for denier 15/1g was Rs 168, making Kadiyala wish he had accepted the contract to produce 5,000 kgs of 15/1g at Rs 182 back in April. Now he was left with having to decide how much of deniers 15/1g and 84/21fd to produce during May at the prices Rs 168 and Rs 124, respectively. Also for his attention were a set of related memoranda (Exhibits 1–4).

EXHIBIT 1   Memorandum 1

TO: N. S. Kadiyala, Deputy General Manager

FROM: ———, Production Head, Drawtwisting

DATE: April 30

RE: Available drawtwisting hours for the May production of deniers 15/1g and 84/21fd

We have had an unfortunate mechanical breakdown in the drawtwisting area. The effect of this breakdown is that total drawtwisting capacity for May will be significantly reduced (by about a third). As a result, we can allocate no more than 1,000 hours of drawtwisting time in May to the production of deniers 15/1g and 84/21fd.

EXHIBIT 2   Memorandum 2

TO: N. S. Kadiyala, Deputy General Manager

FROM: ———, Production Head, Spinning

DATE: April 27

RE: Renting additional spinning hours

Last month, you complained that we should be allocating additional spinning machine hours to deniers 15/1g and 84/21fd. We now have the opportunity to rent additional spinning time from a competitor. We have yet to discuss price or amount, pending your input. In order to rent the additional capacity for May, we need to let them know something as soon as possible.

EXHIBIT 3   Memorandum 3

TO: N. S. Kadiyala, Deputy General Manager

FROM: ————, Special Assistant to the General Manager

DATE: April 29

RE: Denier 44/10sd

We need additional spinning capacity for denier 44/10sd due to a recent surge in demand. 15/1g and 84/21fd are among those deniers that have been identified as prime candidates to lose allocated capacity. To help us in making our final decision, would you estimate the impact of such a move on deniers 15/1g and 84/21fd?

EXHIBIT 4   Memorandum 4

TO: N. S. Kadiyala, Deputy General Manager

FROM: ————, Marketing Department

DATE: April 30

RE: Price of denier 84/21fd

There appears to be a possibility that the price of denier 84/21fd, relatively stable for some time now, may experience a significant jump in the upcoming month, possibly by as much as 25 percent. Perhaps you should consider boosting your production of denier 84/21fd in response to this very real possibility.

James Vaughan looked over the balcony railing to the sea beyond. As he settled comfortably into the rattan chair, he watched the sweat roll down the side of his glass. He sniffled repeatedly. After three months in the Caribbean, James had become somewhat acclimatized, but the effects of a summer cold lingered. With a sigh, he thought of his imminent return to the United States for the second year of his MBA program. San Huberto was his last assignment for the summer.

The evening's sea breeze blew across the balcony of the Gran Hotel San Huberto, and James thought about the recommendations he would make about pricing strategy to his summer employer, Lesser Antilles Lines (LAL). LAL was a very successful containerized shipping firm moving cargo between Ft. Lauderdale, Florida, and about 15 Caribbean islands. Vaughan was hired to investigate eight potential new markets in the Caribbean and Central America. On his way back to Ft. Lauderdale, he received a call asking him to stop in San Huberto. Because LAL was embroiled in a particularly vicious price war, San Huberto was the only market in which LAL was not producing impressive earnings. Vaughan was asked to survey the scene and evaluate LAL's pricing strategy for the island.

Lesser Antilles Lines

LAL was born in the early 1960s when a Florida construction firm successfully bid on a contract to build sidewalks on a Caribbean island. Much to the manager's disgust, transporting equipment and materials to the particular location was virtually impossible. Although the occasional vessel might call at the port, voyages were infrequent and unreliable. In true West Indian style, vessel operators' attitudes toward scheduling were relaxed and unhurried. The construction firm was unwilling to tolerate the vagaries of local shipping, so it purchased an old barge and began regular "sailings" between Ft. Lauderdale and the island. In a short time, grocery wholesalers, hardware stores, and other businesses on the island requested that their goods be transported on the barge for a fee. They claimed that such a service was better than any other available at that time. LAL "came of age" when revenues from the shipping service began to approach those from the construction end of the business.

In 20 years, LAL's service network grew from 1 island to 15. Revenues in 1985 were almost $50 million. LAL specialized in serving the small islands that historically received little attention from established shipping lines. By offering

This case was prepared in conjunction with James V. Gelly (Darden, Class of 1987).

reliable and frequent transportation in previously neglected regions, LAL garnered impressive market shares and, by providing the highest levels of service to even the smallest customers, the firm defended its market share in spite of intense competition. LAL became something of a legend in the region for its punctuality—it was said that you could set your watch by LAL's vessels.

Maritime Trade

Ocean shipping always played a central role in the world economy, with virtually all internationally traded goods transported by sea. Maritime trade was divided into two categories, bulk and general cargo. The bulk category accounted for roughly 75 percent of total world tonnage shipped in 1985 and was principally made up of petroleum, mineral ores, coal, and grain. General cargo, which comprised the remaining 25 percent of total world tonnage shipped, referred to manufactured goods and consumer products. Because general cargo represented relatively high-value goods, fast and efficient transportation was required to move them. LAL competed in this higher-value general cargo industry, commonly known as the liner trade.

Containerized Transportation.   Before the 1950s, general cargo was moved by the "break-bulk" method. Individual boxes, drums, crates, and sacks were loaded on and off ship by crane and by hand; stevedores and longshoremen supplied labor at the ports of origination and destination. This system was not an efficient one, however. Ocean transportation was a labor-intensive industry—in the early 1960s, a modern liner spent approximately half the year in port being loaded and unloaded.

Although a simple concept, "containerization" did not begin until the mid-1950s when Malcolm McLean, the owner of a Virginia-based trucking firm, began shipping entire trailer-loads of goods. After removing the wheels from 35-foot trailers commonly seen on U.S. highways, McLean shipped full, sealed trailers, rather than individual parcels that were formerly the unit of transportation. Containerization quickly transformed the liner industry. By the mid-1980s, the industry was almost completely standardized, with the Trailer Equivalent Unit (TEU) the unit of measure. A TEU could be moved "intermodally" (by road, rail, and sea) with a minimum of labor and without disturbing the contents (see Exhibit 1).

Competitive Environment in the Mid-1980s.   The liner industry traditionally operated within conferences, which were international groups of private liner companies that collectively agreed on routes, schedules, and rates. Some have observed that conferences resembled institutionalized price-fixing. The conference shipping system became increasingly unstable in the late 1970s and early 1980s. Having once controlled 80 to 90 percent of traffic volume in certain trades, the conferences' control dropped to less than 50 percent by the mid-1980s. As containerization spread, productivity increased, and prices adjusted downward. Furthermore, adaptable firms withdrew from the conferences to take advantage of new trade patterns.

EXHIBIT 1   A Liner Loaded with Containers

By 1985, the world shipping industry was in a severe slump. Subsidized shipyards in most industrialized countries caused new-vessel prices to drop, and the supply of vessels outstripped demand. The contraction in world petroleum consumption caused tremendous under-utilization of bulk vessels, and tanker ships were laid up or scrapped at unprecedented rates. Overcapacity struck the liner industry, also, as the growth in vessel capacity outpaced the growth in demand. Because the industry was one of high fixed costs, freight rates were cut to keep cargoes, and revenues—in real terms—dropped well below 1970s levels.

The market value of all types of vessels fell to a fraction of their replacement cost. Shipyards began offering liberal financing for new construction contracts. As both market value and replacement costs fell, the liner industry became easy to enter. Even as large shipping firms filed for bankruptcy, new firms announced their entry into already overcrowded routes.

Caribbean Environment

The small island-states in the Caribbean were among the last to convert to containerization. Because they were developing countries with near-subsistence economies, they could not afford the cost of modernizing port infrastructures, and many were forced to borrow heavily from developmental agencies to support a shift to containerization.

LAL successfully anticipated the move toward containerization in the Caribbean and was one of the first firms there to convert completely to containerized operations. LAL was also the first to introduce a regular, reliable container service in many markets, and the firm dredged harbors and installed cranes in ports where such improvements were not forthcoming.

Demand Characteristics.   Imports of Caribbean islands reflected the structure and development of the underlying economies. Because many countries were underdeveloped, imports consisted mainly of corrugated tin roofing, lumber, foodstuffs, tools, clothing, and vehicles. The small islands were almost totally dependent on imports for manufactured goods. Countries with tourist industries imported goods to which American and European vacationers were accustomed. In this region, the local importer of goods bore the entire cost of transportation, which was often included on invoices as a surcharge. Exports consisted of agricultural products, such as copra and tropical fruit, as well as hand-crafted items. Balance of payments constraints were chronic.

Because many Caribbean economies claimed tourism as their only industry, increased demand for shipping depended on natural population growth and the size of the tourist sector. Demand could not drop below a critical level of importation, however, because these less-developed economies had no alternative but to import essential commodities.

One of the most important aspects of the Caribbean liner industry was the almost perfect price inelasticity of demand—the price of shipping services could change dramatically in either direction and have almost no effect on the amount of services demanded. Transportation costs played such a small part in the retail price of most imported goods that even a 50 percent reduction or rise in freight charges had little impact on demand. For example, assume a grocery wholesaler paid $2,000 per TEU in freight charges to import frozen chicken parts. A TEU could hold as much as 40,000 pounds of chicken, so the transportation cost per pound was $0.05. Assume a cut in freight rates per TEU of $1,000; the $0.025 savings per pound would have little effect on sales of frozen chicken. Also, Caribbean importers were notorious for absorbing any such savings. Thus, necessity, as well as pricing practices, caused Caribbean demand for shipping services to be almost perfectly price inelastic.

San Huberto.   Discovered in the 16th century, San Huberto (see Exhibit 2 for a map of the Caribbean) was colonized by the English in the 1630s. In 1788, St. Hubert's, as it was then called, was ceded to Spain. After a century of neglect, the island was claimed by a Latin American country and its name changed to its Spanish form, San Huberto. Since World War II, Spanish had been the official language on San Huberto, although Caribbean-English or patois was the language for over three centuries.

EXHIBIT 2   Map of the Caribbean

In 1985, the majority of San Huberto's 34,000 inhabitants were English-speaking blacks, the descendants of plantation slaves brought from Jamaica. Unemployment among them was over 35 percent. By the mid-1980s, a substantial tourist industry evolved in response to the island's duty-free status, and San Huberto had two industries, subsistence farming and modern, international resort-class tourism. An estimated 100,000 tourists visited the island each year, and the volume of consumer durables moving in and out of San Huberto was considerable. Catering to wealthy Colombians, Salvadoreans, Costa Ricans, Guatemalans, and Hondurans in search of duty-free bargains and white-sand beaches, San Huberto offered numerous hotels, restaurants, and stores selling such luxuries as perfume, appliances, and jewelry.

Virtually all goods imported to San Huberto originated in the United States. Dominant users of the container service between the United States and San Huberto were the local importers of food, pharmaceuticals, consumer durables, clothes, alcohol, and hotel supplies. Importers wishing to arrange transportation typically contacted the shipping agent representing a given liner firm. The shipping agent was knowledgeable about sailing schedules, prices, and capacity, and, in a small market such as San Huberto, he or she might also serve as salesman, marketing manager, and even the dock-side supervisor.

The most important facet of the San Huberto market was the island's shallow-draft port. (Draft refers to the depth to which a ship extended under water.) Because the maximum draft of San Huberto's port was only 16 feet, the number and size of vessels able to call there were quite limited. Of firms operating in those waters, only LAL and Kronos Lines (KL) were equipped with the shallow-draft class of vessel required to call on San Huberto. In effect, the San Huberto shipping market was an oligopoly simply because of its remote location and physical limitations.

LAL entered the San Huberto market in 1980, at which time KL had a monopoly on service to the United States. LAL chose Stanley Montagu, one of the island's best-known agents, to help it gain a share of the market serving the United States. Montagu operated a small agency begun by his grandfather in the 1880s and had historically acted as agent for the yachters who called at San Huberto. Although he was a first-rate agent, Montagu had to work hard to gain share for LAL. As a member of the island's black community, he was only slowly gaining the business of the predominantly Spanish-speaking hoteliers, retailers, and restaurateurs.

Although they were the only two firms offering a U.S.–San Huberto connection, LAL and KL became bitter rivals. Begun in the 1960s, KL was owned and operated by Anatoly Rapport, a flamboyant southern European of uncertain origin with a reputation for being cheap, tough, and ruthless. KL operated 4 vessels (versus LAL's 11) and competed in several of the same markets as LAL. KL was a good example of the tough "niche" player that offered service to only a few markets, but was renowned for the tenacity with which it clung to those markets. KL met with some bad luck when one of its vessels was seized by the Venezuelan government for alleged smuggling operations and two others were detained by the Colombian government. These problems did not limit KL's ability to service the islands, however. TransCaribe, which had strong ties with many of the major importers, was the agent KL used in San Huberto for the past 15 years.

San Huberto Market Data

Vaughan's first initiative after arriving in San Huberto was to determine the exact size of the market. This task entailed eight hours of studying shipping manifests (the records of each vessel's cargo), which he found in a cardboard box in a disordered "file-room." After poring over the last three months' shipping manifests in the hot, airless room, Vaughan estimated a total of 3,900 TEUs per year imported into San Huberto. While his total ignorance of Spanish worried him a little, he believed the number to be accurate. On the basis of these same manifests, Vaughan was able to calculate that LAL had a 40 percent unit share of the market.

He then began the extensive series of interviews that served as market research. His custom during the summer was to identify himself as a consultant for an unidentified shipping firm and attempt to interview importers, exporters, and shipping agents to get a feel for the more subjective dimensions of the market. The task in San Huberto was difficult, because he could not communicate with many of the businessmen to whom he spoke, and he was forced to hire an employee at his hotel to translate for him at considerable expense. Vaughan learned first that LAL's choice of Montagu, based on Montagu's abilities, was a wise one, but that the racial and language barrier on San Huberto might work against the agent. Many of the importers stated that they preferred to work with KL's agent, TransCaribe, but could not offer any economic reason for the preference. Montagu, however, was respected by the entire San Huberto market and had made real inroads during the six years that LAL served San Huberto.

Based on his interviews, Vaughan believed that KL had built up a certain loyalty among the major importers during its long period of monopoly in San Huberto. He learned, however, that the usual practice in San Huberto was for importers to divide their orders between both shipping lines in varying proportions. This double-sourcing was considered a legacy from the not-too-distant past of infrequent and unreliable transportation.

Vaughan wanted to know which shipping firm importers would prefer if LAL's and KL's rates were identical, so in his interviews he collected subjective estimates of LAL's market share on that basis. He was surprised to learn that, at equal freight rates, KL was likely to retain a 60 percent market share. The more experienced shipping agents seemed to feel that each difference of $100 per TEU in freight rates would equal about a 10 percent loss of share for the more expensive firm. Exhibit 3 shows a graph of the relationship between LAL market share and the difference in price that these assumptions implied.

EXHIBIT 3   LAL Share as a Function of Price Differential

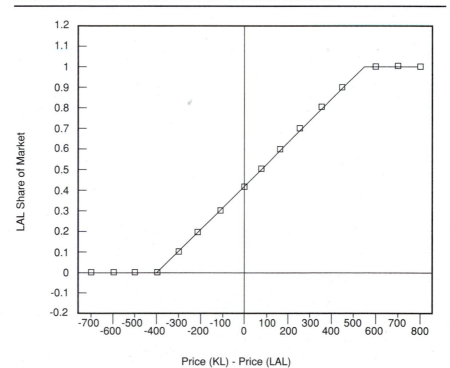

Price (KL) - Price (LAL)

Vaughan was surprised at these results, but the pattern recurred throughout his interviews. LAL, at equal freight rates, would still enjoy only a 40 percent market share; to gain share, LAL would have to set its price below KL's. This conclusion apparently explained LAL's poor profit performance in San Huberto. In trying to gain share, Montagu seemed to touch off the vicious price war of the last year. Because lower freight rates would not stimulate more volume (due to the severe price inelasticity of demand), cutting prices led to shrinking contributions for both firms. Vaughan wondered if Montagu's strategy was either appropriate or wise. His stated objective was to dominate KL and to "run them out of the market," but KL did not seem capable of being pushed around. Indeed, KL had met every one of LAL's price changes shortly after Montagu announced them.

After some work with LAL's controller, Vaughan worked out the various costs associated with shipping one TEU. The costs were for rental on containers, handling expenses in Ft. Lauderdale, vessel costs, and handling costs at LAL's "hub" port of San Juan, Puerto Rico. The firm's TEUs originated in Ft. Lauderdale, were shipped to Puerto Rico on LAL's large "line haul" vessels, were off-loaded in San Juan, and were then reloaded onto smaller "feeder" vessels that sailed to small islands throughout the Caribbean.

LAL's variable cost per TEU in 1986 was:

	Cost per TEU
Trailer rental	$246
Ft. Lauderdale variable handling	308
San Juan variable handling	287
Total	$841

The firm's marketing managers in San Juan believed that KL's cost per TEU was about 5 percent greater than LAL's ($883) because of inefficiencies and KL's smaller-scale operation. The two firms called at the port of San Huberto with the same frequency (i.e., bi-monthly).

James constructed a matrix showing both LAL's and KL's contribution, given the different pricing combinations covered in his market-share analysis. His assumptions for the matrix (shown in Exhibit 4) were as follows:

$$
\begin{aligned}
\text{Market size} &= 3{,}900 \text{ TEU per year} \\
\text{Market share}_{LAL} &= 0.40 + (P_{KL} - P_{LAL})(1/1{,}000) \\
\text{Market share}_{KL} &= 0.60 + (P_{LAL} - P_{KL})(1/1{,}000) \\
\text{Contribution}_{LAL} &= (P_{LAL} - \$841)(3{,}900)(\text{Market share}_{LAL}) \\
\text{Contribution}_{KL} &= (P_{KL} - \$883)(3{,}900)(\text{Market share}_{KL})
\end{aligned}
$$

After completing the matrix, Vaughan learned that KL had just announced that it would match LAL's most recently posted freight rate of $800 per TEU to San Huberto. Studying his findings, he wondered what strategy recommendations he could make to Montagu regarding future LAL prices.

Ехнвіт 4   Contribution Matrix

KL Price

KL Price	800	900	1000	1100	1200	1300	1400	1500	1600	1700	1800	1900
1900	0	0	0	0	0	0	397	793	1190	1587	1983	2380
	-160	230	620	1010	1400	1790	1962	2056	2072	2010	1870	1652
1800	0	0	0	0	0	358	715	1073	1431	1788	2146	2503
	-160	230	620	1010	1400	1611	1744	1799	1776	1675	1496	1239
1700	0	0	0	0	319	637	956	1275	1593	1912	2230	2549
	-160	230	620	1010	1260	1432	1526	1542	1480	1340	1122	826
1600	0	0	0	280	559	839	1119	1398	1678	1957	2237	2517
	-160	230	620	909	1120	1253	1308	1285	1184	1005	748	413
1500	0	0	241	481	722	963	1203	1444	1684	1925	2166	2406
	-160	230	558	808	980	1074	1090	1028	888	670	374	0
1400	0	202	403	605	807	1008	1210	1411	1613	1815	2016	2016
	-160	207	496	707	840	895	872	771	592	335	0	0
1300	163	325	488	651	813	976	1138	1301	1464	1626	1626	1626
	-144	184	434	606	700	716	654	514	296	0	0	0
1200	247	371	495	618	742	865	989	1113	1236	1236	1236	1236
	-128	161	372	505	560	537	436	257	0	0	0	0
1100	254	339	423	508	592	677	762	846	846	846	846	846
	-112	138	310	404	420	358	218	0	0	0	0	0
1000	183	228	274	319	365	411	456	456	456	456	456	456
	-96	115	248	303	280	179	0	0	0	0	0	0
900	33	40	46	53	60	66	66	66	66	66	66	66
	-80	92	186	202	140	0	0	0	0	0	0	0
800	-194	-227	-259	-291	-324	-324	-324	-324	-324	-324	-324	-324
	-64	69	124	101	0	0	0	0	0	0	0	0
	800	900	1000	1100	1200	1300	1400	1500	1600	1700	1800	1900

LAL Price

Note: −194 is KL contribution.
           −64 is LAL contribution.

163

LIGHTWEIGHT ALUMINUM COMPANY: THE LEBANON PLANT

Paul Smith, manager of the Lebanon, Indiana, alloy production plant of Lightweight Aluminum Company, was the last to reach the conference room for the November monthly production planning meeting. The others, including Lonny Gorban, operations research specialist and primary developer of the scrap blending/purchasing linear programming (LP) model the plant was considering for adoption, were already present. In preparation for the meeting, Smith had asked Gorban to use his LP model to determine how best to accomplish December's planned production of two key alloys, and to circulate the results. Smith could tell from the disgruntled looks on the faces of those present that the meeting was not apt to be a smooth one.

Alloy Production

An *alloy* is a mixture of two or more metals, or metals and other substances. Aluminum alloys consist primarily of aluminum, with smaller quantities of other metals, such as manganese and zinc, and/or substances, such as silicon. The proportions of the component materials determine the alloy's physical properties and characteristics.

At Lightweight, aluminum alloys were produced by melting down component materials in large furnaces. In their molten states, the materials combined, and, when cooled, became the desired alloys. It was possible to produce alloys of a specific composition by combining component materials in their pure forms. For example, a sufficient amount of pure zinc could be added to a furnace load to produce an alloy containing 2 percent zinc. At the time of the case, however, metals (and other substances) in their pure form tended to be quite expensive. An alternative, more economical approach was to use scrap alloys. For example, scrap containing 2 percent zinc could be combined with an equal amount of scrap containing 4 percent zinc to produce an alloy containing 3 percent zinc.

In deciding which scrap alloys to combine, and in what quantities, to produce an alloy of specified composition, several factors had to be considered. Most obviously, the proportion of each component material in the finished product had to fall within the required specifications. These specifications were typically stated in the form of ranges on the allowable proportions of each material. For example, it might be specified that zinc comprise no less than 2 percent nor more than 4 percent of a particular alloy. Another factor that had to be considered was the proportion of each type of scrap lost during the melting process,

---

EXHIBIT 1   Specification of Alloys AL311 and AL262—December 1985

Alloy	Silicon Percent	Specifications Manganese Percent	Zinc Percent	Required	Allotted Furnace Production Hours*
AL311	8.0–9.0	0.1–0.3	2.0–3.0	2,000	400
AL262	4.0–6.0	1.0–1.2	1.5–2.5	3,000	500

*Expressed in thousands of pounds.

---

typically expressed as the percentage retained after melting. Still another factor was the *charge rate,* the rate at which each type of scrap melted, typically expressed as lbs./hr. (pounds per hour).

Production Planning at the Lebanon Plant

Each month, the first step in the production planning process was to determine how many pounds of each alloy to produce in the upcoming month. Next, a set number of furnace hours was allocated to each alloy. From the scrap currently in inventory and what was available for purchase, it was then decided (at the monthly production planning meeting) which scraps should be used to produce which alloys and in what quantities. The cast house (or production) superintendent knew what was in inventory; the scrap buyer had a good feel for what was available on the market and at what price. With the aid of the plant manager, the production plan and its associated purchasing schedule were developed.

The scrap blending/purchasing LP model had been built over the course of the previous year to facilitate determining the best production and purchasing plan, given the number of furnace hours allocated to each product. Formulating a production plan for December was to be the model's first test, although it was generally felt that the model would probably require some additional fine tuning, and hence its recommendation for December would probably not be implemented.

Early in November, it had been decided to produce two important alloys in December: AL311 was allocated 400 hours of furnace time, and AL262 was allocated 500 hours. Gorban had taken the specs for these two products (Exhibit 1), along with the scrap availability data (Exhibit 2, gleaned from discussions with the cast house superintendent, John Forrester, and the scrap buyer, Melissa Johnson), and run them through the LP model. The results (Exhibit 3) had been circulated to Smith, Forrester, Johnson, and chief accountant Arthur Miller prior to the November production meeting.

The meeting

"I presume that you have all received and had a chance to look at the December production and purchasing plan determined by the LP model," Smith began. "Let's start by getting your reactions. John?"

EXHIBIT 2   Scrap Availability—December 1985

Scrap	Percent Si	Percent Man	Percent Zi	Metal Available[1]	Cost[2] ($)	Melt Cost[3] ($)	Percent Retained	Charge Rate[4]
Scrap 1 . . . . 0.0	0.0	0.0	4,000[5]	$360	$41	95%	8.0
Scrap 2 . . . . 10.0	0.4	2.5	1,750[5]	330	35	85	7.5
Scrap 3 . . . . 0.2	1.0	0.3	800[5]	310	40	85	7.5
Scrap 4 . . . . 0.3	4.0	3.0	600[6]	290	67	87	6.5
Scrap 5 . . . . 4.0	1.5	0.4	200[6]	260	41	75	2.5
Scrap 6 . . . . 3.0	0.8	5.0	1,000[6]	300	22	93	7.0
Silicon 100.0	0.0	0.0	—	600	43	90	3.0
Manganese 0.0	100.0	0.0	—	525	36	92	6.0
Zinc 0.0	0.0	100.0	—	450	31	90	4.0

[1]Expressed in thousands of pounds.

[2]Expressed as dollars per thousand pounds at the current market price.

[3]Expressed in dollars per thousand pounds at the current market price.

[4]Expressed in thousands of pounds per hour.

[5]Currently in inventory.

[6]None currently in inventory; listed amount is pounds available at the market price.

John Forrester, cast house superintendent

"I wish I could be more positive, Paul, but I have a number of problems with the solution proposed by the LP model. First of all, it has us buying and using Scrap 5. The throughput on that stuff is terrible. The workers end up spending most of the day standing around. If you're interested in improving productivity, that's one way *not* to do it. Furthermore, as you all know, using dirty scrap makes it that much sooner that we have to shut the furnace down and clean the whole thing out.

"Secondly, do we really want to use up all of Scraps 2 and 3 in December? Suppose we come along in January and decide to produce an alloy for which one or both of them is perfect? It strikes me as irresponsible and shortsighted to get rid of our entire inventory of versatile scraps.

"But thirdly, and most importantly, I don't think the solution being proposed by the model is optimal, and I think I can prove it. According to my calculations, the LP solution plan has us producing AL311 at a cost of about $850,000. I think we can produce it for less by doing the following: use 1,200,000 lbs. of Scrap 1; 800,000 lbs. of Scrap 6; and throw in 150,000 lbs. or so of silicon and 3,000 lbs. of zinc. I think you will find that this plan produces more than enough AL311 for less money. The rationale is simple: Scraps 1 and 6 are perfect for AL311, except for the lack of silicon. While silicon is expensive, the additional cost is more than offset by the savings that accrue from using Scraps 1 and 6, which are relatively cheap. I don't know if there is an error in the model, or a bug in the software, but something isn't right. I sent these numbers to Lonny yesterday; maybe he can shed some light on them."

Smith spoke before Gorban had a chance to respond. "Perhaps we should let everybody have their say before giving Lonny a chance to respond. Melissa?"

Melissa Johnson, scrap buyer

"The model results look fine to me, Paul, but I do have a couple of nagging concerns. The most important is the precision with which LP treats some of the inputs. For example, I told Lonny that I could get a million pounds of Scrap 6 at $300 per thousand pounds, but that was a loose approximation, both in terms of quantity and price. In actuality, I might be able to get a lot more, and, since the LP solution has us using all one million pounds, is it safe to assume that we would like to get our hands on more? At the same time, the $0.30 per pound is not firm; it's an estimate based on talking with several vendors. Once word gets around that we're buying, the price might easily go up. At what point does it become prohibitively expensive?"

Arthur Miller, accountant

At this point, Miller interrupted. "While we are on the subject of prices, this is probably as good a point as any to question the use of market replacement cost versus actual purchase price to value the scraps in inventory. While I am fully aware of the danger of applying standard costing in decision making, there are times where it is an accurate estimate of the value of raw materials, specifically when we are not going to sell them on the open market. Pretending that we are by assuming market replacement cost is only deceiving ourselves."

"Art, on that very point," Forrester interrupted. "I don't understand why we're assigning any cost at all to the stuff in inventory. The money has already been spent, the stuff is just sitting there waiting to be used. It sure seems like a sunk cost to me."

"Hold on a minute," Smith interrupted. "This seems to be getting out of hand. Maybe we should slow down a bit and give Lonny a chance to respond."

Lonny Gorban, operations research specialist

For a moment, Gorban was silent, trying to decide where to begin. He had, in fact, received Forrester's "better" plan the day before and had rerun his model to check it out (see Exhibit 4). He could address Forrester's plan and then proceed to each of the other issues raised. Alternatively, there was an issue he himself wanted to raise, namely the arbitrary tightening of the allowable maximum proportions of key elements in the production of alloys.

For example, the maximum allowable proportion of manganese in AL311 was actually 0.5 percent, not the 0.3 percent used to determine the production plan. The tightening of the upper bound was done to minimize the chance that the finished product would not meet specs. This could happen if, for example, the stated proportion of a particular material in a component scrap was incorrect. Minimum allowable amounts were of less concern, since a shortfall could always be corrected by adding material in its pure form to the furnace load. However, if a maximum limit was exceeded, the furnace (which was considered "off-analysis") had to be drained and the process of making the alloy restarted. The cost of draining a furnace load

EXHIBIT 3 Results

Memorandum

To: Forrester, Johnson, Miller, Smith

From: Gorban

Date: November 10

Re: LP model for production planning

Below and attached is a spreadsheet model for December's production schedule. The model is a linear program and has been optimized using an LP software package called *What's Best!* Formulas for selected cells are included in footnotes.

	A	B	C	D	E	F	G	H	I
2									
3	I. INPUT								
4									
5	Exhibit 1: Specification of Alloys AL311 and AL262—December								
6									
7		Silicon		Manganese		Zinc			
8	Product	Min	Max	Min	Max	Min	Max	Required	Hours
9	—	—	—	—	—	—	—	—	—
10	AL311	8.0%	9.0%	0.1%	0.3%	2.0%	3.0%	2,000	400
11	AL262	4.0%	6.0%	1.0%	1.2%	1.5%	2.5%	3,000	500
12									
13	Exhibit 2: Scrap Availability— December								
14								Charge	
15		Percentage of				Total	Percent	rate	
16	Scrap	Silicon	Manganese	Zinc	Available	cost	retained	per 1,000 tons	
17	—	—	—	—	—	—	—	—	
18	SCRAP1	0.0%	0.0%	0.0%	4,000	$401	95%	0.125	
19	SCRAP2	10.0%	0.4%	2.5%	1,750	$365	85%	0.133	
20	SCRAP3	0.2%	1.0%	0.3%	800	$350	85%	0.133	
21	SCRAP4	0.3%	4.0%	3.0%	600	$357	87%	0.154	
22	SCRAP5	4.0%	1.5%	0.4%	200	$301	75%	0.400	

Exhibit 3 *Continued*

	A	B	C	D	E	F	G	H	I
23	SCRAP6	3.0%	0.8%	5.0%	1,000	$322	93%	0.143	
24	Silicon	100.0%	0.0%	0.0%	—	$643	90%	0.333	
25	Manganese	0.0%	100.0%	0.0%	—	$481	90%	0.250	
26	Zinc	0.0%	0.0%	100.0%	—	$561	92%	0.167	
27									
28	II. LINEAR PROGRAMMING MODEL								
29									
30	A. Decision Variables								
31									
32		Input			Output				
33	Scrap	AL311	AL262		AL311	AL262			
34	—	—	—		—	—			
35	SCRAP1	1,005	216		955[1]	205[2]			
36	SCRAP2	613	1,137		521	967			
37	SCRAP3	0	800		0	680			
38	SCRAP4	0	562		0	489			
39	SCRAP5	105	95		79	71			
40	SCRAP6	367	633		342	588			
41	Silicon	105	0		95	0			
42	Manganese	0	0		0	0			

EXHIBIT 3 *Continued*

	A	B	C	D	E	F	G	H	I
43	Zinc	10	0		10	0			0
44		—	—		—	—			
45	TOTAL	2,206[3]	3,442		2,000	3,000			
46									
47	B. Objective Function								
48									
49	TOTAL COST		$2,064,371[4]						
50									
51	C. Constraints								
52									
53	SCRAP AVAILABILITY								
54						Shadow		Range	
55		Required		Available	Slack	price	Decrease	Increase	
56		—		—	—	—	—	—	
57	SCRAP1	1,220[5]	<	4,000[6]	2,780	$0.00	2,780	********	
58	SCRAP2	1,750	<	1,750	0	$17.41	388	226	

[1] +G18*B35

[2] +G18*C35

[3] @SUM(B35..B43)

[4] @SUMPRODUCT(F18..F26,B35..B43)+@SUMPRODUCT(F18..F26,C35..C43)

[5] +B35+C35

[6] +E18

EXHIBIT 3 *Continued*

	A	B	C	D	E	F	G	H	I
59	SCRAP3	800	<	800	0	$6.06	155	312	
60	SCRAP4	562	<	600	38	$0.00	38	********	
61	SCRAP5	200	<	200	0	$7.64	101	68	
62	SCRAP6	1,000	<	1,000	0	$76.02	177	103	
63									
64									
65	SPECIFICATIONS, AL311								
66					Slack	Shadow price	Decrease	Increase	
							Range		
67					—	—	—	—	
68	Production	2,000[7]	>	2,000[8]	0	$444.64	256	398	
69	Silicon								
70	Max	160[9]	<	180[10]	20	$0.00	20	********	
71	Min	160	>	160	0	$292.34	95	20	
72	Manganese								
73	Max	6	<	6	0	$1,535.56	1	1	
74	Min	6	>	2	4	$0.00	********	4	
75	Zinc								
76	Max	40	<	60	20	$0.00	20	********	
77	Min	40	>	40	0	$187.68	10	20	
78	Hours	339[11]	<	400[12]	61	$0.00	61	********	

171

EXHIBIT 3 *Concluded*

	A	B	C	D	E	F	G	H	I
79									
80									
81	SPECIFICATIONS, AL262								
82						Shadow		Range	
83					Slack	price	Decrease	Increase	
					—	—	—	—	
84	Production	3,000	>	3,000	0	$437.04	189	110	
85	Silicon								
86	Max	120	<	180	60	$0.00	60	********	
87	Min	120	>	120	0	$300.12	69	33	
88	Manganese								
89	Max	36	<	36	0	$264.05	6	1	
90	Min	36	>	30	6	$0.00	********	6	
91	Zinc								
92	Max	71	<	75	4	$0.00	4	********	
93	Min	71	>	45	26	$0.00	********	26	
94	Hours	500	<	500	0	$46.38	18	29	

[7] +E45
[8] +H10
[9] @SUMPRODUCT(B18..B26,E35..E43)
[10] +C10*E45
[11] @SUMPRODUCT(H18..H26,B35..B43)
[12] +I10

172

EXHIBIT 4 Optimized Spreadsheet with Forrester's Solution for AL311

	A	B	C	D	E	F	G	H
28	II. LINEAR PROGRAMMING MODEL							
29								
30	A. Decision Variables							
31								
32		Input			Output			
33	Scrap	AL311	AL262		AL311	AL262		
34								
35	SCRAP1	1,200	471		1,140	448		
36	SCRAP2	0	1,273		0	1,082		
37	SCRAP3	0	800		0	680		
38	SCRAP4	0	600		0	522		
39	SCRAP5	0	109		0	82		
40	SCRAP6	800	200		744	186		
41	Silicon	150	0		135	0		
42	Manganese	0	0		0	0		
43	Zinc	3	0		3	0		
44								
45	TOTAL	2,153	3,454		2,022	3,000		
46								
47	B. Objective Function							
48								
49	TOTAL COST		$2,082,167					
50								
51	C. Constraints							
52								
53	SCRAP AVAILABILITY							
54							Range	
55		Required		Available	Slack	Shadow price	Decrease	Increase
56								
57	SCRAP1	1,671	<	4,000	2,329	$0.00	2,329	*********
58	SCRAP2	1,273	<	1,750	477	$0.00	477	*********
59	SCRAP3	800	<	800	0	$7.64	613	165
60	SCRAP4	600	<	600	0	$8.08	142	38
61	SCRAP5	109	<	200	91	$0.00	91	*********
62	SCRAP6	1,000	<	1,000	0	$71.78	200	217

EXHIBIT 4 *Concluded*

	A	B	C	D	E	F	G	H
						Shadow	Range	
					Slack	price	Decrease	Increase
65	SPECIFICATIONS, AL311							
66								
67					—	—	—	—
68	Production	2,022	>	2,000	22			
69	Silicon							
70	Max	157	<	182	25			
71	Min	157	>	162	(4)			
72	Manganese							
73	Max	6	<	6	0			
74	Min	6	>	2	4			
75	Zinc							
76	Max	40	<	61	21			
77	Min	40	>	40	0			
78	Hours	315	<	400	85			
79								
80						Shadow	Range	
81	SPECIFICATIONS, AL262				Slack	price	Decrease	Increase
82								
83					—	—	—	—
84	Production	3,000	>	3,000	0	$433.60	83	227
85	Silicon							
86	Max	120	<	180	60	$0.00	60	********
87	Min	120	>	120	0	$88.36	37	40
88	Manganese							
89	Max	35	<	36	1	$0.00	1	********
90	Min	35	>	30	5	$0.00	********	5
91	Zinc							
92	Max	54	<	75	21	$0.00	21	********
93	Min	54	>	45	9	$0.00	*********	9
94	Hours	500	<	500	0	$60.50	32	27

was estimated at $2,000, regardless of the particular alloy being produced. Since almost all of the molten conglomerate drained from the furnace could be reused, the material loss of a furnace being off-analysis was considered negligible.

Gorban felt that the 0.3 percent figure was much too restrictive. Using it, the odds of any of the roughly 10 December furnace loads of AL311 going off-analysis were virtually negligible. By relaxing it, the alloy could be produced much more economically. Gorban had spent considerable time with the production engineering staff collecting information on alloys similar to AL311. From this, he had developed the following estimates of the probability of the actual manganese proportion exceeding 0.5 percent given where the target was set:

Maximum Manganese Target	Probability of Manganese Exceeding 0.5%
0.5%	40%
0.4	15
0.3	1

Now, however, did not seem the best time to raise this issue. Gorban wondered how he should proceed.

CASE 34
LOREX PHARMACEUTICALS

Carter Blakely, manager of quality assurance for the manufacturing division of Lorex Pharmaceuticals, was pleased with the progress made so far toward the production of the company's newest product, Linatol. Linatol was a highly promising medicine for the treatment of high blood pressure developed and patented by Lorex several years ago. After eight years of thorough product testing, including clinical studies of the drug's effectiveness on humans, the Food and Drug Administration (FDA) had approved Linatol only a week ago. The manufacturing division had been able to prepare a production line during the past week and now one-shift production was scheduled to begin on Monday. The marketing division at Lorex had decided that the initial offering of Linatol would be in sealed 10-ounce bottles, packaged in cases of 12 bottles each. The wholesale price had been set at $186 per case. The one task remaining for Blakely on this Friday afternoon was the selection of a target amount to which each of the 10-ounce bottles of Linatol would be filled.

The Manufacturing of Linatol

Linatol was blended in 5,000-liter batches using a process and formula that were kept confidential by the company. The product was then bottled on one of the company's semiautomatic filling lines. These lines consisted of an automatic filling mechanism for liquids, a capping and sealing component, and an electronic sensor capable of measuring the volume of liquid in each bottle. Bottles that were filled properly were conveyed to a packaging machine that would load and seal cartons of 12 bottles each. At top speed, the line chosen for Linatol could fill and package 1,000 bottles per hour. Because of unavoidable delays and setup requirements, the production rate was expected to average 500 cases over an eight-hour shift. These rates were slower than most of the other filling lines in use, but the relatively low production volumes of Linatol dictated that it be filled on one of the older, slower lines, which was not needed for any other product.

The entire line was operated by two employees who earned $12.80 per hour, including fringe benefits. Every product was charged an overhead burden to cover the huge expense of maintaining an antiseptic filling room. For the line on which Linatol would be bottled, the overhead was charged at a rate of $89.50 per hour.

The cost of the materials used by the filling line (bottles, caps, cap seals, labels, and packaging) was estimated to be $1.10 per bottle.

Those bottles not filled to the 10-ounce requirement were identified by the electronic eye and automatically directed for special handling. A team of filling-room

EXHIBIT 1   Linatol Projected Operating Profit (5,000 liters; i.e., 169,088 ounces)

Item	Cost
Revenue:	
Commercial*	$218,405
Seconds (15% rejects)	30,834
Total	$249,239
Costs:	
Active ingredients	$67,662
Blending direct labor	432
Blending indirect labor	170
Blending overhead	1,698
Filling materials	18,235
Filling direct labor	566
Filling overhead	1,978
Seconds packaging labor	147
Total	$90,888
Gross margin	$158,351

*At a 10.2-ounce target, one batch yields 1,381.44 cases. At an 85% acceptance rate, 1,174.22 of the cases are sold
in the commercial market, and 207.22 are sold as seconds. This fill target and acceptance rate are for planning
purposes only. The actual target and acceptance rate will be determined after the filling-line test.

attendants periodically labeled these underfilled bottles as seconds and hand-
packaged them for sale to secondary markets (such as government hospitals) at
80 percent of the normal price of $186 per case. Although these attendants
spent most of their time hand-packaging underfilled products, a variety of other
activities kept them busy. Each attendant was capable of labeling and packaging about 12 cases per hour. Attendants made $8.50 per hour, including fringe
benefits.

The initial production of Linatol had been scheduled for one 40-hour-per-
week shift on the filling line for the foreseeable future. The actual batch blend-
ing of Linatol would be scheduled accordingly. An approximate operating profit
statement for Linatol (prepared prior to the filling-line test) is given in Exhibit 1.

The Filling-Line Test

Prior to the start-up of production of a new product, the process capability of the
filling line was tested—first with an inexpensive liquid with physical properties
similar to the product and finally with the product itself. Once the filling process
was "perfected," samples of the filled bottles were individually measured. The
results of 144 bottles of Linatol filled during a test are given in Exhibit 2. This
exhibit also shows which of the 144 bottles were selected by the electronic sensor as underfilled. For this test, the filling mechanism was adjusted to fill to a
target of 10.2 fluid ounces. The consistency of amounts in the 144 test bottles
left little doubt that the fill mechanism could be set to any desired target.

Setting the Fill Target

It now remained for Carter Blakely to determine the fill target. The 10.2-ounce target chosen for the test was arbitrary, and certainly no economic justification existed for keeping this target. A rule often used for setting fill targets was to pick a target that was one standard deviation above the required amount. The relevant standard deviation was, of course, the standard deviation of the amounts placed in individual bottles. However, a one-standard-deviation rule, although cloaked with a certain amount of statistical justification, also seemed to ignore the peculiar economics associated with each filling situation. In fact, a one-standard-deviation rule in the past had led to several occasions when the buffer storage area for underfilled bottles had become clogged with rejected bottles, which caused a temporary stoppage of the entire filling line.

EXHIBIT 2   Filling-Line Test Results

9.89*	10.41	10.53	10.20	10.23	10.15
10.17	10.17	10.32	10.04	10.48	10.11
10.29	10.35	10.16	10.16	10.17	10.19
10.00	10.06	10.21	10.22	9.76*	10.22
10.04	10.19	10.09	10.12	10.06	10.10
10.35	10.17	10.02	10.35	10.17	9.99*
10.05	10.07	10.32	10.24	10.04	10.40
10.19	10.27	10.14	10.07	10.41	10.76
10.21	10.13	10.11	10.40	10.27	10.20
9.79*	10.24	10.20	10.29	10.00	10.31
10.53	10.14	10.35	10.21	10.23	10.16
10.47	9.84*	9.96*	10.10	10.11	10.23
10.24	10.36	10.30	10.23	10.19	10.17
10.17	10.11	10.33	10.19	9.97*	10.00
10.15	10.42	10.36	10.19	10.05	10.11
10.06	10.16	10.17	10.29	10.12	10.30
10.13	10.21	10.15	10.25	10.33	10.64
10.04	10.01	10.14	10.18	10.18	10.10
10.20	10.25	10.07	10.42	10.54	10.23
10.37	10.44	10.37	9.85*	9.91*	10.45
10.24	10.44	10.40	10.45	10.28	10.17
10.03	10.44	10.25	10.37	10.23	10.19
10.01	10.13	10.24	10.22	9.98*	9.98*
10.20	10.29	10.03	10.19	9.99*	10.13
Average 10.16	10.22	10.22	10.22	10.15	10.22
Std. dev. 0.17	0.16	0.14	0.13	0.18	0.19
Grand avg. ... 10.20					
Std. dev. 0.16					

*Identified by the sensor as underfilled.

CASE 35
MAXCO, INC., AND THE GAMBIT COMPANY

Part I

Maxco, Inc., and the Gambit Company were fully integrated, major oil companies each with annual sales over $1 billion and exploration and development budgets over $100 million. Both firms were preparing sealed bids for an oil rights lease on block A-512 off the Louisiana Gulf coast. Although the deadline for the submission of bids was only three weeks away, neither firm was very close to a final determination of its bid. Indeed, management at Maxco had yet to decide whether to bid at all, let alone how much to bid. Although Gambit was virtually certain to submit a bid, the level of Gambit's bid was far from settled. This uncharacteristic hesitancy in the preparation of both firms' bids was a direct result of certain peculiarities in the situation surrounding the bidding for block A-512.

Block A-512 lay in the Alligator Reef area immediately to the south of a known oil-producing region (see Exhibit 1). Just to the north were blocks A-497 and A-498, both of which were already under lease to the Gambit Company. On its leasehold Gambit had two completed wells, which had been in production for some time. In addition, Gambit had an offset control well in progress near the boundary between its leasehold and block A-512. When this well was completed, Gambit would have access to direct information concerning the value of any oil reserves lying beneath block A-512. Maxco's nearest leasehold, on the other hand, was some seven miles to the southeast. Any bid submitted by Maxco, therefore, would necessarily be based solely on indirect information.

The Role of Information in Bidding for Oil Rights Leases. In a bidding situation, information concerning either the object of the bidding or the notions of competing bidders is highly prized. This is even more the case in bidding for the rights to oil reserves lying, perhaps, thousands of feet below the surface. There are, of course, various kinds of information available to bidders for oil rights. To summarize these various types of information briefly, two categories—direct and indirect—may be established.

Information obtained by drilling on a parcel of land is called "direct information." Obviously this is the most precise information obtainable concerning the

Copyright © 1993 by the President and Fellows of Harvard College.
Harvard Business School case 174-091
This case was prepared by Donald L. Wallace under the direction of Dr. John S. Hammond III as the basis for class discussion rather than to illustrate either effective or ineffective handling of an administrative situation. Reprinted by permission of the Harvard Business School.

EXHIBIT 1   Subsurface Map of the Alligator Reef Area

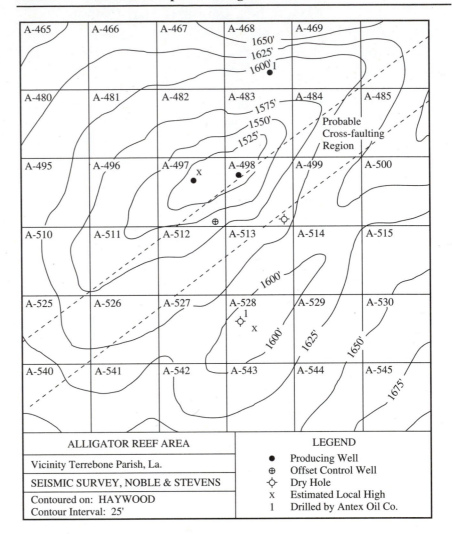

subsurface structure. From core samples taken up during the drilling operation, and from careful laboratory analysis of these samples, considerable information may be accumulated not only about the presence or absence of oil but also about the type, thickness, composition, and physical properties of each of the various geological strata encountered. Such information then provides the driller with a relatively accurate estimate of the oil reserves lying beneath the parcel. Direct information concerning adjacent parcels may be obtained by drilling offset control wells. These wells are offset from the principal producing areas and are located near the boundaries of the leased parcel. Such wells may then provide a particular lessee with precise and valuable information about adjacent parcels.

Indirect information is obtained from sources other than drilling and may be roughly divided into two kinds: scouting and nonscouting. Scouting information is gained by observing the operations of other drillers. By counting the sections of drill pipe—each of known length—introduced into a hole, an observer may infer the depth of the hole. By observing the quantity of cement—required by law—used to plug the various porous strata that are encountered, the thicknesses of these strata may be determined. Normally, however, this type of scouting information will not yield nearly the precision available to the driller himself. It can help in the determination of whether or not oil reserves exist at a particular location, but it is much less useful in determining the size of the reserves.

More definite scouting information may sometimes be obtained by more clandestine means. Eavesdropping on information conversations in public places, subtle forms of bribery and interrogation, even forcible entry onto a competitor's drilling site may provide much more detailed—and more valuable—information. An extreme anecdote tells of two men caught while inspecting a competitor's drilling log—the source document of a driller's direct information. The men were reportedly held at gunpoint for several days in anticipation of the approaching deadline for the submission of bids. Managing to escape, the day before the deadline, the two men were able to report back what they had seen in the log. As a result, the operator whose log had been compromised was forced to raise his bid by $7 million.

Less melodramatic, but highly significant, sources of indirect information are available through means other than scouting. Nonscouting information is obtained, first, from published sources, such as government geological and geophysical surveys, and reports of previous explorations. Second, nonscouting information may be obtained from local seismic surveys conducted either by in-house personnel or private contractors. A third source of nonscouting information is found in the trading of dry hole information. The tradition among drilling operators is to reveal their dry hole experiences. The feeling seems to be that there is far more to be gained from the reciprocal exchange of dry hole information than could be gained from watching a competitor pour a considerable investment into a site that is known to be barren. Finally, nonscouting information may also be obtained from the independent prospectors, promoters, and traders who may have become familiar with certain tracts in the past and are willing to trade this information, again on a reciprocal basis.

As might be suspected in an environment where information has such a high and immediate value, internal security presents a clear and ever-present problem. Bank-type vaults, armed guards, and electrified fences are commonplace. On occasion, entire drilling rigs have been encased in canvas to thwart the efforts of prying eyes. Substantial slow-downs in operations, however, under almost unbearable working conditions have also resulted. Furthermore, a blanket of security must also be placed over the derivation and submission of bids. Information on the level of a particular bid can be even more valuable than information on the value of reserves. When bids were being prepared for the tracts surrounding Prudhoe Bay on Alaska's North Slope, one company packed its entire bidding organization onto a railroad train and ran it back and forth over the same stretch of track until bids had been prepared and submitted and the bidding deadline has passed.

Finally, with information such a prime concern, circulation of false information is often attempted. If an operator is successful in leaking false negative information about a particular parcel, he may be able to later "steal" the parcel with a relatively low bid. On the other hand, to divert attention from a particular parcel, an operator may feign interest in another one by seeming to conduct tests there.

Maxco's Bidding Problem.   Mr. E. P. Buchanan, vice president for exploration and development, had primary responsibility for preparing Maxco's bid. Mr. Buchanan's information on block A-512 was, as indicated previously, indirect in nature. Although some scouting information on Gambit's offset control well was available to him, the primary basis of his information was a private seismic survey, together with published government geological maps and reports. Maxco had acquired the survey data, in a jointly financed effort with Gambit, through the use of a private contractor. The contractor, Noble and Stevens, had prepared a detailed survey of the entire Alligator Reef area several years previously when blocks A-497 and A-498 were up for bid. Under the joint financing arrangement, identical copies of the completed report had then been submitted to both Maxco and Gambit. Such an arrangement, while unusual, was not without precedent in known oil-producing areas. Exhibit 1 represents an updated version of a subsurface map included in Nobel and Stevens' report.

Based on all the information available to him, Mr. Buchanan's judgment concerning the monetary value of the oil reserves under block A-512 was essentially captured by the probability mass function given in Exhibit 2. Furthermore, Mr. Buchanan held that Maxco's bid should be based solely on this monetary value of the oil reserves. Since it was known that no nearby blocks were to be put up for bid for at least 10 years, Mr. Buchanan did not ascribe any informational value to owning a lease on block A-512.

Mr. Buchanan also felt—for the present at least—that Gambit's uncertainty was virtually identical to his own. He was sure, however, that Gambit's well would be completed by the deadline for the submission of bids. At that time Gambit would know the value of the reserves up to perhaps, ±5 or ±10 percent.

For the past several years, Mr. Buchanan had refused to bid on any parcels of land where he felt he was at a distinct disadvantage to a competing bidder. If a competitor had superior (direct) information about a parcel while Maxco had only indirect information, then Mr. Buchanan preferred not to bid at all.

Less than five months ago, however, in an area not far from Alligator Reef, Mr. Buchanan had *lost* a bid on a block adjacent to a Maxco leasehold. Maxco had gone to the expense of drilling an offset control well on its own block and had found a reasonably large oil reserve. Maxco had then lost the bid, however, to a competitor who was operating solely on the basis of indirect information. In addition, the competitor's winning bid had still been low enough to provide for a substantial profit on the venture.

EXHIBIT 2   Probability Distribution of Monetary Values

Monetary Value of Oil Reserves* ($ millions)	Probability
$ 1.7	0.03
2.7	0.06
3.7	0.10
4.7	0.17
5.7	0.28
6.7	0.18
7.7	0.08
8.7	0.04
9.7	0.02
10.7	0.01
11.7	0.01
12.7	0.01
13.7	0.01
	1.00

Mean value = $5.83.

* Net present value at 10%.

Thus Mr. Buchanan was considering a change in his policy. While he very much doubted that anyone else would enter the bidding for block A-512, he was beginning to feel that he himself should do so. If he did decide to bid, he then wondered what sort of bid might be reasonable.

Part II

Gambit's Bidding Problem.   Mr. Buchanan's counterpart in the Gambit Company was a Mr. K. R. Mason; primary responsibility for preparing Gambit's bid thus rested with him.

Until Gambit's well on the Alligator Reef leasehold was completed, Mr. Mason's information concerning block A-512 would be indirect in nature. The primary basis of that information was still the private seismic survey, for which Gambit had contracted jointly with Maxco, together with published government geological maps and reports.

Although Mr. Mason also had detailed production logs on the two producing wells on Gambit's leasehold, he felt that this information was not relevant to the problem of assessing the potential value of block A-512. There was almost certainly some cross-faulting in the Alligator Reef area (see Exhibit 1). Since this cross-faulting would probably terminate the producing area, the principal uncertainty surrounding the value of block A-512 was the precise location of the northernmost cross-fault. Thus, Mr. Mason's judgment was also essentially captured by the probability mass function given in Exhibit 2. Although Mr. Mason's judgment certainly did not coincide precisely with Mr. Buchanan's, the facts available to the two men and the economics in the two companies were largely similar. Neither man's estimate of the situation, therefore, differed significantly from Exhibit 2.

This would, of course, change dramatically when Gambit's offset control well was completed. At that time Mr. Mason would be able to reevaluate the property with a much higher degree of precision.

Normally Mr. Mason would then be in a position to submit a bid relatively close to the true value of the block while still allowing a generous margin for profit. Other bidders, not knowing the true value of the block, would be unable to adopt such a strategy. If they bid at all, they would have to either bid relatively low or risk the possibility of "buying in high" to a disastrously unprofitable situation.

Over the past year, however, several operators in the Louisiana Gulf coast had narrowly lost out when bidding for blocks on which they had direct information. Granted that in no case were extremely large reserves lost; nevertheless, operators bidding with nothing but indirect information had been able to "steal away" substantial reserves from operators who were basing their bids on direct information.

With a view toward reassessing his approach to this kind of situation, Mr. Mason thought that it might be useful to prepare a whole schedule of bids. For each possible "true value" of the reserves, Mr. Mason felt that he should be able to establish an appropriate bid—given that value of the reserves. Thus, Mr. Mason felt that he ought to be able to complete a bid schedule similar to that given in Exhibit 3. He was wondering, however, what a reasonable schedule of bids might be like.

EXHIBIT 3   Gambit's Bid Schedule

If the True Value of the Reserves is:	*Then Gambit's Bid Should Be:*
$1.7 million	$_____ million
$2.7 million	$_____ million
$3.7 million	$_____ million
$4.7 million	$_____ million
$5.7 million	$_____ million
$6.7 million	$_____ million
$7.7 million	$_____ million
$8.7 million	$_____ million
$9.7 million	$_____ million
$10.7 million	$_____ million
$11.7 million	$_____ million
$12.7 million	$_____ million
$13.7 million	$_____ million

CASE 36
THE OAKLAND A'S (A)

Steward Roddey, general manager of the Oakland A's baseball team, stared at the attendance figures he had put together for the recently completed 1980 season (Exhibit 1). It was October 1980, and Roddey was in the middle of a difficult contract negotiation with the agent for Mark Nobel, one of the star players for the A's. Nobel and his agent had argued that, in addition to contributing to the recent success of the A's team, Nobel had also been an attraction at the box office. They claimed that people came to the game specifically to see Nobel pitch, and that Nobel should be compensated accordingly.

Roddey believed there could be some truth to Nobel's claims but wanted to look carefully at last year's figures, nonetheless. He put together the information in Exhibit 1 as a first step, recording everything he thought could possibly influence attendance. The next meeting with Nobel's agent was two weeks away, so Roddey had plenty of time to analyze the data.

Background—Professional Baseball

The Oakland Athletics Baseball Club was one of 28 professional teams that played baseball in the major leagues. Each team played 162 games a season within its league, half of which were played at home. (See Exhibit 2 for final 1980 standings.) At the conclusion of the regular season, the teams with the best won-lost percentages in each of the four separate divisions participated in a post-season single elimination tournament. The first round was a best-of-five game series between the division winners in each league. The two league championship teams then met in a best-of-seven game series called the World Series, the winner of which was designated World Champion.

Each team was owned and operated independently within a framework set forth in the 1921 document, "Major League Agreement." Although gross revenues from the sale of tickets to each game were shared (77 percent to the home team, 20 percent to the visiting team, and 3 percent to the league office), each team was responsible for its own expenses. The largest expense items for the A's were players' salaries, player development, travel, accommodations, and stadium rental. The major expenses associated with actually staging an Oakland home game in the 50,000-seat Oakland-Alameda County Coliseum were also incurred by the A's.

The 1980 Season

The Oakland A's finished second in their division in 1980 with a record of 83 wins and 79 losses, 14 games behind the division-winning Kansas City Royals. Many attributed this turnaround from their 1979 last-place finish (see Exhibit 3)

This case was based on a Supervised Business Study prepared by Ann C. Stephens (Darden, Class of 1982).

EXHIBIT 1   1980 Home Game Data

Date	No. of Tickets Sold	Opposing Team	Position	Games Behind	Day of Week	Average Temp.	Precipitation	Time of Game	Televised	Promotions	Nobel
4/10	24,415	2	5	1	4	57	0	2	0	0	0
4/11	5,729	2	3	1	5	66	0	2	0	0	0
4/12	5,783	2	7	1	6	64	0	1	0	0	0
4/13	6,300	2	5	1	7	62	0	1	0	0	1
4/14	5,260	1	7	2	1	60	0	2	0	0	0
4/15	2,140	1	6	1	2	60	0	2	0	1	0
4/16	2,418	1	4	1	3	61	0	1	0	0	0
4/18	6,570	3	3	1	5	58	0	2	0	0	0
4/19	5,239	3	2	1	6	59	0	1	0	0	1
4/20	9,014	3	1	0	7	57	1	1	1	0	0
(double header)											
5/2	8,636	5	1	0	5	57	0	2	0	0	0
5/3	7,062	5	1	0	6	59	0	1	1	0	0
5/4	18,217	5	1	0	7	58	0	1	0	0	1
(double header)											
5/5	12,605	11	1	0	1	60	0	2	0	0	0
5/6	24,272	11	1	0	2	60	0	2	0	1	0
5/7	4,731	11	1	0	3	60	1	1	0	0	0
5/10	4,929	7	1	0	6	55	1	1	0	0	0
5/11	7,839	7	1	0	7	57	0	1	0	0	1
5/23	4,141	12	4	2	5	56	0	2	0	0	0
5/24	5,061	12	3	2	6	55	0	1	1	0	0
5/25	10,549	12	5	3	7	57	0	1	0	0	1
5/26	21,882	13	4	2	1	58	0	1	1	1	0
5/27	4,488	13	4	3	2	58	0	2	0	0	0
5/28	4,094	13	3	2	3	59	0	1	0	0	1
6/6	15,947	9	3	6	5	59	0	2	0	0	0
6/7	12,990	9	3	6	6	61	0	1	0	0	0

EXHIBIT 1 *Continued*

Date	No. of Tickets Sold	Opposing Team	Position	Games Behind	Day of Week	Average Temp.	Precipitation	Time of Game	Televised	Promotions	Nobel
6/8	18,753	9	3	7	7	63	0	1	0	0	0
6/9	20,162	10	3	7	1	61	0	2	0	0	0
6/10	3,873	10	3	7	2	59	0	2	0	0	0
6/11	5,628	10	3	7	3	60	0	1	0	1	0
6/13	47,768	4	3	7	5	60	0	2	0	0	0
(double header)											
6/14	27,312	4	3	7	6	63	0	1	0	0	1
6/15	46,294	4	3	8	7	64	0	1	0	1	0
6/23	17,666	6	3	9	1	62	0	2	0	1	0
6/24	4,899	6	4	10	2	62	0	2	0	0	0
6/25	6,856	6	4	11	3	63	0	1	0	0	1
6/27	8,482	8	4	11	5	69	0	2	0	1	0
6/28	5,204	8	4	12	6	69	0	1	1	0	0
6/29	7,369	8	4	12	7	63	0	1	0	0	0
7/10	11,337	3	5	12	4	66	0	2	0	0	1
(double header)											
7/11	7,696	3	5	12	5	62	0	2	0	0	0
7/16	7,413	5	5	13	3	65	0	2	0	0	0
7/17	6,370	5	3	12	4	65	1	1	0	0	1
7/18	5,949	11	3	12	5	60	0	2	1	0	0
7/19	6,506	11	3	11	6	65	0	1	1	1	0
7/20	10,606	11	3	11	7	65	0	1	0	1	0
7/21	14,588	7	3	12	1	65	0	2	0	1	1
7/22	8,645	7	3	12	2	63	0	2	0	0	0
(double header)											
7/23	4,765	7	3	12	3	64	0	1	0	0	0
8/4	16,741	2	2	12	1	65	0	2	0	0	0
8/5	4,651	2	2	12	2	67	0	1	0	0	0
8/6	6,697	2	2	12	3	63	0	2	0	0	0
8/8	6,283	1	2	13	5	62	0	2	0	0	0

Exhibit 1 *Concluded*

Date	No. of Tickets Sold	Opposing Team	Position	Games Behind	Day of Week	Average Temp.	Precipitation	Time of Game	Televised	Promotions	Nobel
8/9	13,629	1	2	12	6	63	0	1	0	1	1
8/10	13,062	1	2	13	7	63	0	1	0	0	0
(double header)											
8/19	11,934	9	2	15	2	67	0	2	0	0	0
8/20	7,569	9	2	15	3	65	0	2	1	0	1
8/21	10,947	9	2	15	4	61	0	1	0	0	0
8/22	11,532	10	2	15	5	62	0	2	0	0	0
8/23	10,578	10	2	16	6	64	0	1	0	1	0
8/24	18,745	10	2	17	7	63	0	1	0	1	1
8/25	47,946	4	2	17	1	62	0	2	0	1	0
8/26	32,905	4	2	17	2	62	0	2	0	1	0
9/8	9,731	12	3	19	1	65	0	2	0	0	0
9/9	2,443	12	3	18	2	63	0	1	0	0	0
9/10	3,598	12	2	17	3	64	0	1	0	0	1
9/12	17,440	13	2	17	5	62	0	2	0	0	0
9/13	11,253	13	2	16	6	61	0	1	0	0	0
9/14	10,756	13	2	17	7	63	0	1	0	0	0
9/23	3,069	8	2	15	2	70	0	2	0	0	0
9/24	3,836	8	2	14	3	69	0	2	0	0	0
9/25	3,180	8	2	14	4	64	0	1	0	0	0
9/26	5,099	6	2	14	5	64	0	2	0	0	1
9/27	4,581	6	2	13	6	62	0	1	0	0	0
9/28	10,662	6	2	12	7	65	0	1	0	1	0

Legend:

Opposing team:
1 Seattle
2 Minnesota
3 California
4 Yankees
5 Detroit
6 Milwaukee
7 Toronto
8 White Sox
9 Boston
10 Baltimore
11 Cleveland
12 Texas
13 Kansas City

Position: A's Ranking in American League West.

Day of week: Monday = 1, Tuesday = 2, and so on.

Precipitation: 1 if precipitation; 0 if not.

Time of game: 1 if day game; 2 if night game.

Exhibit 2   Final 1980 Standings

American League
Eastern Division

	W	L	Pct.	G.B.*
Yankees	103	59	.636	—
Baltimore	100	62	.617	3
Milwaukee . . .	86	76	.531	17
Boston	83	77	.519	19
Detroit	84	78	.519	19
Cleveland	79	81	.494	23
Toronto	67	95	.414	36

Western Division

	W	L	Pct.	G.B.*
Kansas City . .	97	65	.589	—
Oakland	83	79	.512	14
Minnesota . . .	77	84	.478	19½
Texas	76	84	.472	20½
Chicago	70	90	.438	26
California	65	95	.406	31
Seattle	59	103	.364	38

National League
Eastern Division

	W	L	Pct.	G.B.*
Philadelphia . .	91	71	.562	—
Montreal	90	72	.556	1
Pittsburgh . . .	83	79	.512	8
St. Louis	74	86	.457	17
Mets	67	95	.414	24
Chicago	64	96	.386	27

Western Division

	W	L	Pct.	G.B.*
Houston	92	70	.568	—
Los Angeles . .	92	70	.568	—
Cincinnati . . .	89	73	.548	3
Atlanta	81	80	.503	11½
San Francisco . .	75	86	.466	17½
San Diego . . .	73	89	.451	20

*G.B. refers to games behind. Because the Yankees won three more games (and lost three fewer) than did Baltimore, Baltimore was three games behind the Yankees.

Source: *New York Times,* October 6, 1980.

to their new manager, Billy Martin.[1] Perhaps the most colorful manager in baseball, Martin had managed six different teams in 12 years. In each instance, he had brought faltering teams to the top of the standings but was fired a short time later.

A second ingredient in the success of the 1980 A's was the remarkable performance of their young pitching staff.[2] Led by Mark Nobel, they had an earned run average[3] of 3.46 (best in the league), compared with 4.74 the year before. Many baseball people attributed this abrupt improvement to the fact that Martin had instructed his pitchers in the art of throwing "spitballs," an effective, but highly illegal, pitch.

---

[1]The manager of a major league team had the responsibility for directing all activities of the team associated with playing and preparing to play the game of baseball. A baseball manager was roughly equivalent to a head coach in other sports.

[2]The pitcher, one of nine players on one side in the game at any one time, started each play by throwing the baseball towards the opposing team's batter. The pitcher had perhaps more influence on the outcome of the game than any one other player. Because he often threw over 100 pitches a game, his arm could not endure more than one game every four or five days.

[3]An earned run average was a measure of the average number of runs per game the opposition scored against each pitcher during a game. It was considered by many to be the most important measure of a pitcher's performance.

EXHIBIT 3   Past Team Performance

Year	W	L	Pct.	Pos.
1968	82	80	.506	6
1969	88	74	.543	2
1970	89	73	.549	2
1971	101	60	.627	1
1972	93	62	.600	1
1973	94	68	.580	1
1974	90	72	.556	1
1975	98	64	.605	1
1976	87	74	.540	2
1977	63	98	.391	7
1978	69	93	.426	6
1979	54	108	.333	7
1980	83	79	.512	2

EXHIBIT 4   Yearly Oakland Attendance

Year	Home	Road	Total
1968	37,466	960,210	1,797,676
1969	778,232	992,124	1,770,356
1970	778,355	971,568	1,749,923
1971	914,993	1,222,741	2,137,734
1972	921,323	1,115,553	2,036,876
1973	1,000,763	1,382,250	2,383,013
1974	845,693	1,526,630	2,372,323
1975	1,075,518	1,436,383	2,511,901
1976	780,593	1,392,109	2,172,702
1977	495,412	1,195,138	1,690,550
1978	526,412	1,381,142	1,908,141
1979	306,763	1,393,196	1,699,959
1980	843,319	1,572,926	2,416,245
Total	10,105,429	16,541,964	26,647,393
Average	777,341	1,272,458	2,049,800

The successes of the A's on the field carried over to the box office. Home attendance in 1980 nearly doubled over the previous season, and road attendance was the highest it had been in the A's history (see Exhibit 4). Total gross revenues from the sale of tickets at home games amounted to $3.085 million, compared with $1.489 million the year before. Ticket prices, lowest in the league, ranged from $2 to $6 (see Exhibit 5) with various discounts (such as half-price night and group rates) offered throughout the year. An aggressive series of promotions numbered 13 in 1980, compared with 4 the previous year (see Exhibit 6).

EXHIBIT 5   Ticket Prices and Starting Times

First deck tickets $6	Single night games . . . . . . 7:30 P.M.
Second deck tickets $5	Single day games . . . . 1:30 P.M.
Third deck tickets $4	Day doubleheaders . . . . 12:30 P.M.
Bleacher tickets $2	Twi-night doubleheaders . . . . 5:00 P.M.

Special Group Plan: A group of 25 or more could receive $1 off the regular full price for each ticket purchased to A's games (Monday excluded).

Source: Company records.

EXHIBIT 6   1980 Promotions

Date	Promotion
4/14	Half-price night
5/6	Drawings for gifts
6/11	Bartenders' & Culinary Union Day—free admission
6/15	T-Shirt Day—free Billy Martin T-shirt
6/23	Bartenders', Beauticians', Cabbies' Night—free admission
6/27	East Bay Merchants' Night—$7,000 merchandise giveaway
7/20	Poster Day
7/21	Family Night
8/9	Cap Day—free caps to those 14 and under
8/23	Farmers' Day—free drawings for produce
8/24	Billy Martin Day
8/26	Old Timers' Day
9/28	Poster Day

Source: American League Office.

Factors Affecting Attendance

Exhibit 1 gives data on the following factors Roddey believed could influence attendance at home games:

Day of the Week.   Roddey was confident that the day of the week on which the game was played influenced attendance. Generally, he thought, weekend games were better attended because more people (especially children when school was in session) had leisure time on weekends.

Team Performance.   Everyone loves a winner, and Roddey believed that the better the A's played, the more people would want to see them play. Especially important was the A's performance relative to the teams in its division. Two measures of this factor are included in Exhibit 1: the A's ranking compared with other divisional teams and the number of games the A's were behind the leading team.[4]

Weather.   The Oakland Coliseum was an open-air stadium, and weather conditions (especially rain) could influence attendance. Included in Exhibit 1 is the average temperature and a record of precipitation during each game.

Double Headers.   Six times during the 1980 home season, the Oakland A's played double headers; that is, two consecutive games on the same day between the same teams. Thus the 75 entries in Exhibit 1 represent 81 home games. One ticket at the same price as a single-game ticket provided admission to both games. Roddey believed this two-for-the-price-of-one bargain increased attendance but was unsure if double headers were actually more profitable than two single games on separate days.

Starting Times.   Baseball could be played in daylight or under artificial lighting at night. Thirty-nine of the A's home dates represented daytime single games or double headers, with the remainder being night games or double headers starting in the late afternoon (see Exhibit 5 for starting times). Roddey was quite familiar with the difference in the composition of day- versus night-game crowds but was not sure if there was any real difference in total attendance. Exhibit 1 contains information on which of the 75 dates were played under the lights.

Starting Pitcher.   Many baseball aficionados thought that the quality of the starting pitcher affected attendance. The starting pitchers for each baseball game were scheduled days in advance, and this information was published in local newspapers. Roddey thought that pitcher Mark Nobel, who might have been considered a star attraction, could conceivably have influenced people to attend those ball games in which he performed. Exhibit 1 gives those games in which Nobel was the starting pitcher.

Opponent.   Although most people came to the ball park to root for the home team, characteristics of the opposing team could also be important criteria in choosing to attend a baseball game. In particular, the New York Yankees—perhaps baseball's most famous team—were known to attract larger crowds than many teams. Roddey was certain that the Yankees had a big effect on the 1980 season attendance since the A's manager Billy Martin had been fired by the Yankees the previous year. Exhibit 1 identifies the opposing team in each contest.

Television.   In the past it had been generally thought that televising a home game would dissuade people from attending the game in person, thus depriving the home team of ticket revenue. Recently, however, the amounts of money

---

[4]"Games behind" may be interpreted as the number of consecutive games the A's would have to win and the division leading team would have to lose before the two would be tied for first place. As an example, if the California Angels were in first place with a record of 42 wins and 34 losses and the A's had won 37 and lost 39, the A's would be 5 games behind the Angels. Comparing the number of games behind to the number of games remaining gave some indication of the chances a team had of eventually winning the division.

local stations offered for broadcast rights to home games had convinced many local teams to televise a portion of the home schedule. Exhibit 1 shows that nine home games were carried on local Oakland station KPIX.

Promotions.   Exhibit 6 lists the kinds of promotions, all designed to bring people into the ball park, run by the A's in 1980. Roddey was fairly confident that they did increase attendance; thus Exhibit 1 includes them as part of the attendance data.

Nobel's Pitch

Mark Nobel's record before 1980 had not been impressive. The 26-year-old had won a total of only 11 games for the A's, although Nobel had been in the major leagues since 1975. An arm injury early in that first year had contributed to his poor performance. He was making only $40,000 a year in 1980, when he turned in a spectacular season. As he entered salary negotiations, he was talking in terms of $600,000 a year.

The major evidence presented by Nobel and his agent in support of his salary demands was performance statistics from the 1980 season. Nobel started 33 games, winning 22 and losing 9. He was the second best pitcher in the American League in four important categories: earned run average (2.53), completed games (24), innings pitched (284⅓), and strikeouts (180). He was voted the Gold Glove Award as best fielding pitcher and finished second in the balloting for the Cy Young Award, given each year to the most outstanding pitcher in each league.

Nobel also argued that he had the ability to attract people to the ball park. He had been quoted in *Sports Illustrated*[5] as saying:

> I'm not saying anything against Rick Langford or Matt Keough [fellow A's pitchers] . . . but I filled the Coliseum last year against Tommy John [star pitcher for the Yankees].

The implication was that Nobel felt he did indeed personally attract people to the games.

The hard numbers behind this argument had been presented to Roddey in a previous negotiation session. The average home attendance for the 16 games that Nobel started was 12,663.6. When Nobel did not start, the average was only 10,859.4. Nobel's agent multiplied the difference in attendance, 1,804.2, by the average ticket price, $3.66, and then by 16; he put forth the resulting figure, $105,650, as a rough measure of the value of Nobel to the Oakland A's as a box-office attraction. The agent also made it clear that this value was above and beyond the value associated with Nobel's ability to help the A's win ball games.

---

[5]Ron Fimrite, "Winning Is Such a Bore," April 27, 1981.

OAKLAND A'S (A) SUPPLEMENT

The following variables were constructed from the data in Exhibit 1 of the "Oakland A's (A)" case (Case 36).

Variable Name	Definition
TIX	Number of tickets sold
OPP	Opposing team (1 through 13)
POS	Position in the division
GB	Games behind
DOW	Day of week (1 = Monday)
TEMP	Temperature (° F)
PREC	Precipitation: 1 if; 0 if not
TOG	Time of game: 1 if day; 2 if night
TV	Television: 1 if televised locally; 0 if not
PROMO	Promotion: 1 if; 0 if not
NOBEL	1 if Mark Nobel started; 0 if not
YANKS	1 if the opposing team was the Yankees; 0 if not
WKEND	1 if Fri., Sat., or Sun.; 0 if not
OD	Opening day: 1 if, 0 if not
DH	Double header: 1 if; 0 if not
O1	Opponent number 1: 1 if; 0 if not
•	
•	
•	
O13	Opponent number 13: 1 if; 0 if not

Exhibit 1 presents the average and standard deviations of these variables, Exhibit 2 presents the correlation coefficients between several pairs of variables, and Exhibit 3 presents the results of various regressive models to explain TIX as a function of various other variables.

This case is based on a Supervised Business Study prepared by Ann C. Stephens, (Darden, Class of 1982).

EXHIBIT 1 **Averages and Standard Deviations**

Variable	Average	Standard Deviation
TIX	11,244.25	9,729.86
OPP	7.05	3.83
POS	2.85	1.34
GB	8.76	6.06
DOW	4.24	2.06
TEMP	62.03	3.32
PREC	0.040	0.20
TOG	1.48	0.50
TV	0.120	0.33
PROMO	0.173	0.38
NOBEL	0.213	0.41
YANKS	0.067	0.25
WKEND	0.520	0.50
OD	0.013	0.12
DH	0.080	0.27
O1	0.080	0.27
O2	0.093	0.29
O3	0.067	0.25
O4	0.067	0.25
O5	0.067	0.25
O6	0.080	0.27
O7	0.067	0.25
O8	0.080	0.27
O9	0.080	0.27
O10	0.080	0.27
O11	0.080	0.27
O12	0.080	0.27
O13	0.080	0.27

EXHIBIT 2   Correlation Coefficients

	TIX	OPP	POS	GB	DOW
TIX	1.000				
OPP	−0.112	1.000			
POS	−0.115	−0.206	1.000		
GB	0.075	0.185	−0.152	1.000	
DOW	−0.007	−0.056	−0.104	−0.123	1.000
TEMP	−0.061	−0.106	0.052	0.657	−0.135
PREC	−0.097	−0.003	−0.182	−0.161	0.176
TOG	0.129	−0.112	0.126	0.091	−0.556
TV	−0.098	0.124	−0.082	−0.169	0.197
PROMO	0.267	−0.025	−0.002	0.118	−0.002
NOBEL	0.076	−0.093	0.033	0.005	0.082
YANKS	0.807	−0.214	−0.051	0.108	−0.005
WKEND	0.058	−0.043	−0.106	−0.145	0.896
OD	0.158	−0.154	0.187	−0.150	−0.014
DH	0.206	−0.249	−0.078	−0.070	0.158

	TEMP	PREC	TOG	TV	PROMO
TEMP	1.000				
PREC	−0.290	1.000			
TOG	0.113	−0.060	1.000		
TV	−0.078	0.134	−0.273	1.000	
PROMO	0.167	−0.093	−0.017	−0.061	1.000
NOBEL	−0.034	0.060	0.086	0.008	0.019
YANKS	0.014	−0.055	0.064	−0.099	0.160
WKEND	−0.178	0.196	−0.306	0.191	0.017
OD	−0.177	−0.024	0.121	−0.043	−0.053
DH	−0.077	0.191	0.012	0.042	−0.135

	NOBEL	YANKS	WKEND	OD	DH
NOBEL	1.000				
YANKS	0.122	1.000			
WKEND	0.109	0.043	1.000		
OD	−0.061	−0.031	−0.121	1.000	
DH	0.206	0.118	0.087	−0.034	1.000

EXHIBIT 3

Model 1: TIX versus NOBEL

Variable	Coefficient	Std. Error	T-Stat.
NOBEL	1,804.207	2,753.164	0.655
CONSTANT	10,859.356	587.342	18.489

R-squared = 0.006
Adjusted R-square = −0.008
Std. deviation of residuals = 9,767.6
Durbin Watson D = 1.196

Model 2: TIX versus 01 through 012, NOBEL

Variable	Coefficient	Std. Error	T-Stat.
NOBEL	323.388	1,755.292	0.184
O1	−4,627.963	3,396.590	−1.363
O2	−1,607.024	3,224.109	−0.498
O3	−3,810.322	3,578.674	−1.065
O4	28,663.478	3,578.674	8.010
O5	−2,177.244	3,526.638	−0.617
O6	−3,412.231	3,358.582	−1.016
O7	−3,628.322	3,578.674	−1.014
O8	−6,516.065	3,358.582	−1.940
O9	1,263.371	3,396.590	0.372
O10	100.833	3,345.816	0.030
O11	−927.898	3,358.582	−0.276
O12	−5,839.463	3,396.590	−1.719
CONSTANT	11,652.167	983.1261	11.852

R-squared = 0.708
Adjusted R-squared = 0.645
Std. deviation of residuals = 5,795.1
Durbin Watson D = 2.291

EXHIBIT 3   *Continued*

Model 3: TIX versus O1 through O12, PREC, TEMP, PROMO, NOBEL, OD, DH

Variable	Coefficient	Std. Error	T-Stat.
PREC	–3,772.043	3,383.418	–1.115
TEMP	–184.293	237.731	–0.775
PROMO	5,398.545	1,780.857	3.031
NOBEL	–403.502	1,518.000	–0.266
OD	15,382.632	5,652.397	2.721
DH	7,645.224	2,429.894	3.146
O1	–7,213.660	2,999.437	–2.405
O2	–3,203.395	3,046.540	–1.051
O3	–5,780.245	3,242.464	–1.783
O4	25,640.501	3,196.000	8.023
O5	–3,444.192	3,056.500	–1.127
O6	–4,568.433	2,988.677	–1.529
O7	–5,075.192	3,190.707	–1.591
O8	–5,973.904	3,329.604	–1.794
O9	1,966.401	2,971.357	0.662
O10	–2,352.715	3,002.119	–0.784
O11	–1,701.151	3,023.445	–0.563
O12	–5,627.881	2,911.665	–1.933
CONSTANT	22,740.489	14,777.323	1.539

R-squared = 0.803
Adjusted R-squared = 0.740
Std. deviation of residuals = 5,011.0
Durbin Watson D = 2.269

Quantitative Business Analysis Casebook

EXHIBIT 3 *Continued*

Model 4: TIX versus OPP, NOBEL

Variable	Coefficient	Std. Error	T-Stat.
OPP	−269.135	297.809	−0.904
NOBEL	1,572.135	2,768.562	0.568
CONSTANT	12,807.161	2,182.002	5.869

R-squared = 0.017
Adjusted R-square = 0.010
Std. deviation of residuals = 9,779.9
Durbin Watson D = 1.146

Model 5: TIX versus PREC, TOG, TV, PROMO, NOBEL, YANKS, WKEND, OD, DH

Variable	Coefficient	Std. Error	T-Stat.
PREC	−3,660.109	3,251.502	−1.126
TOG	1,606.406	1,334.121	1.204
TV	223.421	1,982.301	0.113
PROMO	4,382.173	1,658.644	2.642
NOBEL	−1,244.411	1,546.545	−0.805
YANKS	29,493.164	2,532.314	11.647
WKEND	1,468.269	1,328.585	1.105
OD	16,119.831	5,388.174	2.992
DH	5,815.814	2,375.194	2.449
CONSTANT	5,082.356	2,170.419	2.342

R-squared = 0.742
Adjusted R-squared = 0.706
Std. deviation of residuals = 5273.5
Durbin Watson D = 1.733

EXHIBIT 3   *Continued*

Model 6: TIX versus PROMO, NOBEL, YANKS, DH

Variable	Coefficient	Std. Error	T-Stat.
PROMO	4,195.743	1,737.742	2.414
NOBEL	−1,204.082	1,607.869	−0.749
YANKS	29,830.245	2,641.516	11.293
DH	5,274.262	2,457.377	2.146
CONSTANT	8,363.238	527.298	15.861

R-squared = 0.692
Adjusted R-square = 0.675
Std. deviation of residuals = 5,551.0
Durbin Watson D = 1.96

Model 7: TIX versus PREC, PROMO, NOBEL, YANKS, OD

Variable	Coefficient	Std. Error	T-Stat.
PREC	−1,756.508	3,227.439	−0.544
PROMO	3,758.92	1,687.895	2.227
NOBEL	−209.484	1,549.192	−0.135
YANKS	30,568.223	2,570.535	11.892
OD	15,957.998	5,491.220	2.906
CONSTANT	8,457.002	496.203	17.043

R-squared = 0.709
Adjusted R-square = 0.688
Std. deviation of residuals = 5,434.5
Durbin Watson D = 1.873

EXHIBIT 3   *Concluded*

Model 8: TIX versus GB, TEMP, PREC, TOG, TV, PROMO, NOBEL, YANKS, WKEND, OD, DH

Variable	Coefficient	Std. Error	T-Stat.
GB	156.240	136.632	1.144
TEMP	−440.363	258.493	−1.704
PREC	−5,021.658	3,348.736	−1.500
TOG	1,807.918	1,331.109	1.358
TV	572.777	1,991.314	0.288
PROMO	4,736.968	1,665.964	2.843
NOBEL	−1,353.056	1,537.185	−0.880
YANKS	29,038.808	2,536.088	11.450
WKEND	1,319.888	1,330.660	0.992
OD	14,928.553	5,484.738	2.722
DH	5,968.288	2,362.325	2.526
CONSTANT	30,815.082	16,223.465	1.899

R-squared = 0.753

Adjusted R-square = 0.710

Std. deviation of residuals = 5,237.0

Durbin Watson D = 1.80

CASE 38
THE OAKLAND A'S (B)

Steward Roddey, general manager of the Oakland A's major-league professional baseball team, was in the midst of contract negotiations with Mark Nobel, a star pitcher for the A's. Nobel had had an excellent season in 1980, winning 22 games and losing only 7, and had finished second in the balloting for the Cy Young Award, given each year to the outstanding pitcher in the 14-team American League. His fine performance had been a pleasant surprise to the A's, because Nobel had won only 11 total games for the team since he started playing major-league baseball in 1975.

Roddey knew that such a dramatic improvement in a player's performance would make contract negotiations particularly difficult. Although Nobel had made only $40,000 for the 1980 season, he had begun salary negotiations with a $600,000-a-year request.

The Resurgent Oakland A's

Mark Nobel's surprise performance in 1980 contributed to a fairly successful year for the Oakland team. In contrast to their last-place finish in 1979, the A's finished second in the seven-team American League West Division with a record of 83 wins and 79 losses (see Exhibit 1). The team's performance had rekindled Oakland's interest in baseball, and home attendance was the highest it had been since 1975 (see Exhibit 2 for attendance figures).

EXHIBIT 1   Past Team Performance

Year	W	L	Pct.	Pos.
1968	82	80	.506	6
1969	88	74	.543	2
1970	89	73	.549	2
1971	101	60	.627	1
1972*	93	62	.600	1
1973	94	68	.580	1
1974	90	72	.556	1
1975	98	64	.605	1
1976	87	74	.540	2
1977	63	98	.391	7
1978	69	93	.426	6
1979	54	108	.333	7
1980	83	79	.512	2

*A two-week player strike shortened this season.

EXHIBIT 2   Yearly Attendance

Year	Home	Road	Total
1968	837,466	960,210	1,797,676
1969	778,232	992,124	1,770,356
1970	778,355	971,568	1,749,923
1971	914,993	1,222,741	2,137,734
1972	921,323	1,115,553	2,036,876
1973	1,000,763	1,382,250	2,383,013
1974	845,693	1,526,630	2,372,323
1975	1,075,518	1,436,383	2,511,901
1976	780,593	1,392,109	2,172,702
1977	495,412	1,195,138	1,690,550
1978	526,412	1,381,142	1,907,554
1979	306,763	1,393,196	1,699,959
1980	843,319	1,572,926	2,416,245
Total	10,104,842	16,541,970	26,646,812
Average	777,296	1,272,459	2,049,755

This success on the field translated into increased revenues at the box office. Total gross revenue from ticket sales was $3.1 million in 1980, compared with only $1.5 million the year before. The A's received 77 percent of this home revenue, with 20 percent going to the visiting team and 3 percent to the league office. Ticket prices at the 50,000-seat Oakland-Alameda County Coliseum were the lowest in the league at $2, $4, $5, and $6, with no changes expected for 1981. The actual cost to the A's of staging a game at the Coliseum did not vary significantly with attendance.

Roddey was confident the team would improve on its 1980 performance. Hopes were high that the experience gained in 1980 would enable the relatively young Oakland team to win its division in 1981. The team planned no major personnel changes and was content to give its manager, Billy Martin, full responsibility for guiding the A's. Martin was an experienced manager, with a history of turning losing teams into winners in a relatively short time. The 1981 season would be Martin's second as manager of the A's.

Roddey's enthusiasm for the coming season showed in his personal forecast of 95 wins for 1981. Each year for the last 13, he had recorded a predicted number of wins for the coming season. Although far from perfect (he was 11 games off in 1977), Roddey was nonetheless proud of his record as a forecaster (see Exhibit 3).

Mark Nobel's Contract

Contract talks between Roddey and Mark Nobel's agent had slowed considerably until Nobel's agent brought up the possibility of a bonus clause tied to yearly attendance. One of the negotiating points made by Nobel and his agent

___

EXHIBIT 3   Roddey's Predictions

Year	Predicted Number of Wins
1968	79
1969	90
1970	91
1971	106
1972	89
1973	84
1974	92
1975	91
1976	88
1977	70
1978	67
1979	65
1980	80

___

was that Nobel attracted people to the ballpark. In addition, they were confident that Nobel and the A's were about to have an above-average year both on the field and at the box office. Rather than argue the validity of these contentions, Nobel's agent had suggested that the A's simply pay Nobel a bonus if and when the contingencies occurred.

One plan put forth was for Nobel to receive 50 cents for every ticket purchased over 1 million. Thus, if total attendance at 1981 home games was less than 1 million, Nobel would not receive a bonus. But if attendance reached 1,100,000 in 1981, for example, Nobel would receive a $50,000 bonus in addition to his fixed yearly salary.

A second alternative was for Nobel to receive lump-sum bonuses if and when home attendance reached certain specified levels. One suggestion would have Nobel receiving $50,000 if attendance exceeded 1 million, another $50,000 if attendance reached 1.5 million, and a final $50,000 if attendance reached 2 million.

When contract talks resumed, Roddey wanted to be prepared to respond to the incentive clause suggested by Nobel and his agent. He had checked with the league office and found that such a clause was allowable under the bylaws of major-league baseball. As a result, Roddey believed he needed to bring to the contract talks a measure of the cost to the A's of the two proposed attendance clauses. He knew the negotiations might come down to a choice between a fixed salary and a somewhat lower salary with one of the proposed clauses.

Personally, he found the idea of an attendance-incentive clause rather appealing. He did not think there was much of a chance that the A's would have to pay under such a plan. After all, only twice in the last 13 years had home attendance reached a million, and those had been championship years. And even if the A's did have to pay, it would be in a year when the team could most afford it.

CASE 39
PIEDMONT AIRLINES: DISCOUNT SEAT ALLOCATION (A)

Marilyn Hoppe smiled as she set aside the most recent edition of the *Piedmonitor,* the company's monthly news magazine. The lead article for April 1985 (see Exhibit 1) had done an excellent job of describing the function of Marilyn's Revenue Enhancement Department, and, in general, she was pleased with it. The article was both accurate and informative, and had stressed the importance of revenue enhancement to the financial success of the company. Because of the article, Marilyn believed that it might now be a little easier to obtain the cooperation of other departments in providing the vast array of data and information needed to successfully carry out the revenue enhancement activities.

The major function of the department was to decide exactly how many discount fare seats were to be sold on each of Piedmont's flights. The financial importance of revenue enhancement meant that Marilyn and her department shouldered a considerable burden of responsibility. Although she had every reason to be pleased with her department's performance, she often wondered whether there might be room for improvement. Piedmont's new information system was as good as most in the industry, and the seven analysts were both knowledgeable and quite good at using the information to allocate discount seats. The nagging problem was that the process still relied quite heavily on the judgments of these seven. Although the analysts were indeed well-informed experts with access to huge amounts of data and information, they were still humans making numerous daily decisions in a manner that was not as "scientific" as the article might suggest.

Discount Seat Allocation

The recent practice in the airline industry was to offer a wide variety of discount fares to passengers who were willing to purchase tickets far in advance of a flight's departure. The number of discount seats was limited, however, in order that the remaining seats could be reserved for full-fare (primarily business) travelers who made plans nearer departure time.

Piedmont scheduled 836 daily departures—almost 30,000 flights a month, for which discount seats had to be allocated. The company had committed over $1 million to Marilyn's department for a sophisticated computer system tailored to provide the necessary information to make these decisions. In addition to up-to-the-minute bookings, the department's seven revenue enhancement analysts could find out fares, schedules, how each flight booked a year earlier, and what the competition was doing in each market. They could also obtain bookings

---

Exhibit 1   Revenue Enhancement
These People Make Certain Piedmont Maximizes Its Revenue

Cathy Howe scans the screen of her reservations computer, studying Flight 364 from DCA to GSO.

To determine how the flight has done in the past, she turns to her MAPPER computer and, moments later, has data on the flight for the past 90 days. She then pulls up information from MAPPER for the flight's next 30 days.

Howe can tell you our fares, our schedules, how the flight traditionally booked a year earlier, and what the competition is doing in this market. And she knows the booking trends for this flight for each day of the week.

This historical report coupled with current and future demand data give her enough analytical material to make an important decision for Piedmont. She will allocate the number of seats that Piedmont will sell on this flight at a discount.

And Howe is responsible for making similar decisions on 109 other flights in 16 Piedmont markets.

"If I can produce just $100 additional revenue every day on each of the flights I monitor, Piedmont will realize over a $4 million annual revenue improvement," she said, "and that's why I'm here, to help maximize the revenue on each of these departures."

Major Responsibility

Howe is one of seven revenue enhancement analysts, at the department's new offices at Madison Park, who has become an expert in Piedmont's markets. Each analyst is responsible for monitoring over 100 flights a day in 15 to 20 markets. Not only do they know the history on each of their flights, they are aware of the schedules, the many fares, booking trends, and what the competition is doing in each of these markets.

The person who set up the new departure and is responsible for its day-to-day operation is Marilyn Hoppe, manager–revenue enhancement. She joined Piedmont last summer after 10 years with Republic Airlines.

Input from Others

To ensure a system of checks and balances, Hoppe monitors what the analysts are doing and reviews their regular monthly reports. In addition, input from other departments is vital to the effective operation of Revenue Enhancement, and there are frequent meetings with other areas of the Company.

"What we have is a perishable commodity," Hoppe said. "We are striving to give each individual flight in a given market a careful mixture of discount and full-fare seats and thus increase our revenue."

The department, part of our Marketing Division, works closely with the Pricing, Tariff, and Scheduling departments.

Note: Terms to Know

Capacity control—allocating seats so as to best meet demand while preventing loss of revenue.

Load factor—percentage of seats filled on our flights.

Revenue—money we receive for services.

Revenue passenger miles (RPMs)—one passenger carried one mile.

Yield—the amount of money we receive for carrying one passenger one mile.

Source: *Piedmonitor* 36, no. 3, April 1985.

EXHIBIT 1 *Continued*

"Our Pricing Department develops fare programs, sets our fares, and performs fare analysis," Swenson said. "Tariffs put the fare programs into operation, and Revenue Enhancement determines the appropriate mix of discount and full-fare seats on each flight."

Piedmont has committed over $1 million to the newly created department for a sophisticated computer system, which has been tailored to our needs. The system has been developed specifically for Piedmont with input from many areas of the company, in particular Data Processing, which continues to provide considerable support.

"Trying to manage 836 departures a day—almost 30,000 flights a month—requires a state-of-the-art system," Hoppe said. "The company has provided us with this system so we can scientifically approach our job. Since deregulation, the whole area of pricing has become extremely complicated and competitive. These tools are necessary in order to control our discount programs."

The philosophy of the department is exactly opposite from the way the industry operated prior to deregulation. The theory then was that, in the final days before a flight, airlines should sell all remaining seats at a discount in order to fill the plane.

"But since deregulation, airlines have discovered the opposite to be true. The number of discount seats should be limited, based on the individual market characteristics, and the remaining seats should be reserved for full-fare business travelers who make plans nearer departure time," she said.

Marilyn Hoppe (right) manager–revenue enhancement, Steve Nelson, an analyst, and Mary Cline, secretary for the department, go over future Piedmont flight schedules, which are being transmitted to the department from our reservations system.

EXHIBIT 1   *Continued*

"What we're doing is getting a good base with the lower fares and reserving the remaining seats for higher-yield traffic, people who make plans closer to departure. Our late-booking passengers, usually business travelers, are probably our most valued customers, our frequent fliers. They often must make plans on short notice and, by allocating fewer discount seats, we give them more flexibility," Hoppe said.

The department allocates seats for each class of service so as to best meet demand while preventing loss of revenue. In most cases, this involves providing discount seats to those passengers who book early, but systematically limiting discount seats at a specific period of time before departure.

Discount seats, in fact, are generally available for over 300 days prior to departure and will only be pulled back, if appropriate, 7 to 14 days before departure, Hoppe said. This process is capacity control and results in more revenue.

"We're offering the business person a full schedule from which to choose and the ability to change flights," Hoppe said. "If we didn't offer discounts, fewer people would travel and, in the end, the businessman or woman would have to pay more and would have fewer flights from which to choose."

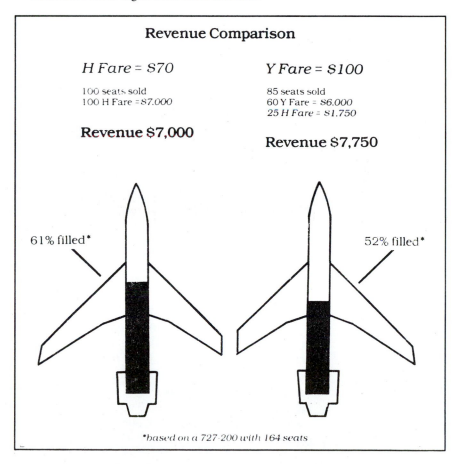

Revenue Comparison

H Fare = $70

100 seats sold
100 H Fare = $7,000

Revenue $7,000

Y Fare = $100

85 seats sold
60 Y Fare = $6,000
25 H Fare = $1,750

Revenue $7,750

61% filled*

52% filled*

*based on a 727-200 with 164 seats

EXHIBIT 1   *Concluded*

"The most successful airlines in the industry, by and large, are using similar techniques employing the same logic. During the last full-blown fare war three years ago, we all learned that we have to restrict discount fares to manage them. By allocating seats we hope to keep our yield up with little impact on load factor," she added.

Revenue Enhancement is already making an impact on Piedmont's financial picture. In 1984, our load factor was 52.42 percent, down 2.4 points from the year before. Yet our total operating revenues grew 36.1 percent to a record $1.3 billion. In 1984, our yield was 17.64 cents per revenue passenger mile, compared with 15.94 cents in 1983.

Monitoring Flights

"Everyone must realize how closely we monitor flights," she emphasized. "You can't determine the performance of a flight by looking only at the number of people who board that flight. Load factor is important, but you also must consider the revenue side. We may have fewer people on a flight but that flight may produce more revenue, because more passengers are paying full fare or another higher-yield fare."

---

trends for each flight for each day of the week. With this information, the analysts determined the number of seats to be sold at a discount.

This discount-seat-allocation decision involved a critical tradeoff: If too many seats were sold at a discount, the airline could lose the difference between the full fare and discount fare for every potential full-fare passenger lost—either because the plane sold out and full-fare customers were turned away, or because customers who might otherwise have paid the full fare "diverted" to the discount fare. The loss caused by diverting was the reason Piedmont often limited the sale of discount-fare seats even in those situations where there was no chance of selling out a flight. If, on the other hand, too few seats were sold at a discount, the airline lost the discount fare for every passenger who would have taken the flight had the discount fare been available but opted instead not to take the flight at all, rather than pay the full fare. This kind of customer was called a "stimulator," because the discount fare stimulated them to take the flight. If a discount fare was not available, potential sales to stimulators were lost. In contrast, a customer who would take the flight at either fare was called a "diverter." A diverter would pay the full fare if no discount seats were available but would divert to the discount fare if it was available.

The seven analysts were repeatedly called on to evaluate the tradeoffs between lost sales due to stimulators turned away and increased revenues from diverters kept at the full fare. Even though large amounts of information were available, striking the proper balance was mostly left to their judgments. Their performance was closely monitored, and all indications were that they were having a positive impact on the company, but Marilyn still wanted to search for ways to improve. Perhaps she could provide some additional guidance for them (maybe in the form of certain decision rules) in making these important deci-

EXHIBIT 2   Flight 224 Historical Bookings and Revenues

	Weekday	*Weekend*	*Total*
Number of flights	56	22	78
Number of sold-out flights	11	2	13
Number of passengers	7,683	2,075	9,758
H passengers	2,017	1,112	3,129
Y passengers	5,666	963	6,629
Segment* revenue	$707,790	$174,140	$881,930
H revenues	$141,190	$77,840	$219,030
Y revenues	$566,600	$96,300	$662,900
Total† revenue	$856,426	$210,710	$1,067,136
H revenues	$145,592	$94,820	$240,412
Y revenues	$710,834	$115,890	$826,724

* Segment revenue refers to the CLT-to-BOS flight only.

†Total revenue includes segment revenues and any additional revenues from Flight 224 passengers connecting to other Piedmont flights.

sions. She decided to start by examining the booking and seat-allocation history of Flight 224 from Charlotte (CLT) to Boston (BOS), a typical Piedmont flight.

Flight 224

Flight 224 was scheduled to leave CLT each day (seven days a week) at 8:30 A.M. and arrive at BOS at 10:20 A.M. Because the flight originated in CLT and terminated in BOS, any passengers with final destinations other than BOS changed planes there and made connections to a separate flight leaving BOS for their final destination. Approximately 25 percent of the flight's passengers had these connecting flights, one-half of which were with airlines other than Piedmont.

All 164 seats on the Boeing 727-200 used for this flight were sold as a single class; that is, there was no first class/coach distinction. All seats were not sold at the same fare, however. A limited number of discount seats called "H-fares," were available for $70. In contrast, the regular fare, called a "Y-fare," was $100. These fares were for the CLT to BOS flight only. Passengers with other final destinations paid a total fare equal to the sum of the fares for each segment of their particular flight. This particular flight had been in existence for only about three months. Marilyn compiled the data given in Exhibit 2, describing the historical bookings and revenues for this flight, and Exhibit 3 shows the company's operating-cost estimates.

After compiling these data, Marilyn met with Cathy Howe, the analyst responsible for Flight 224, to review the decision process used in allocating H-fare seats. They agreed to focus on a particular allocation decision, and Cathy was happy to walk Marilyn through the decision she was about to make regarding Flight 224, which departed a few weeks later on May 8.

EXHIBIT 3   Flight 224 Cost Estimates*

	Cost per Flight
Fuel	$2,240
Maintenance	1,470
Flight crew	770
Ground crew	250
Landing fees	105
Overhead	2,230
Total	$7,065

*Single one-way flight.

EXHIBIT 4   Recent Wednesday Departures of Flight 224

Departure Date	H Bookings	Y Bookings	H Allocation	Total
4/24	42	97	42	139
4/17	44	88	44	132
4/10	45	92	45	137
4/03	52	112	52	164
3/27	35	111	35	146
3/20	46	56	46	102
3/13	52	89	52	141
3/06	57	107	57	164
2/27	26	114	26	140
2/20	28	90	28	118
2/13	50	114	50	164

"The first thing I'd do is check historical bookings for this flight. Since this is a Wednesday flight, I'd put together a relevant history of bookings for previous Wednesday departures of this flight. Here's where I have to be careful to consider all the other factors that can influence booking patterns. For example, the strike at National Airlines meant this flight saw an unusually large number of bookings during early March." A few seconds later, Cathy had a screen full of information on recent Wednesday departures of Flight 224 (Exhibit 4). "See there, our March 6 flight sold out because of that strike, and I seriously doubt that anyone's going to strike right before the departure of this May 8 flight.

"From looking at these data, I'd draw a couple of conclusions. First, you can see that demand for this flight is hard to predict. The flights departing on February 13 and April 3 both sold out, but the load factor [percentage of seats sold] for the March 20 departure was only 62 percent. You can see that, if I set any reasonable allocation, we'd almost certainly sell them all. That 62 percent load factor on March 20 was quite low for this flight, but it still meant we sold 102 seats—most of them at full fare. If I did not limit discount-fare seats for the upcoming May 8 flight, I would predict that total demand for seats would be about 180—much higher than the capacity of the plane. By 'total demand' I mean both stimulators and diverters, anyone willing to take the flight at the discount fare. If pressed to make a judgment on what total demand for discount seats might be, I'd think in terms of the bell-shaped curve and put a 68 percent chance that demand would be between 150 and 210. Looking at the other extreme, if I did not allocate any seats to be sold at the discount fare I would have to think in terms of how many of our potential customers would pay the full fare or how many are stimulators. Because I think the diverter/stimulator mix for this flight is about 60/40, it follows that, if no seats were sold at a discount, 60 percent of the potential demand would remain. This would result in about 108 (180×0.6) full-fare sales. The uncertainty here is a little harder to judge, but I would say that there's a 68 percent chance we would sell between 90 and 126 seats if all seats were offered at the full fare.

"But, quite obviously, it is probably best to set the allocation somewhere between the two extremes of 164 (offer all seats at the H-fare of $70) and 0 (offer all seats at the Y-fare of $100). In reality, I always have the opportunity to reset this allocation at a later date if conditions change. But I still like to set a good initial allocation and then modify it only slightly as the time of departure draws near. One thing we never do, however, is raise the allocation once all discount-fare seats have been sold. This avoids the loss of goodwill associated with selling someone a full-fare seat, because we tell him or her no discount-fare seats are available, and then having that passenger discover that discount-fare seats were sold at a later date."

CASE 40
PIEDMONT AIRLINES: DISCOUNT-SEAT ALLOCATION (B)

As Marilyn Hoppe thought about how to help Cathy Howe plan the number of discount seats to offer on Flight 224, she thought of the problem in terms of how many seats to reserve for the full-fare passengers. Past experience had been that Piedmont had virtually always been able to sell all the discount seats on Flight 224. If we reserve R seats, Hoppe reasoned, then the number of discount seats is simply 164 – R. Suppose we decide R now, well in advance of the flight, and consider it fixed for the remainder of the time before departure?

She thought about what would happen if R were set too low: Suppose it were low by one seat? Then we would lose a full-fare passenger, but that seat would have been filled by a discount passenger. So the cost of R being low by one seat is the difference between full-fare revenue and discount fare, or $30 for Flight 224.

Suppose we set R too high, however, again by one unit only? She reasoned that the seat would go empty, because there would be no full-fare passenger to fly in it. Because the discount passengers would have been restricted, they couldn't fly in it. Thus, she proposed, the cost of being over is the revenue from one discount passenger, or $70.

Marilyn now thought about what to do with these costs. Had these costs been equal, she would have simply used an R that was the mean of the distribution of full-fare demand, or 108. Because it was less costly to reserve too few full-seat fares, however, she believed that she should make R less than 108. The question was: How much less? She seemed to recall a discussion of this somewhere in her past and thought that it was best to make the relative odds of being low match the relative cost of being low. She was not sure, so she looked through a few books to find the result.

In a text on quantitative methods for business, Hoppe found the so-called *newsvendor* problem, which was the question of how many newspapers to buy in the face of uncertain demand. She read that, if she knew the cost of having one newspaper too few (cost of under) and the cost of having one newspaper too many (cost of over), and if the relevant costs were constant per unit, then she should order an amount that corresponded to the critical fractile of her demand distribution. This critical fractile is the ratio of the cost of under to the total of the cost of under plus the cost of over. If she could apply this approach to her problem, the critical fractile would be $30/(30+70) = 0.30$. The task was now a straightforward matter of finding the 30th percentile of Howe's assessed distribution for the number of full-fare passengers. Using a normal distribution with mean 108 and standard deviation 18, Hoppe calculated the result to be 99, to the nearest integer.

Based on this approach, the plan was to reserve 99 seats for full-fare passengers and allocate the other 65 seats to discount fares. Hoppe filed away this result for her next meeting with Howe and thought how impressed her boss would be when he learned about the new approach. She relaxed for a moment with *The Wall Street Journal,* but before 10 minutes had passed she had her notes out again on the table. Yield management made such a huge difference in bottom-line profits in her company that she had better not jump to any hasty conclusions; her reputation would be on the line.

Hoppe noted that this discount allocation of 65 was much larger than had been used before on Flight 224. Numbers don't lie, she thought; there had already been many times in her career when getting the numbers right had saved her. And she had found situations where her own analysis topped existing practice. Here, however, the use of the newsvendor approach was new to her. Could it be directly applied to this situation? After all, the textbook example didn't talk about two types of customers.

She decided a Monte Carlo simulation would help her verify this new result—and allow her to test alternative plans as well. The Case 1 section of Exhibit 1 explains the important cells in the electronic-spreadsheet model she developed.

EXHIBIT 1   A Description of the Monte Carlo Simulation Model

---

Cell *C3:*	Demand, the number of potential customers, drawn from a normal distribution with mean 180 and standard deviation 30, rounded off to the nearest integer.

Case 1

Cell *B6:*	Choose R_1, the seats saved for full fare in Case 1 (59).
Cell *B7:*	$Q_1 = 164 - R_1$ is the number of discount seats available (105).
Cell *B9:*	If $C3 > Q_1$, then from the $C3 - Q_1$ customers that do not fit in the discount seats, determine the potential number of full-fare sales using a binomial distribution with $p = 0.6$.
If $C3 \le Q_1$, then the number of full-fare sales is zero.
Cell *B10:*	Minimum of *B6* and *B9*.
Cell *B16:*	If $C3 > Q_1$, then Revenue $= 70 * B7 + 100 * B10$.
If $C3 \le Q_1$, then Revenue $= 70 * C3$.

Case 2

Cell *D6:*	Choose $R_2 > R_1$, the seats saved for full fare in Case 2 (99).
Cell *D7:*	$Q_2 = 164 - R_2$ is the number of discount seats available (65).
Cell *D9:*	If $C3 > Q_1$, then from the $B7–D7$ additional customers that do not fit in the discount seats for Case 2, determine the number of potential full-fare sales using a binomial distribution with $p = 0.6$ and add to *B9*.
If $C3 \le Q_1$ and $C3 > Q_2$, then from the $C3–D7$ additional customers that do not fit in the discount seats for Case 2, determine the potential full-fare sales using a binomial distribution with $p = 0.6$.
If $C3 \le Q_2$, the number of full-fare sales is zero.
Cell *D10:*	Minimum of *D6* and *D9*.
Cell *D16:*	If $C3 > Q_2$, then Revenue $= 70 * D7 + 100 * D10$.
If $C3 \le Q_2$, then Revenue $= 70 * C3$.

Difference

Cell *C16:*	$B16 - D16$

The simulation first generated the demand (i.e., the number of potential customers) and used this number, along with the number of seats allocated to full-fare customers, to determine the number of discount seats sold. Then the behavior of each remaining potential customer was simulated using a 60 percent probability of diverter to determine how many would buy a full-fare seat if no discount seat were available.

After Hoppe validated the model, she tried the simulation with several different values for R. To her surprise, the best revenues were not from setting R to 99, her critical fractile level. For example, the average revenue at R = 59 was higher than the average revenue at R = 99 (see Exhibit 2). She then expanded the model so that, each time it ran, it would calculate the revenue for an R = 59 strategy (cell *B16* of Exhibit 1), the revenue for an R = 99 strategy (cell *D16*), and the difference in revenue for the two strategies for each trial (cell *C16*). Exhibit 3 shows the distribution of this difference in revenue for the same 2,500 trials used in Exhibit 2. It looked pretty convincing, from this simulation at least, that R = 59 was better than R = 99, but she was not sure that this result might not be "the luck of the draw" resulting from not enough trials.

Next, she set up an experiment to search for the optimal level. She decided to look over the range of R = 30 to R = 80 and to compare the difference in revenues for strategies that varied by increments of five seats. In other words, first she tested R = 30 versus R = 35, then R = 35 versus R = 40, and so on, all the way to R = 75 versus R = 80. The results are contained in Exhibit 4. She puzzled over them for a while, then picked up the paper again. "I'll have to mull this over," she muttered to herself.

EXHIBIT 2   Graphs of Revenues Generated from R = 59 and R = 99 Strategies

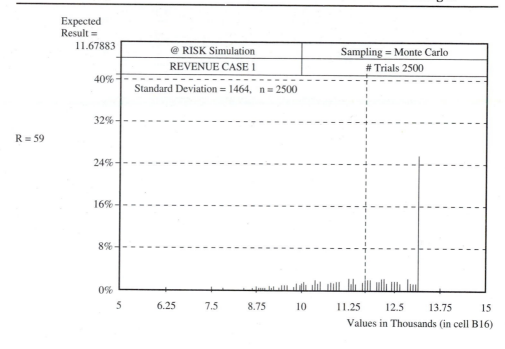

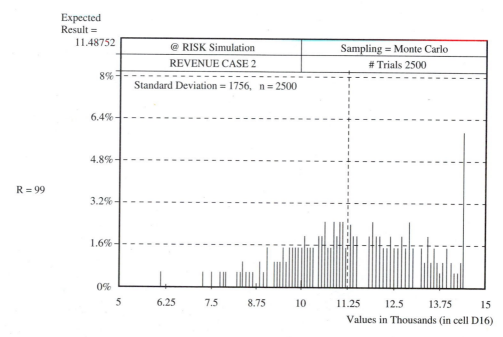

EXHIBIT 3   Monte Carlo Results for Difference (Cell C16) in Revenue for the R = 59 and R = 99 Strategies

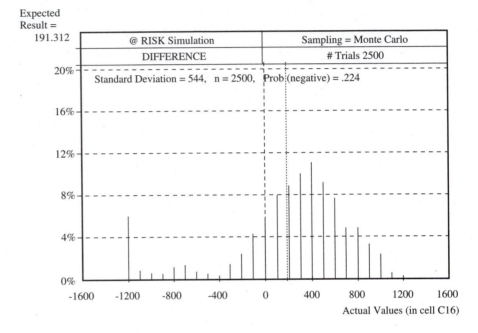

EXHIBIT 4   Simulation Results for Different R-Values and for the Difference between R and R + 5

R, Full-Fare Seats	Revenue for R		Rev. for R + 5		Difference: Revenue for R – Revenue for R + 5	
	Mean	*Std. Dev.*	*Mean*	*Std. Dev.*	*Mean*	*Std. Dev.*
30	11516	1156	11551	1215	−34.8	125
35	11550	1231	11577	1290	−27.5	126
40	11579	1289	11598	1348	−19.5	127
45	11601	1338	11611	1396	−10.3	128
50	11606	1389	11609	1442	−2.9	127
55	11584	1449	11578	1499	6.2	126
60	11617	1501	11607	1549	10.4	126
65	11609	1546	11593	1590	15.9	124
70	11583	1592	11561	1631	21.9	122
75	11553	1636	11528	1672	24.9	121

Number of trials = 16,000.

CASE 41
PROBABILITY ASSESSMENT EXERCISE

The purpose of this exercise is to explore how well you as an individual and your group as a team can assess cumulative probability distributions. As a result, the exercise consists of two parts:

1. Individual assessments, based on your private knowledge only.
2. Group assessment, in which your team pools its knowledge and develops a consensus forecast.

The 10 uncertain quantities, whose cumulative probability distributions are to be assessed, are described in Uncertain Quantities to Be Assessed. In the Individual Questionnaire (Exhibit 1), you are asked to assess five fractiles for each of the 10 probability distributions. When completing this questionnaire, *please do not consult* handbooks, statistical abstracts, or the like. We seek a faithful expression of your current imperfect state of knowledge, rather than the correct answer! After you and the other members of your group have made your individual assessments, please meet as a group, pool your knowledge, arrive at a consensus, and complete the Group Questionnaire (Exhibit 2). In your group, you will be assessing quantities 8, 9, and 10 only. Please do not alter your individual assessments as a result of the discussions in your group.

Be sure to bring the assessment sheet to class.

EXHIBIT 1   Individual Questionnaire

Your Assessments

Please assess the probability distributions of the 10 quantities described on page 2, and complete the table below.

	0.05 Fractile	0.25 Fractile	0.50 Fractile	0.75 Fractile	0.95 Fractile
1. First female driver	_____	_____	_____	_____	_____
2. Japanese 500 companies	_____	_____	_____	_____	_____
3. O'Hare departures	_____	_____	_____	_____	_____
4. U.S. debt	_____	_____	_____	_____	_____
5. 1987 MBAs	_____	_____	_____	_____	_____
6. Airline deaths	_____	_____	_____	_____	_____
7. NYC to Istanbul	_____	_____	_____	_____	_____
8. Area of United States	_____	_____	_____	_____	_____
9. German autos in Japan	_____	_____	_____	_____	_____
10. U.S. trade deficit	_____	_____	_____	_____	_____

Uncertain Quantities to Be Assessed

1. The year in which Mrs. John Howell Phillips of Chicago became the first female licensed driver in the United States.

2. The number of Japanese companies among *Fortune*'s 1990 "Global 500," the world's largest industrial corporations (in sales).

3. The number of passenger arrivals and departures at Chicago's O'Hare airport in 1989.

4. The U.S. national debt as of August 18, 1993.

5. The number of master's degrees in business or management conferred in the United States in 1987.

6. The number of passenger deaths that occurred worldwide in scheduled commercial airliner accidents in the 1980s.

7. The shortest navigable distance (in statute miles) between New York City and Istanbul.

8. The total area of the 48 contiguous states of the United States of America (in millions of square miles).

9. The number of German automobiles sold in Japan in 1989.

10. The total U.S. merchandise trade deficit with Japan (in billions of dollars) in the 1980s.

Source for some questions: "Managing Overconfidence" by J. Edward Russo and Paul J. H. Schoemaker, *Sloan Management Review* (Winter 1992).

EXHIBIT 2   Group Questionnaire

After the members of your group have entered their individual assessments, meet to complete the questionnaire below. The three assessments refer again to the quantities described in Uncertain Quantities, but this time pool the knowledge within the group. After you reach a consensus, each member of the group should enter the data in the table below.

	0.05 Fractile	0.25 Fractile	0.50 Fractile	0.75 Fractile	0.95 Fractile
8. Area of United States	_____	_____	_____	_____	_____
9. German autos in Japan	_____	_____	_____	_____	_____
10. U.S. trade deficit	_____	_____	_____	_____	_____

BRING THIS DATA TO CLASS.

CASE 42
PROBLEMS IN REGRESSION

1. Union Camp—Trenton

An important element in the scheduling procedure of the Union Camp Corporation's corrugated container plant in Trenton, New Jersey, involved forecasting the amount of processing time each job would require at each work center. One piece of information available was the number of thousand square feet (MSF) in the job. Data for 15 randomly selected jobs processed on a particular printing press follow:

MSF	Hours
26.0	2.00
34.2	4.17
29.0	4.42
34.3	4.75
85.9	4.83
143.2	6.67
85.5	7.00
140.6	7.08
140.6	7.17
40.4	7.17
101.0	10.00
239.7	12.00
179.3	12.50
126.5	13.67
140.8	15.08

Can regression be used to provide a forecast? Two jobs waiting to be processed contained 157.3 MSF and 64.7 MSF. What is the probability that the first, larger job will take less than eight hours to process? What is the probability that the second, smaller job will take less than eight hours?

2. South Wales Mining Company

The South Wales Mining Company often needs to make rapid and exact estimates of the weight of a pile of loose materials, such as coal. To help do this more accurately, the company has compiled information about 10 coal piles for which the actual weight was known. The information consists of the diameter of the base of the pile (D), the diameter of the top of the pile (d), and the height of the pile (h). These distances are all given in units of feet, and the weight (W) of the coal pile is given in metric tons.

W	D	h	d
56	20	10	15
93	25	10	20
161	30	12	24
31	15	12	10
70	20	14	13
76	20	14	13
375	40	16	32
34	15	14	8
45	20	8	16
58	20	10	15

How should South Wales Mining combine information in D, h, and d to predict the weight of a pile of coal?

EXHIBIT 1   Graphic for Problem 2

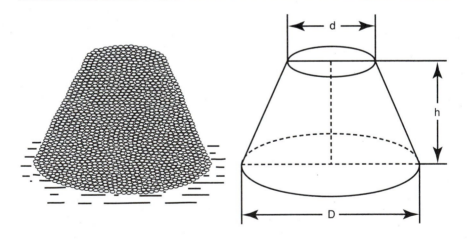

3. Longevity and Handedness

In the early 1990s, two psychologists surveyed the next of kin listed on public death certificate records in two counties in southern California. The survey asked the handedness of the recently deceased family member. Subjects were labeled right-handers if they wrote, drew, and threw a ball with their right hand. All other subjects were labeled as left-handers. Next of kin of young children and homicide victims were not surveyed.

The age of death (AOD) of the 867 right-handers averaged 75.00 years. The AOD of the 82 left-handers averaged 66.03. A dummy variable was created representing the handedness of the subjects:

$$DR = \begin{cases} 1 \text{ if subject was right-handed} \\ 0 \text{ if subject was mixed or left-handed} \end{cases}$$

and a regeression analysis was performed relating AOD to DR. The results appear below:

Regression Statistics

Multiple R	0.1518763
R square	0.0230664
Adjusted R square	0.0220348
Standard error	16.418869
Observations	949

ANOVA

	df	SS	MS	F	Significance F
Regression	1	6027.699921	6027.7	22.35966	2.60415E-06
Residual	947	255291.5539	269.5793		
Total	948	261319.2538			

	Coef.	Std. Error	t Stat	P-value	Lower 95%	Upper 95%
Intercept	66.03	1.813160744	36.41707	2.9E-182	62.4717241	69.588276
X Variable 1	8.97	1.89696739	4.7286	2.6E-06	5.247255964	12.692744

What is your explanation for the rather surprising results?

4. Market Study

In a market-segmentation study, data on net income (I) in thousands, family size (F), and expenditures on consumer durable goods (C) were collected from 20 randomly selected households:

I	F	C
10	4	1960
10	3	2390
15	4	3060
15	5	3220
20	6	3570
20	5	4360
25	7	4970
25	6	5190
30	8	5390
30	7	5550

The company sponsoring the study was interested in isolating the effects of income and family size on the dollar amounts spent for consumer durable goods.

5. Class Participation

There is a popular notion that students sitting on the right side (right from a student's perspective) of the classroom are called on more often than students on the left. Ten students, randomly selected from each side of one of last year's classes, had the following numerical class-participation grades:

Right Side	Left Side
14	8
19	9
19	10
17	20
13	10
13	13
16	17
4	5
12	3
12	8

Use regression with a dummy variable to test the notion that the average class-participation grade is higher on the right side of the class.

CASE 43
ROADWAY CONSTRUCTION COMPANY

In late August, David Black, president of Roadway Construction Company, was preparing his capital-budgeting recommendation for the upcoming fiscal year. Paramount in his mind were the recently announced $9.25 billion Georgia highway program and the opportunities for growth that this program represented for Roadway. The most immediate need would be for another asphalt-manufacturing plant.

The New Highway Program

The August 3 issue of a contracting industry bulletin described the Georgia highway plans as follows:

> It's time to breathe a sigh of relief and celebrate! The state legislature approved on July 27 a funding plan to raise $9.25 billion for road construction over the next 13 1/2 years. . . . The legislation sets up a state highway trust fund to four-lane some 1,800 miles of the intrastate highway system. This will put 90 percent of the state's population within 10 miles of a four-lane highway. . . . Under the program all or portions of seven urban loops will be completed and 10,000 miles of unpaved secondary roads will be paved. . . . The new funding is in addition to the annual state highway construction program, which amounts to approximately $400 million.

Roadway

Roadway Construction Company, a division of Southern Highways, Inc., was a wholly owned subsidiary of a *Fortune* 500 conglomerate whose core business was the refining and marketing of petroleum products. Southern provided corporate management for 20 companies similar to Roadway located in the South from Virginia to California. These divisions were grouped geographically into six regions, each managed by a regional vice president who reported to the president of Southern Highways, Inc.

The Roadway division operated three branches, maintained six operating/marketing offices, and ran eight asphalt-manufacturing plants. It competed with 13 similar contractors, who operated a combined total of 26 asphalt plants. Roadway provided earth grading, drain-pipe installation, stone-base placement, asphalt paving, and curb gutter construction in a 20-county area of eastern Georgia. The work contributed to the completion of federal and state highways; city, county, subdivision, and military-base streets; airport runways; sites for manufacturing plants and commercial building; parking

This case was based on a Supervised Business Study prepared by Douglas L. Schwartz (Darden, Class of 1990).
Copyright © by the University of Virginia Darden School Foundation, Charlottesville, Virginia. All rights reserved.

lots; and residential driveways. Roadway was the primary provider of these services in the area (40 percent market share) and had annual revenues in excess of $40 million.

Roadway's main source of revenue was the manufacture and placement of asphaltic concrete (hot-mixed asphalt), the product that constitutes the traveling surface of asphalt streets and highways, and all other company functions operated to support this primary business. Asphaltic concrete is manufactured by mixing specifically sized and blended crushed stone and sand that have been dried and heated to approximately 300 degrees (F) in a rotating kiln with 4 to 6 percent of liquid asphalt (the residual of the manufacture of all other petroleum products). When placed on the roadway and properly compacted, this mixture produces a smooth and durable riding surface. Roadway manufactured and placed approximately 700,000 tons/year and sold approximately 40,000 tons/year to smaller competitors. This asphaltic concrete was produced from seven nonportable "batch" plants strategically located within the market area and one continuous-type, portable "drum-mix" plant. The basic raw materials of liquid asphalt and crushed stone were purchased; Roadway produced its own sand.

Strategic location was the key competitive consideration in the asphalt-paving business. All competitors could purchase raw materials, manufacture the product, and place the asphalt within the ranges of their manpower, equipment, and management efficiency. Competitive advantage lay in situating the asphalt plant in the optimum location relative to the sources of raw materials and the location of a project. The raw materials and the hot-mixed asphalt were transported by trucks, and because the mixed asphalt had to be placed and compacted before it cooled below 250 degrees, transportation time was limited to between two and six hours, depending on weather conditions.

The Decision Process

The divisions operated with a great deal of autonomy, and most management decisions were made independently by a division president. Through close communication over time with Charlie Meadows, his regional vice president, David Black knew the broad parameters within which he could operate independently. He consulted with Meadows only on decisions outside those established bounds. Generally, nonroutine purchases exceeding $100,000 received fairly close scrutiny and required a financial analysis to determine the net present value (NPV), payback, profitability index (the ratio of the present value of future cash flows divided by the initial investment), and internal rate of return (IRR). Once the available funds were approved, the specific purchases were prioritized, with considerable weight given to the division president's recommendations. On final approval, the actual purchase commitments were made by the division president.

Black was reviewing the asphalt-plant decision in preparation for his meeting with Meadows next month in Marietta, Georgia. At that time Black was expected to make and justify his recommendations.

The New Asphalt Plant

Two asphalt plants were available for expanding Roadway's capacity to meet the needs of the new highway program for the next 10 years: a new portable-drum plant and a used batch plant from one of the other divisions. Each plant would have 150,000 tons/year of asphalt-producing capacity with a mix value of $23/ton. The two options differed primarily in cost and service life.

The batch plant would cost $700,000 (plant, erection, and site preparation), have a five-year life, and have a $100,000 salvage value at the end of the five years. The raw materials for this plant were expected to cost $14.00/ton (sand, crushed stone, and liquid asphalt combined); the operating costs were expected to be $2.50/ton; and the maintenance and repair cost, $1.00/ton.

The drum plant would cost $1.5 million (plant, erection, and site preparation), have a 10-year life, and have a $300,000 salvage value at the end of the 10 years. This plant had a raw-material advantage over any batch plant, because it could utilize up to 30 percent RAP (*r*ecycled *a*sphalt *p*roduct) whereas a batch plant could use only 12–15 percent RAP. Thus raw-material costs for a drum plant were only $12.75/ton. Currently, competitors operated five drum-mix plants in the Roadway market area, which put Roadway at a cost disadvantage when bidding against these competitors. Additionally, because the drum plant was brand-new, maintenance costs would be only $.50/ton and operating costs were expected to be as little as $2.00/ton. The drum plant also had a nonquantifiable advantage as a "striking arm" for new markets because of its highly portable capabilities.

Wear and tear was expected to increase maintenance costs for the plants by 10 percent a year. Operating costs were expected to go up by 4 percent a year over the useful lives of the two plants. Roadway currently used a 12 percent hurdle rate for all capital investments, was taxed at an effective rate of 38 percent, and handled all depreciation on a straight-line basis for making investment decisions.

CASE 44
SHUMWAY, HORCH, AND SAGER (A)

Claire Christensen was involved in a new project in her second year with the management consulting firm of Shumway, Horch, and Sager (SHS). It appeared to be another situation in which she was expected to jump quickly out of the blocks with the project and make some clever money-saving recommendation, then find the follow-on project to produce next month's billable days.

The client was an organization of magazine publishers that had become aware of their inability to predict the circulation of their magazines in the future. The publishers wanted a good forecast for a variety of reasons; for example, to decide how many copies to print. The current concern to be resolved was the establishment of a contracted rate base. This was the number of copies that *Good Housekeeping* guaranteed selling each month and was used to determine the advertising revenue. SHS was hired both to suggest a procedure for one-month-ahead forecasts and to make recommendations on the contracted rate base decision.

Christensen thought she could find a way to forecast each issue's sales. She started by picking the magazine *Good Housekeeping* and probing whether she could forecast January 1988 sales using previous data. She had obtained data on total circulation over the past nine years (July 1979–December 1987) from the Publisher's Statement to the Audit Bureau of Circulation. The 8 1/2 years of data are shown in Exhibit 1. She was aware that about 10 million copies of this magazine generally were printed each month, to ensure that no individual newsstand would run out of the magazine.

Christensen pondered how time patterns in past sales might help her predict the sales of a future issue. (See Exhibit 2 for a graph of the circulation data.) *Good Housekeeping* was not a magazine that she read, but she had seen it while waiting for the dentist, and her aunt had it in her house. She knew that the December issue greatly increased newsstand sales because of its holiday recipes and gift-giving ideas. The January issue always seemed to be low, because people evidently felt they had overspent and overeaten during the holidays and were trying to cut back. Changes in the interests of purchasers and in the content of the magazine were also important forces that could gradually move the sales up or down over time.

Just as Christensen was going to dive into the calculations, a representative from *Good Housekeeping* called to clarify the situation with the contracted rate base. The magazine would realize advertising revenue of $1 times the guaranteed rate base. There was a caveat, however. If they did not meet the base value,

EXHIBIT 1   *Good Housekeeping* **Circulation Figures (July 1979–December 1987)**

Date	Obs.#	Circulation	Date	Obs.#	Circulation
Jul79	1	 5264165		53	 5334053
	2	 5313127		54	 5763516
	3	 5117969	Jan84	55	 5198585
	4	 5098771		56	 5501741
	5	 5187708		57	 5329592
	6	 5645295		58	 5322838
Jan80	7	 5023173		59	 5178815
	8	 5333352		60	 5247590
	9	 5224234	Jul84	61	 5194827
	10	 5079207		62	 5118408
	11	 5167277		63	 5291564
	12	 5006445		64	 5047946
Jul80	13	 5150974		65	 5105056
	14	 5180346		66	 5448542
	15	 5223467	Jan85	67	 5023818
	16	 5153303		68	 5099829
	17	 5247109		69	 5253739
	18	 5789798		70	 5138210
Jan81	19	 5350502		71	 5251664
	20	 5371371		72	 5450869
	21	 5327700	Jul85	73	 5022522
	22	 5269993		74	 5206132
	23	 5240438		75	 5042725
	24	 5273266		76	 5096277
Jul81	25	 5439920		77	 5067717
	26	 5378584		78	 5508198
	27	 5329516	Jan86	79	 5133963
	28	 5292129		80	 5180897
	29	 5378127		81	 5161222
	30	 5736465		82	 5174238
Jan82	31	 5073651		83	 5047775
	32	 5553245		84	 5152063
	33	 5439363	Jul86	85	 5001222
	34	 5363948		86	 5232314
	35	 5367404		87	 5235207
	36	 5316957		88	 5009584
Jul82	37	 5412745		89	 5352370
	38	 5387779		90	 5498755
	39	 5439224	Jan87	91	 5159840
	40	 5341392		92	 5274075
	41	 5396853		93	 5179002
	42	 5961612		94	 5269295
Jan83	43	 5335737		95	 5005048
	44	 5618540		96	 5166569
	45	 5604606	Jul87	97	 5068848
	46	 5343116		98	 5007388
	47	 5294990		99	 5265191
	48	 5327995		100	 5046595
Jul83	49	 5177176		101	 5300978
	50	 5290109		102	 5526153
	51	 5449099			
	52	 5344570			

EXHIBIT 2   Graph of *Good Housekeeping* Total Sales over Time

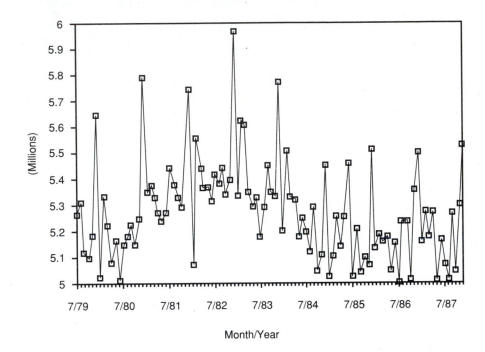

Month/Year

they would refund an amount to their advertisers equal to $1.25 times the short-fall in circulation. For example, if the contracted rate base was 5 million and only 4.5 million copies of the magazine were sold, the magazine would receive $5 million of advertising revenue, but have to refund $1.25 × (500,000) or $625,000. If they exceed the contracted rate base, however, they were not able to collect any revenues for the excess.

The representative said that *Good Housekeeping* had been planning to raise the advertising base rate from its current level of 4.78 million copies to 6.50 million, effective February 1. The magazine was wondering whether or not the date of the increase should be accelerated by one month, to take effect January 1. The representative was calling to ask if Christensen would, as part of her analysis, evaluate the impact of such an acceleration.

Christensen went back again to her forecasting task, realizing that no decision on the contracted rate base could be made without it.

Case 45
Shumway, Horch, and Sager (B)

Christensen started to look at the circulation data of some of the other monthly magazines represented by the client organization (see Exhibits 1–3). The first set of data was for *Working Woman,* which was targeted at women who were in management careers in business. Contents included sections devoted to entrepreneurs, business news, economic trends, technology, politics, career fields, social and behavioral sciences, fashion, and health. It was sold almost entirely through subscriptions, as evidenced by the latest figures reported to the Audit Bureau of Circulation (823.6K subscriptions out of 887.8K total circulation).

The next graph represented circulation data for *Country Living,* a journal that focused on both the practical concerns and the intangible rewards of living on the land. It was sold to people who had a place in the country, whether that was a working farm, a gentleman's country place, or a weekend retreat.

The third set of data was for *Health,* which was a lifestyle magazine edited for women who were trying to look and feel better. The magazine provided information on fitness, beauty, nutrition, medicine, psychology, and fashions for the active woman.

A fourth graph was for *Better Homes and Gardens,* which competed with *Good Housekeeping* and was published for husbands and wives who had serious interests in home and family as the focal points of their lives. It covered these home-and-family subjects in depth: food and appliances, building and handyman, decorating, family money management, gardening, travel, health, cars in your family, home and family entertainment, new-product information and shopping. The magazine's circulation appeared to be experiencing increased volatility over time. Was this the beginning of a new pattern?

The last magazine was *True Story.* It was edited for young women and featured story editorials as well as recipes and food features, beauty and health articles, and home management and personal advice. This journal's circulation appeared to have a definite downward trend over the past nine years. Was the cause a general declining interest in the subject matter, or was this a cycle that would correct itself in the future (like the sine wave Christensen had studied in trigonometry)?

EXHIBIT 1   Graphs of *Working Woman* and *Country Living* Circulations

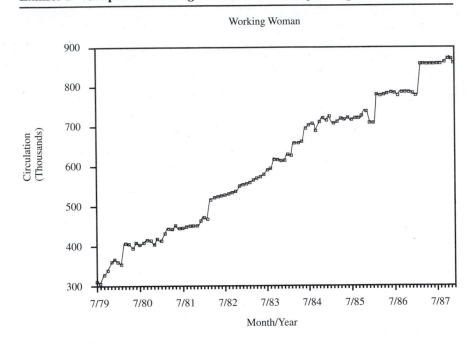

Working Woman

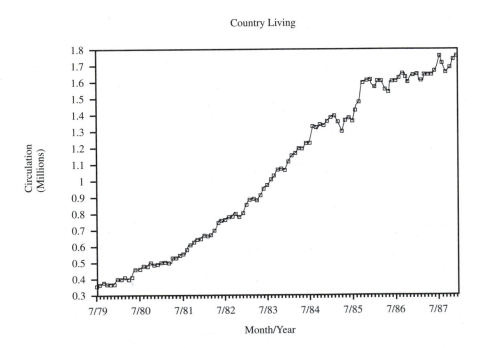

Country Living

EXHIBIT 2   Graphs of *Health* and *BH&G* Circulations

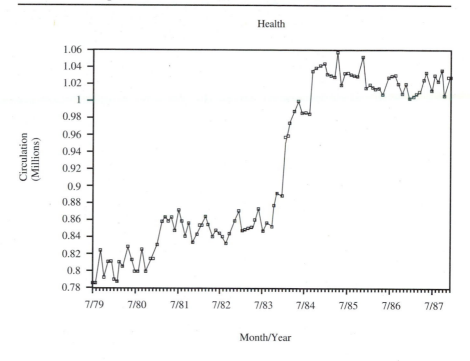

Health

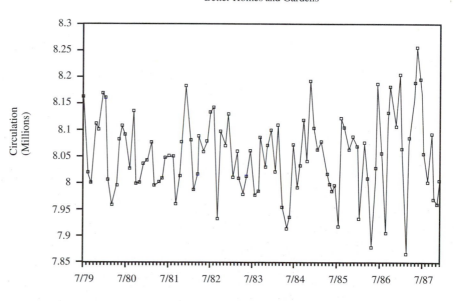

Better Homes and Gardens

EXHIBIT 3   Graph of *True Story* Circulation

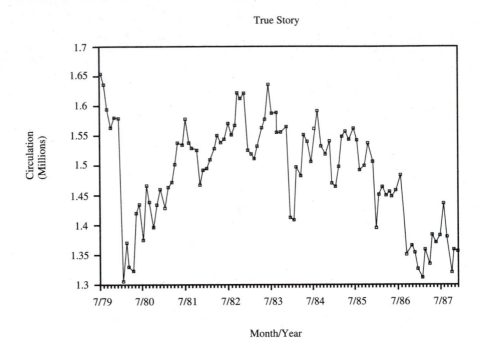

True Story

Month/Year

Case 46
Sleepmore Mattress Manufacturing: Plant Consolidation

W. Carl Lerhos, special assistant to the president of Sleepmore Mattress Manufacturing, had been asked to study the proposed consolidation of plants in three different locations. The company had just added several new facilities as a result of the acquisition of a competitor; some were in markets currently served by existing facilities. The president knew the dollar savings would be fairly easy to calculate for each location, but the qualitative factors and the tradeoffs among them were more difficult to judge. This was the area in which he wanted Carl to spend most of his time.

The major objectives in evaluating a consolidation plan for the sites were to maximize manufacturing benefits, maximize sales benefits, and maximize direct financial benefits. These objectives would be composed of exploiting 13 attributes (see Exhibit 1). After spending some time looking at each attribute individually,

---

Exhibit 1　Hierarchy of Objectives

I.　Maximize Manufacturing Benefits
- *a.*　Labor
- *b.*　Management effectiveness
  1. Talent availability
  2. Plant size
- *c.*　Operability
  1. Product-line complexity
  2. Training
  3. Production stability
- *d.*　Facilities
  1. Layout
  2. Location
  3. Space availability

II.　Maximize Sales Benefits
- *a.*　Maximize service
- *b.*　Maximize quality

III.　Maximize Direct Financial Benefits
- *a.*　Minimize initial cost
- *b.*　Maximize ongoing benefit

EXHIBIT 2   13 Attributes Selected for Evaluation of Consolidation

Rank	Attribute	Worst Outcome	Best Outcome
1	Labor	Create hostile union	Eliminate hostile union
2	Quality	Drastically worsen quality	Strongly improve quality
3	Service	Lose business	Increase business
4	Annual savings	Lost $1 million/yr.	Save $1 million/yr.
5	Initial cost	Cost $5 million	Save $5 million
6	Management talent	Severely worsen management	Strongly improve management
7	Plant size (sales)	Create $35 million plant	Create $15 million plant
8	Plant location	Move from rural area to city	Move from city to rural area
9	Product-line complexity	Increase to full product line	Reduce product line
10	Space availability	Need a new facility (100,000 sq. ft.)	Save an expansion of 100,000 sq. ft.
11	Production stability	Increase demand variability	Decrease variability
12	Training	Train all new labor	Small layoff—no new training
13	Plant layout	Create poor layout	Eliminate poor layout

Carl and the other officers of Sleepmore ranked them in order of most important to least important. They also added the best and worst possible outcomes for each attribute (see Exhibit 2).

Measurements

In each case, the attributes were assigned a number from 0 to 10, with 10 being the best possible outcome mentioned in Exhibit 2. Each location was in a different region, and each of the three locations involved a decision between two alternatives—consolidate the plants there or keep them separate. The plants produced different product lines. Exhibits 3 to 5 give brief descriptions and scores of the three potential consolidation opportunities. Only the "consolidate" alternatives are scored; in other words, each "keep separate" alternative has a default score of five for each attribute (except for the attribute plant size, which was undefined for the pair of plants prior to consolidation). Therefore, the attributes are really scored *relative* to the current situation, in which the plants are separate. The scores Carl assigned were based on subjective assessments after talking with the managers and visiting the sites.

Weights

After Carl had scored each attribute on his scale of 0–10, he faced the more difficult task of deciding how important one attribute was compared with another. The quantitative attributes would be fairly easy to weigh. He knew that the company's discount rate (15 percent), along with its planning horizon (10 years), might help in this regard, but he was not quite sure how.

EXHIBIT 3   Consolidation Evaluated at Site 1: Merge Plant 1A into Plant 1B

Attribute	Plant 1A	Plant 1B	Score for Combining
Labor	Poor	Excellent	9; large improvement
Quality	Poor	Good	9
Service	Poor	Good	8
Annual savings	High overhead	Efficient; merger saves $1 MM/yr.	——
Initial cost	Save $1MM if plant merged	N/A	——
Management talent	Poor	Excellent	9
Plant size (sales)	$3 million	$27 million	——
Plant location	Large city	Rural area	10
Product-line complexity	2 major product lines	2 separate lines	0; very complex
Space availability	N/A	Has extra space; needs 0 new sq. ft.	——
Production stability	Small demand/ high uncertainty	Large demand/low uncertainty	7; reduce variation
Training	N/A	Extra labor available	7.5
Plant layout	Congested plant	Well laid out	7.5

He had heard the president say, "The smaller a plant, the easier it is to manage. If we could improve from a $35 million plant size to a $15 million plant, the gain would be equivalent to a savings from the status quo of $1 million a year in operating costs." Carl made a quick mental calculation, which suggested the weight for plant size would be one-half the weight for annual savings—he'd check it later.

The mattress-manufacturing industry required a lot of space. If a consolidation required a new plant or a significant addition, the hassle of moving, as well as hidden expenses, would be additional negative factors. The cost would be $25/sq. ft. for each additional square foot of space.

To help him in assigning weights to the other, more qualitative attributes, Carl pulled out his notes from a meeting attended by the president, the vice president of operations, and the vice president of human resources. At this meeting, held at the time of the acquisition, the list shown in Exhibit 2 had been generated and the relative importance of each attribute had been discussed.

The vice president of human resources had said, "Labor is the most important because the quality of labor determines the major aspects of plant performance (like quality, profitability, and so on). Experience has shown that a good labor force can overcome many obstacles, but a poor labor force leads to trouble. In fact, I think labor is twice as important as the average of all 13 attributes." Carl wondered about the context for this statement. He verified that

EXHIBIT 4   Consolidation Evaluated at Site 2: Put Plant 2B into Plant 2A

Attribute	Plant 2A	Plant 2B	Score for Combining
Labor	Average	Poor	6
Quality	Average	Average	5
Service	Average	Good	7
Annual savings	Under capacity; merger saves $500K	Under capacity	——
Initial cost	N/A	Save $1MM if merge plant	——
Management talent	Average	Good	6
Plant size (sales)	$5 million	$10 million	——
Plant location	Industrial park	Large city	6
Product-line complexity	2 major product lines	2 different lines	0; very complex
Space availability	Need to add 50K sq.ft. if merge	No room	——
Production stability	Small demand/ high uncertainty	Counter cyclical demand	9; reduce variation
Training	Underutilized labor	Underutilized labor	9; small layoff
Plant layout	Excellent	Poor	9

EXHIBIT 5   Consolidation Evaluated at Site 3: Put Plant 3B into Plant 3A

Attribute	Plant A	Plant B	Score for Combining
Labor	Below average	Good	3; may lose Plant 3A labor
Quality	Average	Average	5
Service	Average	Good	6
Annual savings	Under capacity; merger saves $200K/yr.	Efficient	——
Initial cost	N/A	Save $2MM if merge	——
Management talent	Average	Below average	6
Plant size (sales)	$9 million	$18 million	——
Plant location	Large city	Suburb	4
Product-line complexity	2 major product lines	2 different lines	0; very complex
Space availability	Need 30K sq. ft. if merge	No room	——
Production stability	Small demand/ high uncertainty	Uncertain demand	6; demand not counter-cyclical
Training	Underutilized labor	N/A	3; some labor quits
Plant layout	Good	Cramped	7

the vice president had the ranges of Exhibit 2 in mind: improving labor relations from "create hostile union" to "eliminate hostile union" was twice as valuable as improving the average attribute from worst to best.

The vice president of operations agreed with the comment about labor and said, "I think quality and service, although slightly less important than labor, are two other attributes that deserve more weight than average."

There seemed to be a consensus that management was the next most important qualitative attribute because, like labor, management would determine the fate of the plant. Unlike labor, however, management could be rather easily changed. Overall, this attribute was considered "average" in terms of importance.

The president then argued for consideration of plant location: "Plant location is as important as plant size. Our data show that plants in more congested areas [cities] tend to be less profitable than plants in rural areas."

The vice president of operations said, "Because Sleepmore produces a different product line in different plants, consolidations could drastically increase complexity and reduce long-term efficiency. I move that product-line complexity be considered the next most important qualitative attribute, albeit its importance is about two-thirds the importance of management talent, in my opinion."

The remaining three attributes—stability, training, and layout—were agreed to have individual effects that were relatively small; but their combined effect was considered about twice that of product-line complexity.

The hardest task was to evaluate the tradeoffs that management would be willing to make between quantitative and qualitative factors. In this regard, the president had expressed difficulty to Carl in choosing between a change in the labor from the status quo to eliminate a hostile union and a change in initial cost savings of $7 million.

Decision

Carl had to figure out an effective way to combine all this information about both quantitative and qualitative factors to make decisions whether to consolidate at *each* of the three sites. He wondered how sensitive his decisions would be to the weights he assigned each attribute.

CASE 47
SPRIGG LANE (A)

May 19, 1988, was a beautiful day in Charlottesville, Virginia. Tom Dingledine could see some cows grazing the pasture on the rolling hillside outside his window. He was grateful for the bucolic setting, which was made possible by his doing well with the projects he managed, one of which now required some concentration. Tom was the president of Sprigg Lane Natural Resources, a subsidiary of the Sprigg Lane Investment Corporation (SLIC). The decision at hand was whether to invest in the Bailey Prospect natural gas opportunity.

The Company

Sprigg Lane was a privately held investment corporation founded in 1961. It had become a diversified corporation composed of two major groups. The first was devoted to manufacturing high-quality home furnishings. Its masthead company was Virginia Metalcrafters, which produced handcrafted brass giftware. Other companies in the group included an outdoor lantern company in Maine and an antique reproduction furniture company in Maryland. With the establishment of National Legal Research Group in 1970, another major group—The Research Group—was started. Since then four other research companies had been added in the fields of consumer product marketing, computer software, tax research, and investment financial analysis.

The group's recent formation of Sprigg Lane Development Corporation, which was involved in the purchase and development of real estate, brought the total number of company subsidiaries to nine. SLIC sales for 1987 approximated $30 million and it employed over 525 people.

Drilling and Developing a Well[1]

The most common drilling rig in operation in 1988 was the rotary rig, composed of five major components—the drill string and bit, the fluid-circulating system, the hoisting system, the power plant, and the blowout-prevention system. To facilitate the drilling process, generally a fluid known as drilling mud (composed of water and special chemicals) was circulated around the hole being drilled. In some cases, such as the Bailey Prospect, air was used as the "drilling mud." The major purpose of the drilling mud was to lubricate the drill bit and to carry to the surface the cuttings that could otherwise remain in the hole and clog it.

---

[1]U.S. Department of Energy, *The Oil and Gas Drilling Industry,* 1981, pp. 13–16.

After the well was drilled, and if gas were found, the well had to be completed and prepared for production. A metal pipe of 8.625 inches diameter called "casing" was generally inserted about 1,300 feet into the ground. Then a pipe of 4.5 inches diameter called "production casing" was inserted into the cased hole all the way down through the production zone (about 5,400 feet) and cemented. After the cement set, the production casing was perforated so gas could flow to the surface through it.

The cost to drill an "average" well in Doddridge County, West Virginia, location of the Bailey Prospect, was $160,000. There was some uncertainty, however, in the cost from well to well because of such factors as differing depths of wells and different types of terrain that had to be drilled. Experts in the local area said that there was a 95 percent chance that the cost for any given well would be within $5,400 of the average cost, assuming a normal distribution.

SLIC's Entry into Natural Gas

In January 1987, Tom, who had been working as the CFO of a private oil and gas exploration and development company, met the president of SLIC and joined the company to find some investment opportunities for it. Tom became convinced that the company could enjoy higher potential returns (30–40 percent after tax) from natural resource exploration than from other investment opportunities, including real estate, which were yielding 15–20 percent. Although natural resource exploration was clearly riskier, Tom felt the risk could be managed by drilling only sites that were surrounded on three to four sides by existing wells. Through further research, he found two other factors that helped reduce the risk: first, contracts with the pipeline distributors typically locked in the natural gas selling prices for four years; and second, well operating expenses were covered by contracts that only allowed increases every three years, with the increase capped at 15 percent per three-year period. Tom thought that the annual increase in the total well cost would be equivalent to one-half the rate of inflation.

The president of SLIC was so impressed with Tom's presentation on the entire subject that he offered him the job as president of a new division to be called Sprigg Lane Natural Resources (SLNR). Tom took the offer, and in his first year on the job (1987), SLNR had drilled four wells. It had not been difficult operationally to drill the four wells, but it had been challenging to find enough high-quality investment opportunities. Tom considered wells to be "good" if they met all the following criteria: (1) payback of initial cash investment in 42 months or less, (2) at least 25 percent internal rate of return (IRR) on an after-tax basis, and (3) at least 15 percent IRR on a pretax basis.

In the first five months of production, one of the wells had already paid back 52 percent of its initial investment—well ahead of its target 28-month payout. The other wells were also doing well, and all of them were at least on schedule for meeting their targeted return on investment. Even though things had gone favorably for Tom so far, he knew the pressure was still on him to make good decisions because SLNR was planning to drill 20 more wells in 1988.

Investment Strategy

SLNR acted as the managing general partner in the gas-drilling ventures it formed, which gave it full responsibility for choosing sites and managing the well if gas were found. SLNR gathered information from the state of West Virginia and from other companies drilling in the vicinity of a well (if they were willing to engage in "information trading"). Tom would then put together a package of 10 wells that he considered good investments, based on all the information he had gathered. The total initial investment for a typical package would be around $1.6 million. SLNR would retain about 25 percent ownership and sell the rest to several other general partners.

As managing general partner, SLNR was responsible for hiring a general contractor who would actually hire a firm to do the drilling, and SLNR's geologist, Brad Thomas, would determine whether there really was enough gas to make it worth completing a well. If the decision was to go ahead, the general contractor would also be in charge of the day-to-day operations of a well. SLNR had entered into a joint venture with Excel Energy of Bridgeport, West Virginia, in which they agreed that Excel would act as the general contractor for all the wells on which SLNR acted as managing general partner.

The first-year production level varied significantly from well to well. Tom found the uncertainty could be described with a lognormal probability distribution with a mean of 33 million cubic feet and a standard deviation of 4.93 million cubic feet.

The Bailey Prospect

Exhibit 1 is a copy of the spreadsheet Tom had developed to analyze one well, called the Bailey Prospect, as a potential member of the package of 10 wells he was currently putting together. As Tom thought about the realization of this one well, he knew the Bailey Prospect was surrounded by producing wells from the target gas-producing formation. It was virtually certain, therefore, that SLNR would hit the formation and decide to complete the well; but there was a 10 percent chance that either an operational failure would cause zero production or that the gas formation would be depleted because of the surrounding wells, resulting in essentially zero production. In either of these cases, the pretax loss would be $160,000. In the more likely case, there would be gas produced and Tom would then find out how much the well would produce in the first and subsequent years. He would also learn what the Btu content (see Exhibit 2 for an explanation of the more commonly used abbreviations and terms in the well-drilling business) was for the gas, which would affect the total revenue generated by the well.

Revenues and Expenses. The spreadsheet was basically an income statement over the well's life. The price per mcf was calculated by multiplying the contracted price per MMBtu times the Btu content divided by 1,000. The production in mcf was then estimated for the first year and calculated for each succeeding year, based on the percentage decline values given in the

EXHIBIT 1 Bailey Prospect Base-Case Spreadsheet

WELL ASSUMPTIONS

TOTAL WELL COST	$160.000
INTANGIBLE COST (%OFTOTAL)	72.50%
MONTHLY OPERATING COSTS	$300
ANNUAL LEASE EXPENSE	$3,000
INFLATION FACTOR WELL EXP	1.75%

PRODUCTION DATA
ENOUGH (0 = NO, 1 = YES)?	1
1st YEAR Mcf	33,000

PRODUCTION DECLINE AFTER . . .
YEAR 1	22.50%
YEAR 3-5	17.50%
YEAR 6-14	12.50%
YEAR 15-24	10.00%
	5.00%

ENVIRONMENT

FEDERAL TAX RATE	34.00%
STATE TAX RATE	9.75%
SEVERANCE TAX RATE	3.40%
COUNTY TAX RATE	4.50%
SECTION 29 TAX CREDIT	$0.7600
% QUALIFIED	100.00%
GNP DEFLATOR	3.50%
ROYALTIES	15.2344%

GAS PRICE DATA
CURRENTPRICE($/MMBTU)	$1.90
BTUCONTENT(BTU/FT3)	1,155
1ST YEAR OF PRICE INCREASE	5

RESULTS

EQUITY PAYOUT (AFTER-TAX) =	23.26 MO.
INTERNAL RATE OF RETURN (CF AFTER-TAX) =	41.07%
INTERNAL RATE OF RETURN (PBT) =	16.65%
NET PRESENT VALUE (CFAT) @ 15%	$110,263
CUMULATIVE CASH FLOW AFTER-TAX	$432,235

Spreadsheet — Years 0–12

YEAR	0	1	2	3	4	5	6	7	8	9	10	11	12
INITIAL INVESTMENT	(160,000)												
PRICE PER MCF		2.19	2.19	2.19	2.19	2.27	2.35	2.43	2.52	2.61	2.70	2.79	2.89
PRODUCTION(MCF)		33,000	25,575	21,099	18,462	16,154	14,135	12,721	11,449	10,304	9,274	8,347	7,512
GROSS REVENUE		$72,419	$56,124	$46,303	$40,515	$36,691	$33,228	$30,952	$28,832	$26,857	$25,017	$23,304	$21,707
LESS: ROYALTIES		11,033	8,550	7,054	6,172	5,590	5,062	4,715	4,392	4,092	3,811	3,550	3,307
NET REVENUE		$61,386	$47,574	$39,249	$34,343	$31,101	$28,166	$26,237	$24,440	$22,766	$21,206	$19,753	$18,400
OPERATING EXPENSES		6,600	6,716	6,833	6,953	7,074	7,198	7,324	7,452	7,583	7,715	7,850	7,988
SEVERANCE & COUNTY TAX		5,721	4,434	3,658	3,201	2,899	2,625	2,445	2,278	2,122	1,976	1,841	1,715
DEPRECIATION	116,000	6,286	6,286	6,286	6,286	6,286	6,286	6,286					
PROFIT BEFORE TAX	(116,000)	$42,779	$30,139	$22,472	$17,904	$14,843	$12,057	$10,182	$14,710	$13,061	$11,514	$10,062	$8,698
DEPLETION		9,208	7,136	5,887	5,151	4,665	4,225	3,936	3,666	3,415	3,181	2,963	2,760
STATE INC. TAX	(11,310)	2,042	1,289	830	555	369	199	83	587	484	387	296	210
FEDERAL INC. TAX	(35,595)	(18,247)	(15,853)	(14,484)	(13,821)	(12,937)	(12,141)	(11,631)	(9,231)	(8,796)	(8,393)	(8,022)	(7,679)
PROFIT AFTER TAX	(69,095)	$49,777	$37,567	$30,238	$26,018	$22,746	$19,775	$17,795	$19,688	$17,958	$16,339	$14,825	$13,407
AFTER TAX CASH FLOW	(113,095)	$65,270	$50,989	$42,411	$37,455	$33,697	$30,285	$28,016	$23,354	$21,373	$19,520	$17,788	$16,167
CUMUL. AFT TAX CASH FLOW	(113,095)	(47,825)	$3,164	$45,575	$83,030	$116,727	$147,013	$175,029	$198,383	$219,756	$239,276	$257,064	$273,232
NPV THROUGH YEAR N	(113,095)	(56,339)	(17,784)	$10,102	$31,518	$48,271	$61,364	$71,896	$79,531	$85,606	$90,432	$94,255	$97,277

Spreadsheet — Years 13–25

YEAR	13	14	15	16	17	18	19	20	21	22	23	24	25
INITIAL INVESTMENT													
PRICE PER MCF	2.99	3.10	3.20	3.32	3.43	3.55	3.68	3.81	3.94	4.08	4.22	4.37	4.52
PRODUCTION(MCF)	6,761	6,085	5,476	5,202	4,942	4,695	4,460	4,237	4,025	3,824	3,633	3,451	3,279
GROSS REVENUE	$20,220	$18,835	$17,545	$17,251	$16,962	$16,678	$16,399	$16,124	$15,854	$15,588	$15,327	$15,071	$14,818
LESS: ROYALTIES	3,080	2,869	2,673	2,628	2,584	2,541	2,498	2,456	2,415	2,375	2,335	2,296	2,257
NET REVENUE	$17,140	$15,966	$14,872	$14,623	$14,378	$14,137	$13,901	$13,668	$13,439	$13,214	$12,992	$12,775	$12,561
OPERATING EXPENSES	8,127	8,270	8,414	8,414	8,414	8,414	8,414	8,414	8,414	8,414	8,414	8,414	8,414
SEVERANCE & COUNTY TAX	1,597	1,488	1,386	1,363	1,340	1,318	1,296	1,274	1,252	1,231	1,211	1,191	1,171
DEPRECIATION													
PROFIT BEFORE TAX	$7,415	$6,208	$5,072	$4,846	$4,624	$4,405	$4,191	$3,980	$3,773	$3,569	$3,367	$3,170	$2,976
DEPLETION	2,571	2,395	2,231	2,193	2,157	2,121	2,085	2,050	2,016	1,982	1,949	1,916	1,884
STATE INC. TAX	129	52	(21)	(35)	(48)	(61)	(73)	324	312	300	288	276	265
FEDERAL INC. TAX	(7,364)	(7,074)	(6,808)	(6,737)	(6,668)	(6,599)	(6,532)	(9,381)	(9,316)	(9,252)	(9,190)	(9,127)	(9,067)
PROFIT AFTER TAX	$12,080	$10,836	$9,670	$9,424	$9,182	$8,945	$8,711	$10,987	$10,761	$10,539	$10,320	$10,105	$9,894
AFTER TAX CASH FLOW	$14,651	$13,211	$11,901	$11,618	$11,339	$11,065	$10,796	$13,037	$12,777	$12,521	$12,269	$12,022	$11,778
CUMUL. AFT TAX CASH FLOW	$287,882	$301,113	$313,014	$324,632	$335,971	$347,036	$357,832	$370,869	$383,646	$396,166	$408,435	$420,457	$432,235
NPV THROUGH YEAR N	$99,658	$101,528	$102,990	$104,232	$105,286	$106,180	$106,938	$107,735	$108,414	$108,992	$109,485	$109,905	$110,263

EXHIBIT 2   **Explanation of Commonly Used Terms**

Btu	British thermal unit—amount of heat required to raise the temperature of 1 pound of water by 1 degree Fahrenheit.
MMBtu	1 million Btus.
Decatherm	1 MMBtu.
FT^3	1 cubic foot.
mcf	1,000 cubic feet.
Intangible well costs	Any expense for something that could not be used again (e.g., fees to the drilling crew, cement costs). A purchase of metal pipe, on the other hand, would represent a tangible cost.
Severance	Sales tax to state on gas or oil withdrawn and sold.
Depletion	Generally the concept is similar to depreciation. It compensated the company for the money spent to acquire the right to drill. Generally accepted accounting principles only recognized cost depletion, which amortized the cost on a unit of production basis (e.g., number of mcf produced this year divided by the total mcf in the ground times the cost). The IRS, however, allowed the company to calculate depletion under the more favorable of two methods. One of these being cost depletion, the other is called "percentage depletion." The latter was in the spreadsheet and was almost always more favorable.

assumptions. The gross revenue was just the product of the price per mcf times the mcf of gas produced in a given year. Out of the gross revenue came a 15.23 percent royalty payment to the owner of the mineral rights, leaving net revenue. Several expenses were deducted from net revenue to arrive at the profit before tax:

1. Monthly operating costs of $300 were paid to Excel Energy in addition to a budgeted amount of $3,000 for other operating expenses that might occur on an annual basis. These costs were increased annually by the well-expense inflation factor.

2. Local taxes of 4.5 percent times the gross revenue were paid to the county and a severance tax (see Exhibit 2) of 3.4 percent times the gross revenue was paid to the state of West Virginia.

3. Depreciation expense for year 0 equaled the intangible drilling cost, which was 72.5 percent of the total well cost. The remainder of the initial drilling cost was depreciated on a straight-line basis over seven years.

To compute profit after tax, the following equations applied:

$$\text{Profit after tax} = \text{Profit before tax} - \text{Depletion} - \text{State income tax} - \text{Federal income tax}$$

$$\textit{Where: } \text{Depletion} = \text{minimum of } 0.5 \times (\text{Profit before tax})$$
$$\textit{or } 0.15 \times (\text{Net revenue})$$

EXHIBIT 3   Interest Rates and Yields

	Bills	Notes and Bonds					Moody's*	
	1-Yr	*3-Yr*	*5-Yr*	*7-Yr*	*10-Yr*	*30-Yr*	*Aaa*	*Baa*
1985	7.81	9.64	10.12	10.5	10.62	10.79	11.37	12.72
1986	6.08	7.06	7.30	7.54	7.68	7.78	9.02	10.39
1987	6.33	7.68	7.94	8.23	8.39	8.59	9.38	10.58
1988 Jan	6.52	7.87	8.18	8.48	8.67	8.83	9.88	11.07
Feb	6.21	7.38	7.71	8.02	8.21	8.43	9.40	10.62
Mar	6.28	7.50	7.83	8.19	8.37	8.63	9.39	10.57
May 18	7.34	8.23	8.66	8.90	9.20	9.30	10.22	11.45

*Based on yields to maturity on selected long-term corporate bonds.

Sources: *Federal Reserve Bulletin,* June 1988, and *The Wall Street Journal,* May 19, 1988.

$$\text{State income tax} = \text{State tax rate} \times (\text{Profit before tax} - \text{Depletion})$$
$$- 1/2 \times (\text{Severance tax})$$

$$\text{Federal income tax} = \text{Federal tax rate} \times (\text{Profit before tax} - \text{Depletion} - \text{State}$$
$$\text{income tax}) - \text{Section 29 credit}$$

Section 29 of the federal tax code had been passed by Congress in 1978 to stimulate drilling for a particular kind of natural gas that was especially difficult to extract from the ground, namely, that found in rock called "devonian shale," which composed the Bailey Prospect. This rock consists of many very small pockets where the gas resides until it is ferreted out. It provided, in 1988, a tax credit of $0.76 per decatherm. This tax credit rate was increased each year with inflation, but its future value was in the hands of Congress and thus far from certain.

Initial Results and Investment Considerations. To find the net present value (NPV), Tom added back the depreciation and depletion to the profit after tax to come up with the yearly cash flows. These flows were then discounted at the company's hurdle rate of 15 percent for projects of this risk (see Exhibit 3 for a table listing rates of return for investments of varying maturities and degrees of risk) to calculate the NPV through any given year of the well's life. His pro forma analysis indicated the project had an IRR of 41.1 percent and an NPV of $110,263.

Tom was feeling good about the Bailey Prospect, even though he knew he had made many assumptions. He'd used 1155 BTU/FT^3 to estimate the heat content of the gas because it was the expected (mean) value, when in reality he knew it could be as low as 1,055 or as high as 1,250, with the most likely value (mode) being 1,160. He also guessed that inflation, as measured by the gross national product (GNP) deflator (a measure similar to the consumer price index or CPI), would average 3.5 percent over the 25-year project life, but he thought

EXHIBIT 4   Historical and Forecast Data

Historical Natural Gas Prices

Year	Wellhead Price ($/MCF)	Year	Wellhead Price ($/MCF)
1987	1.78	1975	$0.44
1986	1.94	1974	0.30
1985	2.51	1973	0.22
1984	2.66	1972	0.19
1983	2.59	1971	0.18
1982	2.46	1970	0.17
1981	1.98	1969	0.17
1980	1.59	1968	0.16
1979	1.18	1967	0.16
1978	0.91	1966	0.16
1977	0.79	1965	0.16
1976	0.58	1964	0.15

ALL YEARS: MEAN=$0.976 STD DEV=$0.922
LAST 8 YEARS: MEAN=$2.189 STD DEV=$0.412

Source: *Basic Petroleum Data Book,* January 1988, Section VI, Table 2.

Percentage Change from Previous Period in GNP Deflator

Year	Percent Chg	Year	Percent Chg
1987	3.0%	1969	5.6%
1986	2.6	1968	5.0
1985	3.2	1967	2.6
1984	3.7	1966	3.6
1983	3.9	1965	2.7
1982	6.4	1964	1.5
1981	9.7	1963	1.6
1980	9.0	1962	2.2
1979	8.9	1961	1.0
1978	7.3	1960	1.6
1977	6.7	1959	2.4
1976	6.4	1958	2.1
1975	9.8	1957	3.6
1974	9.1	1956	3.4
1973	6.5	1955	3.2
1972	4.7	1954	1.6
1971	5.7	1953	1.6
1970	5.5		

LAST 16 YEARS: ARITHMETIC MEAN=6.31%, STD DEV=2.45%
LAST 25 YEARS: ARITHMETIC MEAN=5.39%, STD DEV=2.51%
LAST 35 YEARS: ARITHMETIC MEAN=4.5%, STD DEV=2.59%
25-YEAR MOVING AVERAGE: MEAN=4.91%, STD DEV=0.46%

Source: *Economic Report of the President,* 1988, p. 253

(Continued)

EXHIBIT 4   *Concluded*

Forecasts for Percentage Change in GNP Deflator

	1988	1989	1990	Avg 1988–90
Data Resources*	3.1	3.8	4.5	3.8
Wharton†	3.8	4.5	4.5	4.3
UCLA‡	2.7	2.8	3.9	3.1

*Data Resources, Inc., November 1987, p. 99.
†Wharton Econometrics, September 1987, p. 9.7–9.8.
‡UCLA National Business Forecast, December 1987, p. 47.

he ought to check a couple of forecasts and look at the historical trends. See Exhibit 4 for both forecasts of GNP deflator values as well as historical GNP deflator values and historical natural gas prices. Tom's idea was to use the GNP deflator to forecast natural gas prices after the four-year contract expired and to increase the value of the natural gas tax credit on an annual basis.

Further Questions and Uncertainties. When Tom showed the results to Henry Ostberg, a potential partner, Henry was impressed with the "expected" scenario but asked, "What is the downside on an investment such as this?" Tom had done his homework and produced Exhibits 5 and 6. Exhibit 5 showed the results if there was not enough gas to develop. Exhibit 6 showed what would happen if there was enough gas, but all other uncertain quantities were set at their 1 chance in 100 worst levels. Henry was somewhat disturbed by what he saw but said, "Hey, Tom, we're businessmen. We're here to take risks; that's how we make money. What we really want to know is the likelihood of this sort of outcome."

Tom realized he had not thought enough about the probabilities associated with potential risks that a project of this kind involved. He also put his mind to work thinking about whether he had considered all the things he had seen that could change significantly from one project to another. The only additional uncertainty he generated was the yearly production decline, which could vary significantly for a given well. He had used what he considered the expected values in this case, but now he realized he ought to multiply each one by some uncertain quantity, with a most likely value of 1.00, a low of 0.50, and a high of 1.75, to allow for the kind of fluctuation he had seen.

Tom wondered what would be the most effective way to incorporate all six of the uncertainties (total well cost, whether the well produced gas or not, first-year

EXHIBIT 5 Spreadsheet with No Gas Produced

WELL ASSUMPTIONS

TOTAL WELL COST	$160,000
INTANGIBLE COST (%OFTOTAL)	72.50%
MONTHLY OPERATING COSTS	$300
ANNUAL LEASE EXPENSE	$3,000
INFLATION FACTOR WELL EXP	1.75%

PRODUCTION DATA
ENOUGH(0 = NO, 1 = YES)?	0
1st YEAR Mcf	33,000

PRODUCTION DECLINE AFTER . . .
YEAR 1	22.50%
YEAR 2	17.50%
YEAR 3-5	12.50%
YEAR 6-14	10.00%
YEAR 15-24	5.00%

ENVIRONMENT

FEDERAL TAX RATE	34.00%
STATE TAX RATE	9.75%
SEVERANCE TAX RATE	3.40%
COUNTY TAX RATE	4.50%
SECTION 29 TAX CREDIT	$0.7600
% QUALIFIED	100.00%
GNP DEFLATOR	3.50%
ROYALTIES	15.2344%

GAS PRICE DATA
CURRENTPRICE($/MMBTU)	$1.90
BTUCONTENT(BTU/FT3)	1,155
1ST YEAR OF PRICE INCREASE	5

RESULTS

EQUITY PAYOUT (AFTER-TAX) = ERR MONTHS	ERR
INTERNAL RATE OF RETURN (CF AFTER-TAX) =	ERR
INTERNAL RATE OF RETURN (PBT) =	ERR
NET PRESENT VALUE (CFAT) @ 15%	($95,304)
CUMULATIVE CASH FLOW AFTER-TAX	($95,304)

Years 1–12

YEAR	1	2	3	4	5	6	7	8	9	10	11	12
INITIAL INVESTMENT	($160,000)											
PRICE PER MCF	2.19	2.19	2.19	2.19	2.27	2.35	2.43	2.52	2.61	2.70	2.79	2.89
PRODUCTION (MCF)	0	0	0	0	0	0	0	0	0	0	0	0
GROSS REVENUE	$0	$0	$0	$0	$0	$0	$0	$0	$0	$0	$0	$0
LESS: ROYALTIES	$0	$0	$0	$0	$0	$0	$0	$0	$0	$0	$0	$0
NET REVENUE	0	0	0	0	0	0	0	0	0	0	0	0
OPERATING EXPENSES	0	0	0	0	0	0	0	0	0	0	0	0
SEVERANCE & COUNTY TAX	0	0	0	0	0	0	0	0	0	0	0	0
DEPRECIATION	160,000	0	0	0	0	0	0	0	0	0	0	0
PROFIT BEFORE TAX	($160,000)	$0	$0	$0	$0	$0	$0	$0	$0	$0	$0	$0
DEPLETION	(15,600)	0	0	0	0	0	0	0	0	0	0	0
STATE INC. TAX	(49,096)	0	0	0	0	0	0	0	0	0	0	0
FEDERAL INC. TAX		0	0	0	0	0	0	0	0	0	0	0
PROFIT AFTER TAX	($95,304)	$0	$0	$0	$0	$0	$0	$0	$0	$0	$0	$0
AFTER-TAX CASH FLOW	($95,304)	$0	$0	$0	$0	$0	$0	$0	$0	$0	$0	$0
CUMUL. AFT TAX CASH FLOW	($95,304)	($95,304)	($95,304)	($95,304)	($95,304)	($95,304)	($95,304)	($95,304)	($95,304)	($95,304)	($95,304)	($95,304)
NPV THROUGH YEAR N	($95,304)	($95,304)	($95,304)	($95,304)	($95,304)	($95,304)	($95,304)	($95,304)	($95,304)	($95,304)	($95,304)	($95,304)

Years 13–25

YEAR	13	14	15	16	17	18	19	20	21	22	23	24	25
INITIAL INVESTMENT													
PRICE PER MCF	2.99	3.10	3.20	3.32	3.43	3.55	3.68	3.81	3.94	4.08	4.22	4.37	4.52
PRODUCTION (MCF)	0	0	0	0	0	0	0	0	0	0	0	0	0
GROSS REVENUE	$0	$0	$0	$0	$0	$0	$0	$0	$0	$0	$0	$0	$0
LESS: ROYALTIES	$0	$0	$0	$0	$0	$0	$0	$0	$0	$0	$0	$0	$0
NET REVENUE	0	0	0	0	0	0	0	0	0	0	0	0	0
OPERATING EXPENSES	0	0	0	0	0	0	0	0	0	0	0	0	0
SEVERANCE & COUNTY TAX	0	0	0	0	0	0	0	0	0	0	0	0	0
DEPRECIATION	0	0	0	0	0	0	0	0	0	0	0	0	0
PROFIT BEFORE TAX	$0	$0	$0	$0	$0	$0	$0	$0	$0	$0	$0	$0	$0
DEPLETION	0	0	0	0	0	0	0	0	0	0	0	0	0
STATE INC. TAX	0	0	0	0	0	0	0	0	0	0	0	0	0
FEDERAL INC. TAX	0	0	0	0	0	0	0	0	0	0	0	0	0
PROFIT AFTER TAX	$0	$0	$0	$0	$0	$0	$0	$0	$0	$0	$0	$0	$0
AFTER-TAX CASH FLOW	$0	$0	$0	$0	$0	$0	$0	$0	$0	$0	$0	$0	$0
CUMUL. AFT TAX CASH FLOW	($95,304)	($95,304)	($95,304)	($95,304)	($95,304)	($95,304)	($95,304)	($95,304)	($95,304)	($95,304)	($95,304)	($95,304)	($95,304)
NPV THROUGH YEAR N	($95,304)	($95,304)	($95,304)	($95,304)	($95,304)	($95,304)	($95,304)	($95,304)	($95,304)	($95,304)	($95,304)	($95,304)	($95,304)

EXHIBIT 6 Spreadsheet with Gas Found but All Other Uncertainties Set at 1 Chance in 100 Worst Level

WELL ASSUMPTIONS

TOTAL WELL COST	$166,237
INTANGIBLE COST (%OFTOTAL)	72.50%
MONTHLY OPERATING COSTS	$300
ANNUAL LEASE EXPENSE	$3,000
INFLATION FACTOR-WELL EXP	1.34%

PRODUCTION DATA

ENOUGH(0 = NO, 1 = YES)?	1
1st YEAR Mcf	24,000

PRODUCTION DECLINE AFTER . . .

YEAR 1 =	37.20%
YEAR 2 =	28.93%
YEAR 3-5 =	20.67%
YEAR 6-14 =	16.53%
YEAR 15-24 =	8.27%

ENVIRONMENT

FEDERAL TAX RATE	34.00%
STATE TAX RATE	9.75%
SEVERANCE TAX RATE	3.40%
COUNTY TAX RATE	4.50%
SECTION 29 TAX CRED	$0.7600
% QUALIFIED	100.00%
GNP DEFLATOR	2.67%
ROYALTIES	15.2344%

GAS PRICE DATA

CURRENTPRICE($/MMBT)	$1.90
BTUCONTENT(BTU/FT3)	1.060
1ST YEAR OF PRICE INCREASE	5

RESULTS

EQUITY PAYOUT (AFTER-TAX) =	65.08 MONTHS
INTERNAL RATE OF RETURN (CF AFTER-TAX) =	-183.03%
INTERNAL RATE OF RETURN (PBT) =	-185.22%
NET PRESENT VALUE (CFAT) @ 15%	($30,191)
CUMULATIVE CASH FLOW AFTER-TAX	($18,096)

Years 0–12

YEAR	0	1	2	3	4	5	6	7	8	9	10	11	12
INITIAL INVESTMENT	($166,237)												
PRICE PER MCF		2.01	2.01	2.01	2.01	2.07	2.12	2.18	2.24	2.30	2.36	2.42	2.49
PRODUCTION (MCF)		24,000	15,073	10,712	8,498	6,742	5,349	4,465	3,727	3,110	2,596	2,167	1,809
GROSS REVENUE		$48,336	$30,356	$21,574	$17,116	$13,941	$11,356	$9,731	$8,340	$7,147	$6,124	$5,248	$4,498
LESS: ROYALTIES		7,364	4,625	3,287	2,607	2,124	1,730	1,483	1,270	1,089	933	800	685
NET REVENUE		40,972	25,732	18,287	14,508	11,817	9,626	8,249	7,069	6,058	5,191	4,449	3,813
OPERATING EXPENSES		6,600	6,688	6,777	6,868	6,960	7,052	7,147	7,242	7,339	7,437	7,536	7,637
SEVERANCE & COUNTY TAX		3,819	2,398	1,704	1,352	1,101	897	769	659	565	484	415	355
DEPRECIATION	120,522	6,531	6,531	6,531	6,531	6,531	6,531	6,531					
PROFIT BEFORE TAX	($120,522)	$24,023	$10,115	$3,275	($242)	($2,774)	($4,855)	($6,197)	($832)	($1,845)	($2,729)	($3,502)	($4,179)
DEPLETION		6,146	3,860	1,637	(121)	(1,387)	(2,427)	(3,099)	(416)	(923)	(1,365)	(1,751)	(2,090)
STATE INC. TAX		921	94	(207)	(303)	(372)	(430)	(468)	(182)	(211)	(237)	(260)	(280)
FEDERAL INC. TAX		(13,569)	(10,372)	(8,469)	(7,348)	(6,380)	(5,595)	(5,107)	(3,690)	(3,336)	(3,035)	(2,779)	(2,562)
PROFIT AFTER TAX		$30,525	$16,533	$10,314	$7,529	$5,365	$3,597	$2,476	$3,456	$2,624	$1,907	$1,288	$753
AFTER-TAX CASH FLOW	($117,504)	$43,202	$26,924	$18,482	$13,939	$10,509	$7,701	$5,908	$3,040	$1,702	$543	($463)	($1,337)
CUMUL. AFT TAX CASH FLOW	($117,504)	($74,302)	($47,378)	($28,896)	($14,957)	($4,448)	$3,253	$9,161	$12,201	$13,903	$14,445	$13,983	$12,646
NPV THROUGH YEAR N	($117,504)	($79,937)	($59,579)	($47,427)	($39,457)	($34,232)	($30,903)	($28,682)	($27,688)	($27,204)	($27,070)	($27,170)	($27,419)

Years 13–25

YEAR	13	14	15	16	17	18	19	20	21	22	23	24	25
INITIAL INVESTMENT													
PRICE PER MCF	2.55	2.62	2.69	2.76	2.84	2.91	2.99	3.07	3.15	3.24	3.32	3.41	3.50
PRODUCTION (MCF)	1,510	1,260	1,052	965	885	812	745	683	627	575	527	484	444
GROSS REVENUE	$3,854	$3,303	$2,831	$2,666	$2,511	$2,365	$2,227	$2,098	$1,976	$1,861	$1,753	$1,651	$1,555
LESS: ROYALTIES	587	503	431	406	383	360	339	320	301	283	267	251	237
NET REVENUE	3,267	2,800	2,399	2,260	2,128	2,005	1,888	1,778	1,675	1,577	1,486	1,399	1,318
OPERATING EXPENSES	7,739	7,842	7,947	7,947	7,947	7,947	7,947	3,973	3,973	3,973	3,973	3,973	3,973
SEVERANCE & COUNTY TAX	304	261	224	211	198	187	176	166	156	147	138	130	123
DEPRECIATION													
PROFIT BEFORE TAX	($4,776)	($5,303)	($5,771)	($5,897)	($6,016)	($6,129)	($6,234)	($2,361)	($2,455)	($2,543)	($2,626)	($2,704)	($2,778)
DEPLETION	(2,388)	(2,651)	(2,885)	(2,949)	(3,008)	(3,064)	(3,117)	(1,180)	(1,227)	(1,271)	(1,313)	(1,352)	(1,389)
STATE INC. TAX	(298)	(315)	(329)	(333)	(336)	(339)	(342)	(151)	(153)	(156)	(158)	(160)	(162)
FEDERAL INC. TAX	(2,379)	(2,224)	(2,094)	(2,043)	(1,996)	(1,950)	(1,908)	(1,258)	(1,220)	(1,185)	(1,151)	(1,120)	(1,090)
PROFIT AFTER TAX	$289	($112)	($462)	($572)	($677)	($775)	($868)	$229	$146	$69	($4)	($72)	($137)
AFTER-TAX CASH FLOW	($2,098)	($2,764)	($3,347)	($3,521)	($3,685)	($3,839)	($3,985)	($952)	($1,081)	($1,202)	($1,317)	($1,425)	($1,526)
CUMUL. AFT TAX CASH FLOW	$10,547	$7,784	$4,437	$916	($2,769)	($6,609)	($10,593)	($11,545)	($12,626)	($13,829)	($15,145)	($16,570)	($18,096)
NPV THROUGH YEAR N	($27,760)	($28,151)	($28,562)	($28,939)	($29,281)	($29,591)	($29,871)	($29,929)	($29,987)	($30,042)	($30,095)	($30,145)	($30,191)

249

production of gas, the Btu content, rate of production decline, and the average inflation over the next 25 years) into his investment analysis. He remembered doing "what if" tables with Lotus™ back in business school, but he had never heard of a six-way table. As he skimmed back through his quantitative methods book, he saw a chapter on Monte Carlo simulation and read enough to be convinced that this method was ideally suited to his current situation.

When Tom told Henry about this new method of evaluation he was contemplating, his partner laughed and said, "Come on, Tom, it can't be that hard. What you're talking about sounds like something they'd teach brand-new MBAs. You and I have been doing this type of investing for years. Can't we just figure it out on the back of an envelope?" When Tom tried to estimate the probability of his worst-case scenario, it came out to 0.00000001 percent—not very likely! There was no way he was going to waste any more time trying to figure out the expected NPV by hand based on all the uncertainties, regardless of how intuitive his friend thought it should be. Consequently, Tom thought a little more about how Monte Carlo simulation would work with this decision.

In his current method of evaluating projects, he had used the three criteria mentioned earlier (< 42-month payback of initial cash investment, > 15 percent IRR on pretax basis, and > 25 percent IRR on after-tax basis). He could see that calculating the average IRR after several Monte Carlo trials wouldn't be very meaningful, especially since there was a 10 percent chance that you would spend $160K on a pretax basis and get no return! It would be impossible to find an IRR on that particular scenario. He did feel he could calculate an average NPV after several trials and even find out how many years it would take until the NPV became positive. As he settled into his chair to finish reading the chapter, which looked vaguely familiar, he looked up briefly at the verdant hillside and wondered for a moment what resources were under the hill.

CASE 48
T. ROWE PRICE ASSOCIATES

Peter Gordon's day had begun as usual with *The Wall Street Journal*. As was his custom, he had started reading at the back, but he had not yet finished "Heard on the Street" when his direct lines to Salomon Brothers and Chemical Bank lit up almost simultaneously. It was 8:45 A.M. on Tuesday, June 21, 1983.

The trader at Salomon Brothers was offering to sell $50 million of a new issue of M-S-R Bond Anticipation Notes at 99.50. Salomon was co-manager of the deal, and Gordon had noticed the tombstone in the *Journal* that morning (Exhibit 1). Gordon put the Salomon call on hold, picked up the Chemical Bank line, and heard Chemical's trader offer him $52,780,000 of Montgomery County, Maryland, notes at 7.04 percent. Because he expected to receive $49,950,000 in cash on July 1 when several notes already in his portfolio matured, Gordon asked both traders if they would be willing to sell for delivery on that date. When they agreed, he said he would respond to their offers by 9:30 A.M. He had 45 minutes in which to choose the better investment.

The Municipal Bond Market

Although corporate bonds were more widely followed by the investing public, the municipal bond market was considerably larger. States, local governments, and municipal agencies offered $57.3 billion in new bonds in 1982, twice the amount of new corporate issues. "Munis" were distinguished from corporate bonds and U.S. Treasury instruments by the advantageous feature that interest income from municipal bonds was not subject to federal taxation. Consequently, the individual and corporate investor could frequently earn a better return by investing in municipal securities, which, although they earned lower rates of interest, produced a tax-free income stream. See Exhibit 2 for the yields of a selection of corporate, Treasury, and municipal bonds.

Municipal securities were of two major types—general obligation bonds (GOs) and revenue bonds. GOs were issued by state and local governments to raise funds for municipal capital improvements, such as school construction or renovation, street and highway development, or municipal building construction. Such bonds were backed by the "full faith and credit" as well as the taxing power of the state or municipality that issued them.

Revenue bonds, which composed more than three-quarters of the municipal market, were secured by the revenues of the projects to which they supplied capital. These projects included municipal utility projects (water, sewer, gas),

---

This case was prepared in conjunction with Edward R. Case (Darden, Class of 1984).

Exhibit 1 M-S-R Tombstone

This announcement appears as a matter of record only.

New Issue

$447,200,000
M-S-R Public Power Agency
(California)

$215,000,000 San Juan Project Bond Anticipation Notes, Series A
$232,200,000 San Juan Project Revenue Bonds, Series A

A Joint Exercise of Powers Agency consisting of the Modesto Irrigation District, the City of Santa Clara and the City of Redding

The Series A Notes and Series A Bonds are dated June 15, 1983 and due July 1, as shown below. The Series A Notes are not subject to redemption prior to maturity. The Series A Bonds are subject to redemption as described in the Official Statement.

In the opinion of Bond Counsel, under existing laws, regulations, rulings and court decisions, interest on the Series A Notes and Series A Bonds is exempt from present federal income taxes and State of California personal income taxes.

Neither the faith and credit nor the taxing power of the State of California or any political subdivision thereof or M-S-R or any member of M-S-R is pledged to the payment of the Series A Notes or Series A Bonds.

$215,000,000 6¾% Bond Anticipation Notes due July 1, 1986—Price 99.50%

Amount	Due	Coupon Rate	Price	Amount	Due	Coupon Rate	Price
$1,030,000	1988	7¼%	100%	$1,285,000	1991	8 %	100%
1,105,000	1989	7½	100	1,385,000	1992	8¼	100
1,190,000	1990	7¾	100	1,500,000	1993	8½	100
				1,625,000	1994	8¾	100

$ 3,700,000 9 % Term Bonds due July 1, 1996—N.R.*
$ 4,395,000 9¼% Term Bonds due July 1, 1998—Price 100%
$ 15,205,000 9⅝% Term Bonds due July 1, 2003—N.R.*
$ 159,210,000 9⅞% Term Bonds due July 1, 2020—Price 100%
$ 40,570,000 6 % Term Bonds due July 1, 2022—Price 64%

(Accrued interest to be added)

* Not Reoffered.

The Series A Notes and Series A Bonds are subject to the approval of legality by Orrick, Herrington & Sutcliffe, A Professional Corporation, San Francisco, California, Bond Counsel. Certain legal matters will be passed upon for M-S-R by McDonough, Holland & Allen, Sacramento, California, A Professional Corporation, Special Counsel to M-S-R. Certain legal matters will be passed upon for the Underwriters by their counsel, Brown, Wood, Ivey, Mitchell & Petty, San Francisco, California.

Smith Barney, Harris Upham & Co.
Incorporated

E. F. Hutton & Company Inc. — Merrill Lynch White Weld Capital Markets Group
Merrill Lynch, Pierce, Fenner & Smith Incorporated

Salomon Brothers Inc

Bear, Stearns & Co. — A. G. Becker Paribas Incorporated — Blyth Eastman Paine Webber Incorporated — Boettcher & Company — Alex. Brown & Sons — Clayton Brown & Associates, Inc.
Dillon, Read & Co. Inc. — Donaldson, Lufkin & Jenrette Securities Corporation — Drexel Burnham Lambert Incorporated — A. G. Edwards & Sons, Inc. — Ehrlich-Bober & Co., Inc. — The First Boston Corporation
Goldman, Sachs & Co. — Kidder, Peabody & Co. Incorporated — Lazard Frères & Co. — Lehman Brothers Kuhn Loeb Incorporated — Miller & Schroeder Municipals, Inc. — John Nuveen & Co. Incorporated
Oppenheimer & Co., Inc. — Prudential-Bache Securities — Refco Partners — L. F. Rothschild, Unterberg, Towbin — Shearson/American Express Inc. — Thomson McKinnon Securities Inc.
Van Kampen Merritt Inc. — Wertheim & Co., Inc. — Dean Witter Reynolds Inc. — Bateman Eichler, Hill Richards Incorporated — William Blair & Company — J. C. Bradford & Co.
Crowell, Weedon & Co. — Glickenhaus & Co. — Interstate Securities Corporation — Matthews & Wright, Inc. — McDonald & Company
Moseley, Hallgarten, Estabrook & Weeden Inc. — MuniciCorp of California — Wm. E. Pollock & Co., Inc. — Prescott, Ball & Turben, Inc.
Rauscher Pierce Refsnes, Inc. — M. L. Stern & Co., Inc. — Sutro & Co. Incorporated — Tucker, Anthony & R. L. Day, Inc. — Underwood, Neuhaus & Co. Incorporated
Robert L. Adler & Co., Inc. — Advest, Inc. — American Securities Corporation — Bancroft, O'Connor, Chilton & Lavell, Inc.
Barr Brothers & Co., Inc. — Bevill, Bresler & Schulman Incorporated — California Municipal Investors Inc. — Craigie Incorporated — Dain Bosworth Incorporated
Fahnestock & Co. — First of Michigan Corporation — Gabriele, Hueglin & Cashman, Inc. — Gibralco, Inc. — Hanifen, Imhoff Inc.
Herzfeld & Stern — Howard, Weil, Labouisse, Friedrichs Incorporated — Hutchinson, Shockey, Erley & Co. — Johnson, Lane, Space, Smith & Co., Inc. — Kirchner, Moore & Company
J. J. Lowrey & Co. — Mabon, Nugent & Co. — Moore & Schley Municipals, Inc. — E. A. Moos & Co. Incorporated — Morgan, Olmstead, Kennedy & Gardner Incorporated — R. H. Moulton & Company
The Ohio Company — Piper, Jaffray & Hopwood Incorporated — Arch W. Roberts & Co. — Roosevelt & Cross Incorporated — Rotan Mosle Inc. — Seattle-Northwest Securities Corporation
Spelman & Company, Inc. — Stephens Inc. — Stone & Youngberg — Wedbush, Noble, Cooke, Inc. — Westcap Securities Inc. — Wheat, First Securities, Inc. — Birr, Wilson & Co., Inc.
R. L. Crary & Co., Inc. — Davis, Skaggs & Co., Inc. — Diversified Securities, Inc. — First Affiliated Securities — Emmett A. Larkin Company, Inc.
Philip V. Mann & Co., Inc. — J. A. Overton & Co. — San Diego Securities Inc. — Western Pacific Securities Inc. — Thomas F. White & Co., Inc. — Wulff Hansen & Co.

June 21, 1983

Source: *The Wall Street Journal,* June 21, 1983.

EXHIBIT 2   Relative Yields, June 21, 1983

Treasuries

3-month T-bill 8.76%
1-year T-bill 9.23
5-year T-note 10.74
30-year bond 11.11

Corporates

30-year AAA utility 12.30
30-year AAA corporate 11.65

Municipals

6-month project note 4.90
30-year prime G.O. 9.10
30-year hospital revenue bond 10.00

---

transportation facilities (airports, seaports, toll roads), and hospitals. In addition, there were special tax revenue bonds secured by the income from taxes on alcoholic beverages or cigarettes. Revenue bonds had more risk than GOs, because, in the event of a default, the municipality that issued them had no responsibility for repayment.

Municipal bonds competed in the capital market for the same investors' funds as did corporate bonds. In fact, the structure of the municipal bond market was very similar to that of the corporate bond market. Most of the major investment banks underwrote and sold municipal as well as corporate securities. A secondary market also existed in which the bonds that were originally sold by underwriters were reoffered for sale by purchasers. The *Blue List* of current municipal offerings, which Standard & Poor's published daily, was the most complete source of information about bonds for sale in the secondary market. Exhibit 3 is a copy of a *Blue List* page.

The value of a bond is determined by price, the number of years to maturity, and coupon. A 10 percent coupon pays 10 percent per year of the par (face) value in two equal, semiannual payments. The owner of a 10 percent bond with $5,000 par value would receive $250, one-half of the annual coupon, every six months until the bond "matured." On the maturity date, the owner would receive the final coupon payment plus the par value of the bond for a total of $5,250.

Municipal bonds were traded either on the basis of price, which was stated as a percentage of par value, or on the basis of yield to maturity. A bond that traded at a price of 100, therefore, traded at par, while a discount bond that traded at 98.50 sold for 98.5 percent of its par value, or $985 per thousand of face value. Similarly, a premium bond that traded at 101 would cost $1,010 per thousand of face value. The yield to maturity of a bond was expressed as twice the six-month discount rate that set the bond's net present value to zero. For example, an eight-year bond whose coupon was 8.70 percent and was selling for 99 1/4 would

EXHIBIT 3 **Example of *Blue List* Information**

50	VIRGINIA ED.LOAN AU.	7	6/ 1/86		100	SEARSBKI
250	VIRGINIA ED.LOAN AU.	8.10	6/ 1/89		8.00	FIRMERNB
5	VIRGINIA ED.LOAN AU.	8.40	6/ 1/90		99 1/2	CRAIGIE
40	VIRGINIA ED.LOAN AU.	8.40	6/ 1/90		100	FIRMERNB
90	VIRGINIA ED.LOAN AU.	8.40	6/ 1/90		100	HORNERBA
320	VIRGINIA ED.LOAN AU.	8.70	6/ 1/91		100 5/8	ABROWNBA
500	VIRGINIA ED.LOAN AU.	8.70	6/ 1/91		99 1/4	CRAIGIE
250	VIRGINIA ED.LOAN AU.	8.90	6/ 1/92		100	HORNERBA
60	VIRGINIA ED.LOAN AU.	9.10	6/ 1/94		9.00	ABROWNBA
100	VIRGINIA ED.LOAN AU.	9	3/ 1/95		99	AGEDARDS
10	VIRGINIA HSG.DEV.AUTH.	5	10/1/85		7.00	SCOTTSTR
10	VIRGINIA HSG.DEV.AUTH.	6.25	8/ 1/88		8.00	SCOTTSTR
10	VIRGINIA HSG.DEV.AUTH.	6-10	10/1/90		8.50	MERRILNY
45	VIRGINIA HSG.DEV.AUTH.	7.35	8/ 1/93		8.90	BBS
100	VIRGINIA HSG.DEV.AUTH.	7.70	8/ 1/94		8.90	KIDDERPH
10	VIRGINIA HSG.DEV.AUTH.	7.75	8/ 1/95		9.25	SHEARNYB
50	VIRGINIA HSG.DEV.AUTH.	7.60	10/1/95		9.25	HUTTONMD
5	VIRGINIA HSG.DEV.AUTH.	7.60	10/1/95		9.00	KIDDERPH
100	VIRGINIA HSG.DEV.AUTH. (SINGLE FAMILY)	6.40	10/1/96		9.25	THOMSON
5	VIRGINIA HSG.DEV.AUTH.	8.75	9/ 1/06		12.20	RODMANNY
635	VIRGINIA HSG.DEV.AUTH.	6.875	10/1/08		9.50	MATTHEWS
20	VIRGINIA HSG.DEV.AUTH. (SINGLE FAMILY MTGE)	6.20	10/1/09		10.00	DREXNYEX
100	VIRGINIA HSG.DEV.AUTH. (Y/M 10.75) (P/C @ 103)	12.375	11/1/13	C91	10.00	WHEATFST
25	VIRGINIA HSG.DEV.AUTH.FHA INS	5.75	6/ 1/14		9.50	ROGERSLB
1500	VIRGINIA HSG.DEV.AUTH.	0.000	9/ 1/14		3.65	BECKERMU
1000	VIRGINIA HSG.DEV.AUTH.	0.000	9/ 1/14		3 1/2	KIDDERNY
10	VIRGINIA HSG.DEV.AUTH.	6	9/ 1/14		9.50	CRAIGIE
15	VIRGINIA HSG.DEV.AUTH REG	6	9/ 1/14		9.90	MERRILNY
100	VIRGINIA HSG.DEV.AUTH.	0.000	11/1/17		4	BEARSTER
3500	VIRGINIA HSG.DEV.AUTH.	0.000	11/1/17		4 1/4	HUTTONNY
500	VIRGINIA HSG.DEV.AUTH.	0.000	11/1/17		4 1/4	TRIPPCO
5	VIRGINIA HSG.DEV.AUTH.	6.40	11/1/18		9.50	MERRILNY
100	VIRGINIA HSG.DEV.AUTH.	6.20	11/1/20		9.30	MERRILNY
10	VIRGINIA HSG.DEV.AUTH.	6.40	11/1/20		9.40	MERRILNY
5	VIRGINIA HSG.DEV.AUTH.	6.70	11/1/21		9.50	CRAIGIE
5	VIRGINIA HSG.DEV.AUTH.	6.70	11/1/21		9.50	SCOTTSTR
10	VIRGINIA HSG.DEV.AUTH.	7.20	11/1/22		9.50	MERRILNY
25	VIRGINIA HSG.DEV.AUTH.	7.20	11/1/22		9.50	MERRILNY
50	VIRGINIA HWY.COMM.TOLL REV.	4	1/ 1/05		76	BEARSTER
150	VIRGINIA PUB.SCH.AU	5.50	10/1/86		6.40	SOTRBALA
25	VIRGINIA PUB.SCH.AU	5.50	1/ 1/88		7.00	ABROWNBA
5	VIRGINIA PUB.SCH.AU	4.50	1/ 1/89		8.50	THOMSON
5	VIRGINIA PUB.SCH.AU	5	1/ 1/94		8.50	DAVENPOR
20	VIRGINIA PUB.SCH.AU	5.10	1/ 1/94		8.50	DAVENPOR
5	ALBEMARLE CO.	9.25	1/ 1/09		65	DERANDIN
40	ALBEMARLE CO.I.D.A. MBIA (FHA-INS) (MTGE/REV)	11.50	1/ 1/88		7.50	OPCOFTL
10	ALBEMARLE CO.I.D.A. CA @ 71 (HYDRALIC ROAD APT.)	0.000	7/ 1/97	C93	27.15	FISCHER
755	ALEXANDRIA SAN.AUTH. P/R @ 103	6	10/1/89	C86	6.00	CRAIGIE
15	AQUIA SAN.DIST.	6.25	9/ 1/99		9.50	CRAIGIE
25	ARLINGTON CO.HOSP.AU.	5.60	1/ 1/85		6.25	WHEATFST
770	ARLINGTON CO.H.F.A. FHA MBIA	0.000	12/1/05		12.50	OPCONY
5	BRISTOL I.D.A.	14.50	6/ 1/11		12.50	BUCHANAN

Source: *The Blue List of Current Municipal Offerings.*

Exhibit 4   Calculation of Yield to Maturity

On line 7 of Exhibit 3, Craigie Securities offered $500,000 of VELA 8.70s due on 6/1/91 at 99 1/4. The proceeds from the original sale of this issue provided funds for reduced-rate educational loans for Virginia residents. If these bonds had been offered at 99 1/4 on June 1, 1983, what would their yield to maturity have been?

No formula exists for computing yield to maturity. By trial and error, using a calculation similar to the one detailed below, the yield to maturity could be discovered to be slightly less than 8.84 percent. Maybe 8.834 percent is right? The only way to be sure is to discount the bond's cash flows at a six-month rate of 4.417 percent and determine the net present value (NPV).

Date	Cash Flows for a $5,000 Bond	Discount Factor for a Six-Month Rate of 4.417 Percent	Discounted Cash Flow
6/1/83	$(4,962.50)	1.00000	$(4,962.50)
12/1/83	217.50	0.95770	208.30
6/1/84	217.50	0.91719	199.49
12/1/84	217.50	0.87839	191.05
6/1/85	217.50	0.84123	182.97
12/1/85	217.50	0.80565	175.23
6/1/86	217.50	0.77157	167.82
12/1/86	217.50	0.73893	160.72
6/1/87	217.50	0.70767	153.92
12/1/87	217.50	0.67773	147.41
6/1/88	217.50	0.64906	141.17
12/1/88	217.50	0.62161	135.20
6/1/89	217.50	0.59531	129.48
12/1/89	217.50	0.57013	124.00
6/1/90	217.50	0.54601	118.76
12/1/90	217.50	0.52292	113.73
6/1/91	$5,217.50	0.50080	2,612.90
			$(0.35)

Because the NPV is approximately zero with a six-month discount rate of 4.417 percent, an investor would be indifferent between buying this bond or placing $4,962.50 in an alternative investment that paid 4.417 percent semiannually for eight years. The yield to maturity is, then, 8.834 percent (2 × 4.417 percent), the nominal annual rate.

---

have a yield to maturity of 8.834 percent (see Exhibit 4 for the calculation of this figure). Buyers and sellers could quote the price of this bond as either "priced to yield 8.834 percent" or "priced at 99 1/4."

Peter Gordon

Peter Gordon, a vice president of T. Rowe Price Associates (TRPA), managed portfolios of municipal securities for a firm that provided investment research and counsel to individual and institutional investors. TRPA, with total net assets under supervision in excess of $16 billion, was among the largest independent investment advisory firms in the nation. A major portion of these assets was held in nine public, no-load, mutual funds that bore the Price Associates name. TRPA had a reputation for active but conservative investment policies that dated back to the "growth-stock theories" that Mr. T. Rowe Price, a Baltimore financier, developed in the 1930s. Now the firm employed investment analysts, marketing managers and researchers, note, bond, and stock traders, and portfolio managers to oversee its numerous public and private portfolios.

Peter Gordon was responsible for a $1.6 billion investment in municipal bonds and notes and was widely acknowledged to be one of the most successful portfolio managers in his field (see Exhibit 5 for a profile). He was also the first public member ever elected to the Municipal Securities Rulemaking Board, the regulatory agency for municipal bond issuers and dealers. The largest fund under his management, the Tax-Free Income Fund, invested primarily in municipal securities to produce for the fund's shareholders the highest income exempt from federal income taxes that was consistent with the preservation of principal. On June 21, 1983, the net assets of the fund were $982 million. For 1982, the fund had shown a yield of 10.4 percent, while net asset value per share had increased by a record 18.2 percent.

Doing a Deal

Salomon Brothers had offered $50 million worth (par value) of M-S-R Public Power Agency Bond Anticipation Notes. These notes were revenue bonds backed by the income of a power system owned jointly by three California municipalities: the Modesto Irrigation District, the City of Santa Clara, and the City of Redding. The capital raised by these bonds would be used to purchase a share in the ownership of a large coal-fired power plant in Arizona and to pay for power-transmission lines to the three municipalities.

Salomon's price was 99.50 percent, and Salomon offered to deliver the bonds on July 1, 1983, the "settlement date." The bonds would mature on July 1, 1986, and would make semiannual coupon payments on January 1 and July 1. The coupon rate was 6.75 percent.

Because the issue date (the "dated date") was June 15, 1983, if Gordon were to buy the bonds on July 1, he would have to pay 16 days of accrued coupon interest ($147,945.21) to the seller. Gordon would recover this accrued interest as part of the first coupon on January 1, 1984; the amount of the first coupon would thus be $147,945.21 greater than subsequent semiannual coupon payments.

Chemical Bank had offered $52,780,000 worth of Montgomery County Housing Loan Construction Notes, a specialized form of revenue bond, at a yield to maturity of 7.04 percent. These bonds, known in the trade as "monkeys," had a coupon rate of 4.50 percent, would pay interest on January 1 and July 1, and would mature on January 1, 1986. The bonds would raise inexpensive mortgage capital, which the county's housing agency would use to encourage the construction of new, moderately priced, single-family housing. Although Chemical Bank would have preferred to sell the bonds for next-day delivery, the

EXHIBIT 5   Newspaper Article on Peter Gordon

Master trader holds own in bond market

By Michelle Osborn
USA TODAY

BALTIMORE — Meet Peter J.D. Gordon, 36, the tough, confident Scottish-born president of T. Rowe Price Associates Inc.'s fast-growing $1 billion Tax-Free Income Fund, the second-largest municipal bond mutual fund in the USA.

He trades in the bond market from his seventh-floor office in the IBM building here.

He is on the phone much of the day as he picks up information about the market: "The new three, it's at the buck, it's trading extremely well."

He and the brokers speak a shorthand language no outsider can understand: "What do you think of the Lutherans? Do you think they're worth the nine level?"

It's infectious, but Gordon takes care not to get lost in it.

"If you're totally involved in the chitchat of the marketplace, you lose the ability to think," he says.

An inability to think could be a costly proposition for Gordon.

He's a major player in the multibillion-dollar municipal bond market, routinely buying and selling millions of dollars worth of bonds a day for his fund.

The decisions Gordon makes affect the total return on your investment in the fund — both the interest income, or yield, and the fund's per-share net asset value, which is the price you pay to buy into the fund and the money you would get if you sold your shares. (Tuesday, Tax-Free shares closed at $8.96.)

Bond prices fall when interest rates rise and the converse. The share price of the Rowe Price fund follows those fluctuations.

Gordon, though, who's known as an aggressive manager of bond maturity risk, tries to cushion swings in the bond market by lengthening or shortening the maturities of

Tax-exempt bond funds: Here's how they work

Municipal or tax-exempt bond funds, like other mutual funds, pool your money with that of thousands of others who share your investment goals — in this case, tax-free income over a long period.

Like other mutual funds, a bond fund offers a diversified investment portfolio, professional management and liquidity. But with this kind of mutual fund, the share price reflects swings in interest rates: When interest rates go up, bond prices go down and the per-share price of a bond fund tends to follow that drop. When interest rates drop, the share price rises.

T. Rowe Price stresses the importance of total return — interest income or yield, plus appreciation in your original investment.

Reason: As the table at right shows, total return can be negative in a year in which share price falls so much that it offsets the yield. Or total return can soar when share prices rise and that gain is added to yield.

Whether a tax-exempt bond fund is for you depends primarily on your income tax bracket. You should be in at least a 30 percent marginal tax bracket, which means that if your taxable income increases $1,30 cents would be paid in federal taxes.

If your *taxable* income is between $18,201 and $23,500, an 8 percent tax-free yield is equal to an 11.43 percent taxable yield; at $34,101 to $41,500, 8 percent tax-free is the equivalent of a 13.33 percent taxable yield; if your taxable income is $55,301 or more, 8 percent tax-free is equal to a 16 percent taxable yield.

Multimillion-dollar routine

By Bill Perry, UPI, Special for USA TODAY
GORDON: Misses the excitement when he's not at work

How Price fund performs

Here's the performance of the T. Rowe Price Tax-Free Income Fund compared with the total return on municipal bond funds ranked by Lipper Analytical Services Inc.

As of:	Price per share	Annual yield	12-month total return*	Lipper
Dec. 31, 1978	$9.54	5.30%	−2.1%	−3.4%
Dec. 31, 1979	9.20	5.56	+2.0	−1.5
Dec. 31, 1980	8.06	7.75	−5.3	−13.2
Dec. 31, 1981	7.26	9.52	−0.9	−8.4
Dec. 31, 1982	8.58	10.39	+31.0	+39.3
April 30, 1983	9.20	9.70	+35.3	+34.3

* percentage change in share price over a year plus yield
Source: T. Rowe Price Associates Inc.

the bonds in the portfolio.

On this day, he is lengthening the average maturity of the securities he holds to lock in high yields because he believes that another major drop in long-term interest rates — as much as 1 percentage point — is possible by the end of the year.

The fund's seven-day average yield on this trading day is 8.29 percent. By 10 a.m., Gordon already has invested about $28 million in new issues of Ohio housing revenue bonds and Hawaii airport revenue bonds at yields higher than 9 percent.

By tough negotiating in both cases he has purchased the bonds at, in effect, wholesale prices by refusing to pay brokers' commissions.

He doesn't hesitate to throw his weight around in the market. "We came to you first. We may consider buying bonds away from you," he tells one broker, disclosing that he has found other members of the syndicate underwriting the new bond issue who are willing to sell at a cut-rate price. This broker won't give up that commission, and Gordon picks up the bonds from other investment firms.

Some of Gordon's trades take all day to consummate. Some don't get beyond the snap of a finger.

A finger snap this day: Jeffrey J. Alexopulos, Gordon's chief credit analyst, warns him early that a $271 million bond issue by New York City's Metropolitan Transportation Authority has — in Alexopulos' opinion — credit problems.

The existence of in-house credit analysis means Gordon can both avoid overvalued bonds and buy those he thinks are undervalued by rating agencies such as Standard & Poor's Corp. and Moody's Investors Service Inc.

It also means Gordon can get out of issues before problems hit the market. He dumped troubled Washington Public Power Supply System bonds about three years before their credit ratings collapsed.

Gordon is cool, measured. He's a man of few words — and those few often are punctuated with long silences as he punches numbers on his calculator.

He has the guile of a master poker player. But he doesn't play poker. He says he has no need to gamble. The market is more exciting; he sometimes misses it on weekends.

By the time Gordon holds staff meeting at 3:30 p.m., the market's pace has picked up. Gordon already has decided to put more money to work in Ohio housing bonds.

He has plenty of new money to invest: An average of $5 million to $6 million has flowed into the fund daily since the start of 1983.

When the working day ends around 5 p.m., Gordon figures the $51 million in bonds he bought this day will increase the net asset value of the fund by 4 cents a share — if interest rates decline by three-quarters of a percentage point, as he anticipates.

And if rates don't drop? Net asset value would fall 4 cents.

For a typical investor with about $20,000 in the fund, a 4 cent change means a gain or loss of $100.

Since that trading day recently, Gordon decided long-term interest rates were heading up, not down: He has sold about $300 million of bonds and used the proceeds to buy short-term securities to cushion the fund's share price against a decline.

Source: *USA Today,* June 1, 1983.

trader was willing to accommodate Gordon's wishes and sell the bonds with a settlement date of July 1. Since July 1 was also a coupon date, no interest would accrue and the first coupon would be January 1, 1984.

The evaluation of these offers was complicated by the fact that there could be capital gains from the bonds and these gains would be taxable. The M-S-Rs, selling at a discount, would surely have a capital gain of $5 per thousand if the bonds were held to maturity. Gordon expected, however, that the Tax-Free Income Fund would show other, small, realized gains and losses before 1986; such gains and losses were common in successful "actively managed" portfolios. The tax laws allowed such gains to be carried forward or backward; thus, over time, they tended to net out. As a result, Gordon decided to ignore any tax effects in his investment decision.

Gordon also regarded the two securities as having approximately the same degree of credit risk. The M-S-Rs were secured by a "take-or-pay" contract, which required the California utility to repay the project's costs from its revenues even if the project produced no power. Although such contracts had been challenged the previous year in the courts of the state of Washington, the courts of other states such as Texas had upheld the legitimacy of take-or-pay contracts.

TRPA's municipal credit analysts regarded the M-S-R project as sound in spite of its large size. The Montgomery County notes had the advantage of security in the form of liens on the housing projects they financed. Consequently, Gordon believed that the market would not demand a premium for either bond; the M-S-Rs and the Montgomery County notes were equivalent investments from the standpoint of risk.

In the next 45 minutes, Gordon had to decide which bond purchase would be better for his shareholders; but to do so, several calculations would be necessary. First, he would have to find the dollar price of the Montgomery County bonds. Could he, on July 1, afford $52,780,000 in par value when he would only have $49,950,000 in available cash? Second, he would have to calculate the yield to maturity of the M-S-Rs. With these calculations behind him, he would then have to decide how to interpret the respective yields to maturity of the two bonds in light of the facts that (1) similar bonds of similar maturity were selling in the market at yields to maturity of 7 percent, (2) he expected interest rates to decline by year end to a level at which notes like the M-S-Rs and Montgomery County notes could yield 6 percent, and (3) the maturities of the bonds differed by six months.

CASE 49

WACHOVIA BANK AND TRUST COMPANY, N.A. (B):
Piedmont Operations Center Scheduling

A. Mebane Davis was reviewing the staffing needs for the Proof Department. He had recently become the manager of the Piedmont Operations Center of Wachovia Bank and Trust of North Carolina and was anxious to continue the work begun by his predecessor in evaluating a staffing and scheduling problem. As the bank continued to grow, it was necessary to make the staffing and scheduling process more formal to ensure continued cost-effective performance.

Company Background and Operations

Wachovia Bank conducted retail, corporate, and international banking activities and provided a full line of trust services to its customers. It also provided its domestic and international customers a full line of corporate banking services, including cash management, foreign exchange, and money market services. It had total assets of $3.5 billion and net income of $30.5 million.

Because of the statewide nature of Wachovia's business and its rapid growth in recent years, the paper-processing functions of the bank had been divided among five similar operations centers strategically located around the state to provide services to each geographic area. The Piedmont Operations Center in Winston-Salem, North Carolina, was the largest, servicing 58 branches in 10 cities in the surrounding area.

Proof Department

The Proof Department was the heart of the bank's check-clearing operations. The department received and processed checks and other documents to clear them in the shortest possible time to save on float, which averaged $220 million a day systemwide. The department was charged with the responsibility for sorting checks, proving the accuracy of deposits, distributing checks, and listing transactions arising from the daily operations of the bank.

The physical facility consisted of a large room filled with 35 proof machines and several tables. As the couriers arrived, they left their bags of paperwork on a table on one side of the room. The bags were emptied and the contents distributed to one of three tables on the other side of the room according to the type of work; tables were for commercial, personal, and "big-ticket" work. The big-ticket items were always processed first, followed by commercial and then personal items.

This case was based on a Supervised Business Study prepared by Charlotte R. Donnelly (Darden, Class of 1979).

The couriers made several pickups each day, including a visit to each branch shortly after 2:00 P.M. to pick up all the work that was to be included in that banking day. The proof operators were responsible for processing all this work by the end of their day. Work that was accepted at the branches after 2:00 P.M. and was picked up by the couriers at a later time could be left to be done on a subsequent shift. When the proof operators arrived at work in the morning, they finished any personal work left from the day before. The first courier was scheduled to arrive with new work from the branches at about 11:45 A.M., and most of the work arrived between noon and 2:00 P.M.

The department operated from 8:00 A.M. to 6:00 P.M. on Monday and 9:00 A.M. to 6:00 P.M. on Tuesday through Friday. Despite the practice by other banks of handling check processing almost entirely at night, Wachovia believed it was important to give its employees a normal workday.

The volume of items processed in the Proof Department had increased significantly in the last two years, from 38.01 million to 42.975 million. The scheduling problem in the department was magnified because of the uneven nature of the volume. Exhibit 1 contains weekly proof volumes (deseasonalized to take out the yearly seasonal pattern) going back to the beginning of the prior year. This volume pattern led management to use a large part-time staff to cover peak loads. Currently, 14 full-time and 22 part-time proof operators were working at the center. Each operator had an average processing rate of 1,000 items per hour.

Forecasting

The first thing Mr. Davis had to do was forecast demand for next week, week 67 (April 10–14), and then he would need to work out a schedule for the number of full- and part-time staff to meet the predicted demand. A couple of simple forecasting methods had been suggested to him. One was to use the previous week's actual deseasonalized demand for the next week's forecast of the deseasonalized number of checks. Another was to use his predecessor's long-run forecast of weekly volume of 730,000. This number represented the typical deseasonalized volume and was based on years of experience with the operations center. Davis wondered how accurate these simple methods were and whether there might be some other better approach.

He would use his forecast to determine how many hours of additional part-time workers to schedule for the next week. His base schedule, which includes full-time and some part-time workers, was enough to do 600,000 checks; he could add as many additional part-time hours as he wished to the schedule. If he scheduled either full- or part-time hours, he had to pay for them even if the workers completed the check processing early. On the other hand, if the volume of checks was so high that the checks couldn't be processed in the hours he scheduled for the week, he would need to pay overtime wages (which were 50 percent above regular wages) to complete the work for the week. There was no requirement to finish all checks on the day they arrived, but the checks that arrived during the entire week had to be done by Friday afternoon.

EXHIBIT 1   Deseasonalized Weekly Proof Volumes

Week	Volume (000)	Week	Volume (000)
1	633.7	34	809.7
2	628.8	35	778.6
3	725.6	36	818.9
4	670.8	37	789.5
5	718.1	38	791.2
6	752.0	39	842.5
7	714.2	40	875.9
8	740.5	41	847.3
9	817.2	42	894.7
10	721.8	43	855.5
11	710.3	44	836.5
12	741.7	45	763.9
13	827.0	46	820.3
14	824.9	47	780.2
15	726.2	48	828.7
16	813.4	49	838.2
17	780.7	50	910.7
18	828.2	51	921.0
19	804.6	52	711.5
20	816.2	53	694.7
21	836.9	54	811.4
22	735.2	55	733.1
23	800.6	56	749.9
24	814.7	57	733.8
25	757.2	58	849.4
26	849.2	59	846.5
27	696.5	60	802.9
28	796.0	61	823.9
29	802.7	62	814.6
30	833.5	63	777.4
31	807.8	64	797.3
32	785.8	65	781.5
33	760.7	66	931.4

His first task was to get a handle on the forecasting problem; then he could easily use it to find the number of part-time hours to schedule. He first planned to develop a forecast of deseasonalized checks. Then for the week of April 10–14, he could use the seasonal index of 0.975 to adjust the deseasonalized forecast. A seasonal index less than 1 meant that the week had an expected volume less than the average week.

CASE 50
WACHOVIA BANK AND TRUST COMPANY, N.A. (B): SUPPLEMENT

Three procedures were suggested for forecasting the weekly work-load requirements of the Piedmont Operations Center Proof Department.

Method 1.   This simple forecasting scheme uses the previous week's volume to forecast each succeeding week's volume. Based on the data in Exhibit 1, the forecast for week 13 would be 741.7 (the volume for week 12). This procedure would then use the volume of week 66 to forecast the volume during week 67.

Method 2.   This approach uses a forecast suggested by Mr. Mebanes' predecessor for each week in the future. This estimate of 730.0 reflects the prior experience during the entire time that the predecessor was on the job and would not need to be changed each week.

Method 3.   This method is something of a compromise between the previous two. With Method 1, each forecast is equal to the previous actual volume. With Method 2, the forecast is based on the long-run experience with the volume of checks and doesn't change from period to period. With this compromise method, each forecast is calculated by putting some weight (alpha) on the previous actual volume and some weight (with a total weight of one) on the previous long-run forecast:

Next forecast = Alpha * (Volume) + (1 – Alpha) * (Previous forecast)

where alpha is the weight given to the most recent actual volume. This method is called "exponential smoothing."

If equal weights are used, this forecasting method is described by the following equation:

$$F_{t+1} = 0.5 * (X_t) + 0.5 * (F_t)$$

where X_t is the volume in period t and F_t is the forecast in period t. Of course, to evaluate whether the forecast is working, we want to see whether F_{t+1} is close to X_{t+1}, not X_t.

Exhibit 1 shows a spreadsheet that calculates these forecasts. Notice that this forecasting method uses the forecast given by Mr. Mebanes' predecessor to start but updates the forecast each period using the new observation of volume.

This method calculates in week 12 a forecast of 735.4 for the volume of checks in week 13. Continuing the process for all of the data, the forecast for week 67 would be 860.4.

EXHIBIT 1   Spreadsheet

	A	B	C	D	
1		ALPHA =	0.5		
2					
3	WEEK #	VOLUME	AVERAGE	FORECAST	BACKGROUND
4	1	633.7	**730.0** ←		
5	2	628.8	679.4	730.0	730.0
6	3	725.6	702.5	679.4	
7	4	670.8	686.6	702.5	
8	5	718.1	702.3	686.6	
9	6	752.0	727.2	702.3	
10	7	714.2	720.7	727.2	
11	8	740.5	730.6	720.7	
12	9	817.2	773.9	730.6	
13	10	721.8	747.9	773.9	
14	11	710.3	729.1	747.9	
15	12	741.7	**735.4** ←	729.1	+C1*B15
16	13	827.0	781.2	735.4	+(1-C1)*C14
17	14	824.9	803.0	781.2	
18	15	726.2	764.6	803.0	
19	16	813.4	789.0	764.6	
20	17	780.7	784.9	789.0	
21	18	828.2	806.5	784.9	
22	19	804.6	805.6	806.5	
23	20	816.2	810.9	805.6	
24	21	836.9	823.9	810.9	
25	22	735.2	779.5	823.9	
26	23	800.6	790.0	779.5	
27	24	814.7	802.4	790.0	
28	25	757.2	779.8	802.4	
29	26	849.2	814.5	779.8	
30	27	696.5	755.5	814.5	
31	28	796.0	775.7	755.5	
32	29	802.7	789.2	775.7	
33	30	833.5	811.3	789.2	+C33
34	31	807.8	809.6	**811.3** ←	
35	32	785.8	797.7	809.6	
36	33	760.7	779.2	797.7	
37	34	809.7	794.4	779.2	

(Continued)

Exhibit 1   *Concluded*

38	35	778.6	786.5	794.4
39	36	818.9	802.7	786.5
40	37	789.5	796.1	802.7
41	38	791.2	793.6	796.1
42	39	842.5	818.1	793.6
43	40	875.9	847.0	818.1
44	41	847.3	847.1	847.0
45	42	894.7	870.9	847.1
46	43	855.5	863.2	870.9
47	44	836.5	849.9	863.2
48	45	763.9	806.9	849.9
49	46	820.3	813.6	806.9
50	47	780.2	796.9	813.6
51	48	828.7	812.8	796.9
52	49	838.2	825.5	812.8
53	50	910.7	868.1	825.5
54	51	921.0	894.5	868.1
55	52	711.5	803.0	894.5
56	53	694.7	748.9	803.0
57	54	811.4	780.1	748.9
58	55	733.1	756.6	780.1
59	56	749.9	753.3	756.6
60	57	733.8	743.5	753.3
61	58	849.4	796.4	743.5
62	59	846.5	821.5	796.4
63	60	802.9	812.2	821.5
64	61	823.9	818.0	812.2
65	62	814.6	816.3	818.0
66	63	777.4	796.9	816.3
67	64	797.3	797.1	796.9
68	65	781.5	789.3	797.1
69	66	931.4	860.4	789.3
70				860.4

CASE 51
WAITE FIRST SECURITIES

Harold Gagnon, one of Waite First's most important customers, was on the line to Brenda Hagerty, a Waite First account representative. "Happy New Year, Brenda. Listen, good news this early in the year. Our firm did very well last year, and I just learned that my year-end bonus gives me $30,000. I want to use that money to buy a stock to add to my portfolio."

"Well, I believe there are still some good bargains in the market, Harold. I'm glad to hear you had a good year, but I think the good times for the market are still to come. I can recommend several promising stocks."

"You may want to suggest others later, but right now I need you to give me some advice about three stocks I have been following recently: Hilton, Texas Instruments, and Giant Food."

"Those are quite different companies, Harold. Hilton should be in a position to do well now that we are pulling out of the recession with some momentum. Texas Instruments may find a new resurgence in the electronics industry. As for Giant, you can't find anything more basic than selling groceries. I could find more information about these three companies for you and see whether our analysts are recommending them."

"Never mind that. I've already done a lot of research on my own and am convinced that the timing is good for any one of these companies. But I want to be careful to add something to my portfolio that has a lower amount of risk. As you know, I'm 10 years from retirement, and there are already a number of high-flying stocks in my portfolio. I only intend to buy one of these three stocks, and I don't want to see my retirement funds evaporate. Don't get me wrong, I'm bullish on the market but you and I both know that it's all but impossible to predict the market. The S&P can go up or down. I just think it makes sense for me right now to find a stock that does pretty well in both an up and a down market.

"Several of my associates here at the office have told me that the way to build a portfolio is to use beta analysis. Now I don't know the first thing about calculating a beta or any other Greek letter. But as I understand it, the beta of a stock indicates how risky it is, at least relative to the market as a whole. Can you find the beta value for these stocks?"

"Well, I think I can, Harold."

"I'm a little mistrustful of this beta business myself. My friends throw the term around as though any sophisticated investor wouldn't think of trading without examining the beta value. They think it's all you need to know to tell how risky a stock is. But the other day they were talking about two stocks with about the same beta value and one of the stocks seemed a lot more risky to me than the other. Can you do a little research for me and explain how I ought to interpret the beta and how much trust I ought to put into it as a risk measure?"

"Sure, Harold. I believe we have a recent memo on that. In fact, as I look at your account on my screen, I can see a beta calculation for your stock portfolio. We are experimenting with putting the beta calculation in the account information on a few of the larger accounts. I see that you are holding six stocks having roughly equal market value in your portfolio, which in total is worth $305,000 and has a beta of 1.4."

"I'm impressed! You seem to know a lot about me and about beta. Listen, I can't talk any longer now. I have some time tomorrow midmorning. Could I bring the money tomorrow, say around 10:00 A.M., and talk to you more about this beta business and which of the three stocks I should buy now?"

"That fits my schedule; our analyst briefing ends at 10. I can find the beta values for these stocks by then and prepare a little briefing for you on beta."

"Great, Brenda. See you tomorrow."

"Happy New Year, Harold."

As Brenda Hagerty hung up the phone, she had mixed feelings about the conversation. Gagnon was an important account, and there was a good broker's commission in this for her. With a considerable personal portfolio and a position as an influential board member of the local bank, Gagnon could steer considerable business Brenda's way. Hagerty had never calculated betas before, however, nor had she explained any statistical concepts to a customer as perceptive and knowledgeable as Gagnon.

Hagerty's first job was to find recent returns data for the three companies and for the Standard & Poor's 500, which she assumed would be the best surrogate for the market portfolio. She was able to get five years' worth of monthly data (Exhibit 1) by using the recently acquired data base of prices for the New York Stock Exchange. These data were total returns, including dividends.[1] While in the computer reference room, Hagerty ran into Doug Rogers from the research department. After she had explained her problem, Rogers offered to take the data and compute the betas for her.

"Please write down how you do the calculations, so I'll be able to do it myself," Hagerty requested.

An hour later, Rogers appeared at Hagerty's door. "I got tied up and didn't finish the calculations for you," he said. "I did find all the statistics you need for Hilton by hand, however, so you can see how the calculations are done [see Exhibit 2]. The regression line provides a reasonably good fit, as you can see from this scatter diagram I made [Exhibit 3]. I'm sorry, but I've got to get a memo out today and can't finish this for you. You can find the beta estimates in Value Line, rather than calculating them. Or you can let your electronic spreadsheet do the regression calculations."

---

[1]Total returns are defined as: (New price − Old price + Dividends)/Old price. In other words, it is the change in price plus the dividend yield.

"Thanks for your help, Doug. I'm sure I can take it from here."

Hagerty looked at the calculations and immediately searched her bookshelf for the notes from the statistics course she had taken the summer before in preparation for returning to get her MBA. The statistical meaning of beta seemed a little fuzzy to her, and she never had really digested its financial meaning. While looking through her files for the Waite First memo on beta (Exhibit 4), she noticed her watch showed 5:00 P.M. Packing her laptop and calculator, the notes on regression, the beta memo, and the data into her briefcase, she set out for home. One way or the other, she knew she could prepare for Gagnon at home with all of these tools. She just hoped it would not take the whole evening.

EXHIBIT 1   Five Years of Monthly Total Returns

No.	Yr.	Mo.	S&P 500 (%)	HILTON (%)	TI (%)	GIANT (%)
1	1989	1	7.111%	−3.044%	7.012%	−0.619%
2	1989	2	−2.894	−5.340	−8.832	−5.729
3	1989	3	2.081	18.205	−0.800	8.840
4	1989	4	5.009	11.280	0.949	10.660
5	1989	5	3.039	33.138	11.599	4.608
6	1989	6	−0.335	16.006	−11.674	0.000
7	1989	7	8.837	6.345	0.639	28.194
8	1989	8	1.552	0.597	1.587	−13.793
9	1989	9	−0.654	0.474	−3.300	−2.400
10	1989	10	−2.518	−8.737	−17.208	−4.918
11	1989	11	1.654	−2.717	14.290	−3.896
12	1989	12	2.142	−12.000	−1.034	2.703
13	1990	1	−6.882	−25.606	−6.969	−5.702
14	1990	2	0.854	2.444	5.618	−5.607
15	1990	3	2.426	−13.174	3.348	4.455
16	1990	4	−2.689	−14.713	−6.207	2.464
17	1990	5	9.199	20.054	23.529	4.186
18	1990	6	−0.889	−1.354	−5.226	−0.446
19	1990	7	−0.522	−15.011	−19.243	3.498
20	1990	8	−9.431	−23.306	−13.281	−4.673
21	1990	9	−5.118	−15.901	2.000	−12.745
22	1990	10	−0.670	−2.941	−14.667	6.854
23	1990	11	5.993	13.160	32.521	6.878
24	1990	12	2.483	15.058	20.158	12.871
25	1991	1	4.152	−1.879	−1.645	5.351
26	1991	2	6.728	20.000	11.037	−2.092
27	1991	3	2.220	−6.322	−3.482	-0.427
28	1991	4	0.032	3.988	0.940	0.996
29	1991	5	3.860	16.342	−2.795	2.137
30	1991	6	−4.789	−14.541	−14.556	−1.674

EXHIBIT 1   *Concluded*

No.	Yr.	Mo.	S&P 500 (%)	HILTON (%)	TI (%)	GIANT (%)
31	1991	7	4.486	–0.776	–2.256	–3.268
32	1991	8	1.965	–1.515	–2.692	-18.584
33	1991	9	–1.914	–3.077	–10.103	0.543
34	1991	10	1.183	12.063	11.947	1.795
35	1991	11	–4.390	–10.652	–11.289	–5.882
36	1991	12	11.159	3.514	10.314	9.659
37	1992	1	–1.992	6.914	15.854	0.166
38	1992	2	0.959	2.035	5.263	4.688
39	1992	3	–2.183	6.268	–12.520	–6.965
40	1992	4	2.789	10.456	6.130	–8.364
41	1992	5	0.096	–5.728	8.664	–3.529
42	1992	6	–1.736	–4.922	–6.166	0.610
43	1992	7	3.940	1.471	19.217	–0.994
44	1992	8	–2.402	–1.622	–7.761	–1.852
45	1992	9	0.911	4.121	12.764	–10.692
46	1992	10	0.211	–7.124	13.256	0.958
47	1992	11	3.026	6.932	0.000	18.310
48	1992	12	1.011	–7.219	–4.723	6.548
49	1993	1	0.705	11.354	15.818	–2.034
50	1993	2	1.048	–4.167	4.630	–2.874
51	1993	3	1.870	5.163	3.416	15.976
52	1993	4	–2.542	–7.494	–2.146	4.286
53	1993	5	2.272	12.123	13.596	0.493
54	1993	6	0.076	–7.769	8.193	–2.941
55	1993	7	–0.533	–6.957	1.252	4.747
56	1993	8	3.443	7.353	13.958	–9.223
57	1993	9	–0.999	7.397	–6.133	–1.604
58	1993	10	1.939	–4.337	–13.079	5.652
59	1993	11	–1.291	–1.760	–2.095	–3.627
60	1993	12	1.009	32.787	–0.887	10.753

EXHIBIT 2   Doug Rogers' Calculations for the Regression Equation

$$\text{Hilton} = a + b \text{ (S\&P 500)}$$

$$\sum y = 0.6534 \qquad \sum y^2 = 0.83473$$

$$\sum x = 0.5609 \qquad \sum x^2 = 0.08641$$

$$\sum xy = 0.15213$$

$$\hat{b} = \frac{\sum xy - \sum x \sum y / 60}{\sum x^2 - (\sum x)^2 / 60}$$

$$= \frac{0.15213 - (0.5609)\,(0.6534)/60}{.08641 - (0.5609)^2/60}$$

$$= 1.80$$

$$\hat{a} = \bar{y} - \hat{b}\,\bar{x}$$

$$= \cdot\frac{6534}{60} - 1.80 \left[\frac{.5609}{60} \right]$$

$$= -0.006$$

$$\text{Hilton} = -0.006 + 1.80 \text{ (S\&P500)}$$

EXHIBIT 3   Scatter Diagram with Regression Line

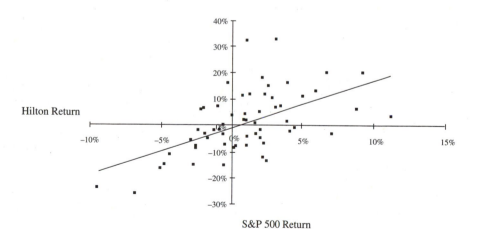

S&P 500 Return

Exhibit 4

TO: Investment Advisors
FROM: Research Department
DATE: December 4, 1993
SUBJECT: Risk Evaluation with Beta Coefficients

Due to numerous requests for a discussion of "beta" as a measure of market-associated risk, this short memo has been prepared for use by our staff.

The relationship between a security's return prospects and those of the market portfolio is often represented by a straight line. The chart below shows a scatter diagram of returns on an individual security plotted against the return on the S&P 500. A point in the diagram represents the stock return (% change in price) and the S&P 500 return in one time period (week, month, or quarter).

The line that provides the best fit to the data may be found by regression analysis. Mathematically, this is the line for which the sum of the squared vertical distances between the points and the line is smallest, hence it is called the "least squares estimate."

The beta coefficient is the slope of the regression line. It indicates the responsiveness of the security's return to that of the market portfolio. A beta of 1 means that, if the market portfolio return exceeds expectations by 1%, then the return of the security is estimated also to exceed expectations by 1%, and if the market portfolio return is lower than expected by 1%, then the return of the security is estimated to be 1% lower than expected. A beta of 2.0 indicates that the stock is "twice" as sensitive as the market portfolio to events that affect the market; if the market portfolio return is 1% above (or below) expectations, the return of this security is 2% above (or below) expectations. A beta less than 1.0, on the other hand, implies that the return of the security will rise (or fall) less, on average, than the return of the market portfolio.

The price of the stock is affected by events peculiar to the company as well as events that affect the market as a whole. Consequently, the actual returns do not all fall on the regression line, but are scattered around it. The standard deviation of the residuals (often called the standard error of the estimate) measures the dispersion of the points about the line. Residual standard deviation is important because it measures a security's nonmarket risk. The greater the residual standard deviation, the greater is the effect on price of company-specific events. Often standard errors are also reported for beta and alpha (the vertical intercept) as measures of the statistical accuracy of these estimates. The R^2 statistic represents the percentage of price fluctuations of a security that are explained by the comovement of the market price.

EXHIBIT 4   *Concluded*

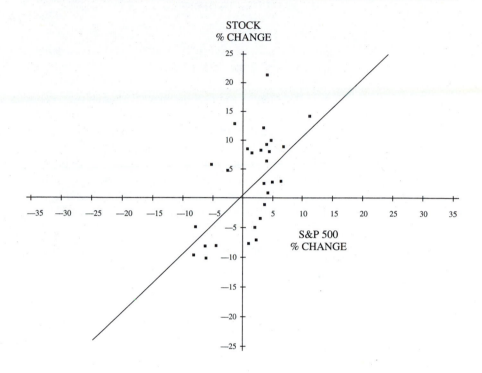

CASE 52
THE WALDORF PROPERTY

As Steve Miller, vice president of land development for Pflug Enterprises, turned his monthly desk calendar, he noted that only two weeks remained in the feasibility period of the Waldorf contract. Failure to terminate the agreement with the Acton Land Development Partnership by February 16, 1989, would, in effect, convert Pflug's refundable deposit of $150,000 into an irrevocable down payment of $150,000. While the Waldorf property was a desirable tract of undeveloped land in a particularly attractive area on the outskirts of suburban Washington, D.C., it did appear to be overpriced in light of potential limitations to the amount of usable acreage. Within the next several days, Miller would have to make a recommendation to Pflug's Management Committee about the continuation, cancelation, or renegotiation of the contract.

Pflug Enterprises

The origins of Pflug Enterprises could be traced to 1964 and the founding of a general contracting company in northern Virginia, which undertook a wide variety of projects from high-rise office buildings to warehouse/industrial facilities. With the launching of the BuildAmerica Condominium concept in 1974, Pflug diversified into real estate development. In subsequent years, Pflug added Skyjet, a helicopter charter service, split the BuildAmerica activity into a development component and a property-management component, and engaged in a number of development partnerships.

BuildAmerica Condominiums addressed the largely neglected needs of the group of small-business owners who required industrial space of a size inefficient for a stand-alone structure. An industrial condominium was an ideal solution for such small- to medium-sized businesses. Since 1974, BuildAmerica had developed 900,000 square feet of condominium space with a total gross sales value of more than $50 million. Exhibit 1 details these projects.

Industrial firms were the primary targets of BuildAmerica Condominiums, but the Skyline project had broadened the target and mixed a number of retail users in with the traditional industrial base. This approach had proven to be very successful, and, if the Waldorf project were undertaken, it would adopt the mixed-use design.

Pflug Enterprises was still owned and managed by its 53-year-old founder, John R. Pflug. John Pflug was a self-made millionaire widely regarded as a street-smart, tough developer. He had earned his notoriety by surviving the serious downturns in the real estate markets in 1974 and 1981. Although he was a hard negotiator with an often volatile temper, he was considered to be fair in his

This case was based on a Supervised Business Study prepared by Steven R. Scorgie (Darden, Class of 1991).

EXHIBIT 1 BuildAmerica Condominiums

Project	Location	Type	Year	Units	Square Feet per Unit	Total Sq. Ft.	Units Sold	Gross Sales to Date
1	Springfield	Industrial	1974	26	1,800	46,800	26	$ 1,274,000
2	Springfield	Industrial	1976	26	1,800	46,800	26	1,482,000
3	Tysons Corner	Industrial	1977	43	1,800	77,400	43	3,268,000
4	Merrifield	Industrial	1978	21	1,800	37,800	21	1,827,000
5	Alexandria	Industrial	1980	89	1,800	160,200	89	8,970,565
6	Alexandria	Industrial	1981	42	1,800	75,600	42	4,978,686
@Skyline	Baileys Xroads	Mixed	1981	60	1,200	72,000	60	10,000,000
@64	Hampton	Industrial	1984	68	1,800	122,400	57	3,661,550
7	Woodbridge	Industrial	1985	84	1,800	151,200	79	8,360,691
8	Manassas	Industrial	1985	84	1,800	151,200	75	7,757,273

Exhibit 2 Pflug Management Team

Steve Miller, Vice President of Land Development
 Master's degree in Planning from the University of Virginia.
 Knowledgeable about northern Virginia land values.
 Quiet by nature, disliked conflict.
 Although not trained in financial analysis, picked it up quickly and was able to
   explain it effectively.

Bob Pflug, Vice President of Marketing
 First-born son of John Pflug.
 Bachelor's degree in Commerce (Marketing and MIS) from the University of
   Virginia.
 Meticulously attentive to detail and systems.
 Cautious and conscientious in approaching new projects.

Steve Scorgie, Vice President of Finance
 Newest member of the management team.
 Former commercial banker.
 Bachelor's degree in Commerce (Finance) from the University of Virginia.
 Opinionated and prone to quick decisions.

---

dealings and to be someone who would stick to his word. His inclinations were to do without "fancy" analyses and to rely on his frequently repeated maxim: "If the deal doesn't make a 25 percent return, it isn't worth doing."

In addition to John Pflug, the management team was made up of Miller, Bob Pflug (vice president of marketing), and Steve Scorgie (vice president of finance). Exhibit 2 presents brief descriptions of these individuals.

The Waldorf Property

The Waldorf property was a 700,444-square-foot (16.080-acre) tract of retail land with excellent location and visibility in Waldorf, Maryland. During the fall of 1988, Waldorf was emerging as a hot area for retail development. The site was located between two major roads, Route 301 and Old Washington Boulevard. Moreover, the property was treeless and flat, which would reduce the cost of site work.

The property was owned by Acton Land Development Partnership (ALDP), which was associated with Sigal/Zuckerman, an experienced developer of retail shopping centers. When Niel Bien, a Sigal/Zuckerman partner, was asked why his firm was not interested in developing the property itself, he responded, "We have a lot on our plate right now and the property is further out [from residential centers] than our typical development." He went on to add that the property had been on the market for two years and that the two previous contracts on it, the most recent of which was with Hahn Development for the $3.5 million asking price, had been dropped.

Subsequent discussions between Miller and Bob Hahn, president of Hahn Development, revealed that Hahn was very bitter about his experience with the Waldorf Property. He had the property under contract for one year and spent $250,000 on time extensions. The extensions were the result of Hahn Development's preliminary environmental study, which indicated a potential for up to seven acres of wetlands (land reserved for wildlife) that could not be used for development. In addition, the study suggested that benzine gas might be present on the site. Although the benzine issue was quickly cleared up and dismissed, the wetlands issue was more problematical and would require lengthy, bureaucratic investigations. When ALDP denied Hahn's request for a further contract extension to work on the wetlands problem, Hahn dropped the contract.

When asked by Miller about the wetlands, Bien insisted that there were no more than two acres on the site and that, in fact, there might be none.

The exact amount could be determined only by the Corps of Engineers, which had been charged with the preservation of wetlands since the mid 1970s. The corps was also empowered to issue permits to developers that allowed wetlands to be filled in. The permits were freely granted until a 1987 suit filed by an environmental group in California. Since the suit, the corps had been very protective in its wetlands policy. Recently, Congress had passed a bill mandating that any filling-in of wetlands required the creation of the same amount of wetlands reserve elsewhere on the property. Sarah White of the Corps of Engineers indicated to Miller in a phone conversation that a study of the property would take no more than 12 months and that, based on the specific property characteristics and the "results of similar studies in the area," there could be anywhere from zero to five acres of wetlands.

The Contract

In an effort to secure the property for detailed considerations without putting money at risk, Pflug Enterprises signed a purchase and sale agreement with ALDP that contained a provision for a three-month feasibility period. During this period, ALDP would hold in escrow a note from Pflug for $150,000. Prior to February 16, 1989 (the end of the feasibility period), Pflug could terminate the agreement without penalty. On February 16, 1989, the deposit would be converted to a down payment and forfeited if the contract were subsequently broken. As was customary in land transactions of this nature, the closing could be delayed a year (February 16, 1990, at the latest) if the property were indeed purchased.

The purchase price was $3.5 million, the initial asking price. Throughout the discussions leading to the contract, Bien had been firm on the price and had repeatedly emphasized that the $3.5 million was not negotiable. Frustrated by Bien's position on price, but anxious to move ahead with its investigation of the project, Pflug postponed further discussions of price until more was known about the details of the project.

EXHIBIT 3   **Waldorf Project Site Plan**

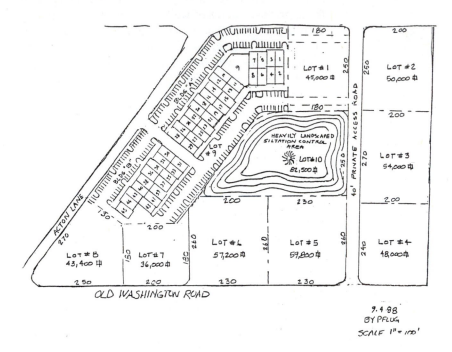

The Development

As the project began to take shape during the early phases of the feasibility period, Pflug determined that 30,400 square feet (0.698 acres) would be needed for roads and buffer areas and that 194,144 square feet (4.457 acres) would be reserved for a BuildAmerica condominium. The remaining 475,900 square feet (10.925 acres) would, after provision for wetlands acreage, be subdivided into commercial lots and sold off to end users. The area set aside for the wetlands would be landscaped into an aesthetically pleasing pool and fountain. Exhibit 3 presents a preliminary site plan with the assumption of 82,500 square feet (1.894 acres) of wetlands.

After a go-ahead decision was made, Pflug management anticipated that the project would extend over a 46-month period. The necessary wetlands study and approval of the site plan by appropriate governmental authorities would require the first 12 months. As the approval process came to a close, various architectural, legal, and building-permit expenses would be incurred. The estimate was that these costs would amount to $297,000 and could actually be paid during the first month of site preparation. Site preparation would then take four months at an estimated cost of $430,000. At the end of site work, the BuildAmerica parcel would be transferred to a partnership (within Pflug Enterprises) at $6 per square foot and the outparcels marketed.

Pflug managers had considerable optimism regarding the sale of the out-parcels. Alan Levine, the commercial sales agent used by Pflug, was sure that he would have all of them sold and ready to close by the time site work was completed. His sales plan called for an average selling price of $10.28 per square foot. Levine generally met his plans, often within a dollar of his estimates, but in the course of a year, the market could shift dramatically and his estimate be substantially off, possibly by $2 per square foot. Sales commissions were 4 percent of the selling price with closing costs paid by the purchaser.

The BuildAmerica Condominiums would comprise 45 units, one 9,000-square-foot unit and 44 standard units with an average of 1,200 square feet per unit. Development was planned to begin immediately after completion of site development and continue for a period of 10 months. Pflug estimated that the architectural, legal, insurance, permit, and inspection costs would amount to $347,000 and that the buildings would cost $2,899,600. The estimates of these development costs were fairly accurate, but a 3 percent contingency was customarily set aside. The development costs would be expended evenly throughout the 10-month construction period.

BuildAmerica Condominiums were generally priced at 10 times the market rental rate. At this price, the mortgage amortization with the ownership advantages was comparable to the rental rate. Karen Palmer, the BuildAmerica sales manager, investigated market rental rates and determined that comparable new construction rentals were $12 per square foot. Her intention was to price the units at $120 per square foot, but she pointed out that the volume of new retail development within a five-mile radius could drive the average selling price $20 per square foot in either direction. More reasonably, the average selling price would be within $6 of the asking price. Palmer had a buyer committed to the 9,000-square-foot unit and expected that four of the standard units would be sold prior to completion of construction, but stated that the number could range between zero and eight units. After completion, she expected the units to sell at a rate of two per month, but acknowledged that the number for any given month could be between zero and four or five. Commissions would be 6.0 percent of gross sales, and closing costs would be 1.5 percent of gross sales. An advertising budget of $80,000 would be allocated and expended evenly over the anticipated 20 months of steady selling to follow completion of the construction.

The site development was expected to be fully financed with prime-plus-one debt (11 percent), and the condominium development with independent financing at prime-plus-two (12 percent). During construction periods, interest would be accrued as principal. Once construction was completed and sales began, the interest would be paid as incurred, and the outstanding principal at the completion of construction would be paid down in proportion to the square feet sold. Each project was evaluated on the basis of cash flow after financing, but before taxes. Taxes were treated on a corporatewide basis. The Pflug Enterprises' cost of capital was 15 percent. Exhibits 4 and 5 present Miller's analyses of the two phases of the project using Pflug's best estimates.

While these figures were positive, the question of the wetlands acreage cast a pall over the entire endeavor. If the Corps of Engineers determined that five acres had to be set aside for wetlands, the land-development project, at the $3.5 million land price, would be a loser.

EXHIBIT 4 Waldorf Land-Development Cash-Flow Projections

	Feb 89	Feb 90	Mar 90	Apr 90	May 90	Jun 90	Total
Land absorption:							
Roads, buffer, wetlands		112,900				194,144	
Feet sold—BuildAmerica						393,400	
Feet sold—out-parcels						0	
Feet remaining	700,444	587,544	587,544	587,544	587,544		
Revenue:							
Gross sales revenue—BuildAmerica						$1,164,864	$1,164,864
Gross sales revenue—out-parcels						4,044,152	4,044,152
Commissions						208,361	208,361
Net sales revenue						5,000,655	5,000,655
Costs:							
Land	$150,000	$3,350,000					3,500,000
Soft costs		297,000					297,000
Hard costs			$107,500	$107,500	$107,500	107,500	430,000
Total cost	$150,000	$3,647,000	$107,500	$107,500	$107,500	$107,500	$4,227,000
Loan balances:							
Opening balance		3,647,000	3,787,931	3,930,154	4,073,680	4,218,522	
Interest		33,431	34,723	36,026	37,342	38,670	180,192
Loan repayment						4,257,192	4,257,192
Ending balance		3,680,431	3,822,654	3,966,180	4,111,022	0	
Cash flow before taxes	($150,000)	$0	$0	$0	$0	$743,464	$593,464

EXHIBIT 5 Waldorf BuildAmerica-Development Cash-Flow Projections

	Jun 90	Jul 90	...	Mar 91	Apr 91	May 91	...	Dec 92	Total
Absorption:									
Feet sold					13,800	2,400	...	2,400	61,800
Feet remaining				61,800	48,000	45,600	...	0	
Revenue:									
Gross sales revenue					$1,656,000	$ 288,000	...	$288,000	$7,416,000
Commissions					99,360	17,280	...	17,280	444,960
Closing costs					24,840	4,320	...	4,320	111,240
Net sales revenue					1,531,800	266,400	...	266,400	6,859,800
Costs:									
Land	$1,164,864								1,164,864
Soft costs		$ 34,700	...	$ 34,700					347,000
Hard costs		289,960	...	289,960					2,899,600
Advertising						4,000	...	4,000	80,000
Total cost	1,164,864	324,660	...	324,660	324,660	4,000	...	4,000	4,491,464
Loan balances:									
Opening balance	1,164,864	1,501,173	...	4,315,581	4,358,736	3,385,426	...	169,271	
Interest	11,649	15,012	...	43,156	43,587	33,854	...	1,693	
Loan repayment					1,016,897	203,126	...	170,964	670,990
Ending balance	1,176,513	1,516,184	...	4,358,736	3,385,426	$3,216,155	...	0	4,757,794
Cash flow before taxes	$0	$0	...	$0	$190,243	$59,274	...	$ 91,436	$1,697,346

279

I N D E X